my life with
WAGNER

my life with

WAGNER

FAIRIES, RINGS, AND REDEMPTION:
EXPLORING OPERA'S MOST ENIGMATIC COMPOSER

Christian Thielemann

PEGASUS BOOKS
NEW YORK LONDON

MY LIFE WITH WAGNER

Pegasus Books LLC
80 Broad Street, 5th Floor
New York, NY 10004

ISBN: 978-1-68177-125-0

10 9 8 7 6 5 4 3 2 1

Printed in the United States of America
Distributed by W. W. Norton & Company, Inc.

For Wolfgang Wagner
with great admiration
and gratitude

Contents

꧁꧂

Foreword

Until I was 15 or 16, I listened to a great deal of Gustav Mahler as well as the music of Richard Wagner. Mahler positively falls into an adolescent's lap. Then, one day, I came across Anton Bruckner, the antithesis of Mahler and a composer who has much in common with Wagner, and I felt that in the long term Mahler and Wagner would not both take up residence in my mind. I had to decide between the more life-affirming or the more life-denying of the two, between Utopia and the enticement of the abyss, between Wagner and Mahler. I came down on the side of Wagner (and Bruckner). And I would do it again and again, although the desire to listen to Mahler still stirs in me quietly from time to time.

The consequences of that decision have left their mark on my life as an artist, and that will be my subject in this book. Why is a life spent with Wagner so worthwhile? And what can be so intriguing about him as a composer? What is it like to conduct Wagner at the Bayreuth Festival Theatre and in other opera houses? What are the component parts of a successful performance? What are the particular features of the individual operas, where does each of them stand in the Wagnerian cosmos? I have asked myself those questions and others besides. I would like to answer them, as far as possible, from the viewpoint of a practising musician, from my life and my professional and personal experience.

In general, conductors do not express themselves in writing. Wagner himself wrote, passionately and exuberantly; he sought for and found himself in writing. Wilhelm Furtwängler has written from the conductor's viewpoint, and very well too; we even have a 'musical phenomenology' from Sergiu Celibidache, and Michael Gielen, Pierre Boulez, Daniel Barenboim and Ingo Metzmacher have all written books on music. But it must be rather unusual for a conductor to devote himself (in the true sense of the word) to a single composer. I want to do that here for two reasons. I have already mentioned the first: my musical thinking and feeling became what it is today through Wagner. Wagner confronted me with myself. The experience was not always one of undiluted pleasure, but it had an enormous influence on welding my feelings together. That distinguished Wagner from many other composers who are also very close to me: Bach, of course, Beethoven, Bruckner, Richard Strauss.

The second reason concerns the hearer. I think all who listen to Wagner (and all who would like to) have a justified, indeed necessary interest in learning what happens in the Wagnerian workshop: the composer's workshop and the workshop of his interpreter. Not all that goes on there is a miracle or a unique event; there are plenty of things that we can know, understand and explain. And I would like to explain them from my own point of view, to counter some new and inaccurate myths, and help to keep the content of Wagner's music from being confused even more with its superficial manifestations. At the time of writing [2012], a tidal wave of publications was about to roll towards us for the 200th anniversary of the composer's birth (22 May 1813), and the literature on him could already fill whole libraries. I am not a musicologist or a sociologist or a historian, I am a musician. But sometimes I feel that I have found the key to Wagner. I would be immensely pleased if reading this book were to open the door to him a little further for others, too.

I

'You haven't been playing the organ, have you?'
My Way to Wagner

I INHERITED A LOVE OF Richard Wagner at birth. I grew up in what would, at the time, have been called a comfortable middle-class parental home, which meant more than flavouring the Christmas goose with marjoram: it implied reliability, a solid principle on which to build in life, something that would prove its value and was worth preserving. I appreciated and surely needed that. Education in a good middle-class household in the early 1960s meant that a child grew up with music, with Bach, Beethoven, Brahms, Bruckner. And in my case with Richard Wagner. Music was simply there from the first, like food on the table, like swimming in the Schlachtensee in summer. Bach's oratorios, Bruckner's symphonies, sonatas by Mozart and Schubert, lieder, chamber music, operatic arias – they all came to my ears from the first day of my life, thanks to the well-stocked collection of records at home, broadcasts of concerts on the radio and, above all, the piano. Both my parents played it very well. I owe it to them that I could sing before I could talk. My mother noted in her diary that when she had been singing me lullabies at bedtime, she happened to hear me singing them again before I went to sleep – without the words, of course. I was about one year old at the time. 'Seems to be musical,' my mother wrote cautiously.

Music is in our family. My father had perfect pitch (and passed it on to me), and there are many musical anecdotes about his own father, my grandfather, a master pastry cook and confectioner, who left Leipzig for Berlin and was soon doing very well there. In the First World War he was drafted in as a scene-shifter at the Unter den Linden Court Opera House, of which Richard Strauss was artistic director at the time. While the other stage hands went home once their work was done, my grandfather stood in the street listening to the operas, and was entranced. *Die Meistersinger von Nürnberg* (*The Mastersingers of Nuremberg*) was one of his favourites – another preference that I have inherited through my father, although after quite a long period of incubation. At first, aged 12 or 13, I thought the third act was deadly boring. All that stuff about

the festive meadow, I thought, those stupid old Mastersingers carrying
on! My father was horrified. Sad to say, he didn't live to see me develop
a special love for Wagner's only comic opera. He died when I was 26.
That evening I had been conducting Smetana's *The Bartered Bride* in
Düsseldorf. I still own the piano on which my father learned to play,
an old Blüthner with a chequered history behind it.

Fortunately my talent was discovered early. I had piano and violin
lessons, and we went to a great many concerts. My parents had a
subscription to the Berlin Philharmonic, and I still remember how
the people sitting in our row would pat me sympathetically: poor boy,
they thought, having to sit patiently through the music again! I must
have been the only child in sight, and they didn't understand how a
red-cheeked five-year-old could perch eagerly on the edge of his seat
while the orchestra in front of us was playing Beethoven. But I wanted
to be there. I didn't want to stay at home with my East Prussian nanny,
I wanted to hear orchestral music, its shimmering colours, the ebb
and flow in which you could lose and at the same time find yourself. Incidentally, whoever the conductor was I thought him a rather
ridiculous figure. What's the idea, I wondered, why is he clenching
his fists and doing a kind of St Vitus's dance? Only with Karajan did
I gradually come to feel that conducting can also seem an organic and
indeed beautiful procedure.

From the first I preferred exuberant music on the grand scale to the
sparse, economical style. I wanted a large ensemble, the full orchestral
sound – to this day I never tire of the *fortissimi* in Richard Strauss's
Ein Heldenleben (*A Hero's Life*). Similarly, I was always fascinated by
slow movements, and liked them better than the fast, jaunty passages.
Quick is easy, I thought, anyone can do it. But slow is difficult, you
have to fill those movements with your own thoughts and ideas, with
colours and nuances. So it was only a question of time before I moved
from the violin to the viola because of its warmer, darker, more velvety
timbre – and from the piano to the organ. On Christmas Eve we usually
went to the Kaiser Friedrich Memorial Church in the Hansa quarter
of Berlin to hear the Organ Mass, with Peter Schwarz playing Part
Three of Johann Sebastian Bach's *Clavier-Übung* (*Keyboard Practice*),
with the wonderful Prelude in E flat major and the triple fugue whose

themes represent the Father, Son and Holy Spirit. When the organ thundered like that I was happy; it was Christmas. To my mind Bach had a wealth, an internal monumentality that attracted me enormously.

At the age of 11 I tried teaching myself the organ in secret. That is to say, the verger of the Church of St John in Schlachtensee unlocked it for me, and I practised chorale preludes on its organ – unsuccessfully, of course. The different manuals, the pedals, the co-ordination of hands and feet: none of it would work. What I did notice, however, was that you couldn't place your fingers as you do on the piano keyboard, and in the end that was what gave me away. My piano teacher, the wife of the Philharmonic's flautist Fritz Demmler, was increasingly unhappy with my technique, and one day cried, out of a clear blue sky, 'You haven't been playing the organ, have you?' So much for any career as an organist. I was forbidden to play the instrument – my parents were firm on that point – and I had to find a new outlet for my unruly tonal fantasies. I soon found it in what, after all, was close to hand: the orchestra. And in the wish to conduct, and in Richard Wagner. I don't know now which came first, the idea of Wagner or the idea of conducting. In my memory they are very closely related. At any rate, in the Wagnerian orchestra, so far as one can speak of *the* Wagnerian orchestra, I think to this day of the register of an organ.

No one had to keep me up to the mark or encourage me where music was concerned, far from it. My grandmother was always saying, 'Do go out into the fresh air, it's such lovely weather!' I wasn't interested in the lovely weather, I wanted to practise and go on practising until six in the evening. Was I supposed to stop work just because the sun was shining outside? That struck me as totally absurd. My sun, my pleasure, my fulfilment were to be found in Bach's *Wohltemperiertes Klavier* (*The Well-tempered Clavier*). I sensed that this was my path. There has never been any alternative to music for me, or even the faintest wish for one.

Experience of Wagner, if anything, reinforced this autistic attitude. On the one hand there was the music that I heard: *Die Walküre* (*The Valkyrie*) in 1966, very early in my life, under Karajan; my first *Lohengrin* at the German Opera House in Berlin in the old Wieland Wagner production, an opera for which, funnily enough, I later acted as répétiteur myself. Every time, these works left me exhausted. Ortrud and Telramund in the second act of *Lohengrin*, on the dimly lit stage: when Telramund sang, *Erhebe dich, Genossin meiner Schmach!* ('Arise, companion of my shame!') it took my breath away for days on end, even if I didn't understand what it was all about. On the other hand, Wagner was ever present in conversations at home, and the tone of voice reserved for him particularly impressed me; it was one of admiration and awe, not at all like my parents' reaction to Haydn, Verdi or Debussy. They certainly did value Haydn and Verdi, but I felt there must be something special about Wagner, and it made me curious. He was surrounded by the mystique of being unsuitable for children, which made him doubly attractive. For a long time I was told, 'You're too young for *Tristan*; we'll wait a bit longer for *Parsifal.*' I was therefore shaken to my depths when I did encounter those two operas at the age of 13 or 14. It was as if I had grown up in a vacuum, a void just waiting to be successively filled by the works of Richard Wagner.

I was enraptured not only by the atmosphere, the musical colours, the instrumentation, but above all by the idea of being overwhelmed by music – and overwhelming others. It was soon clear to me that I wanted to play an active part in this game. So I decided to be a conductor. Like Karajan, whose records I played at home again and again, with the scores on my knees, for preference *Die Ring des Nibelungen* (*The Ring of the Nibelung*), which he recorded in the late 1960s at the Church of Jesus Christ in Dahlem, with the fabulous Thomas Stewart as Wotan and Régine Crespin in the role of Brünnhilde. A distant voice urged me, 'Go out into the fresh air, it's such lovely weather!' No, I thought, leave me alone. What was lovely weather compared to Siegfried's Rhine journey in *Götterdämmerung* (*Twilight of the Gods*)?

I was positively knocked backwards by Wagner, and I knew: this is it. This is what you must do. By this time I had also realized that my parents were Wagnerians through and through. In fact I was surrounded solely by Wagner enthusiasts in my youth – at least, I can't remember any other people or any other subject. That included our music teacher at my high school, who when the conversation turned to the Bayreuth Festival told us how, in his own youth, he had climbed into the Festival Theatre through a lavatory window to get into the dress rehearsals. Later, I looked for that window in vain, but that doesn't necessarily mean anything. There has always been a lot of building work going on at the Festival Theatre. But I immediately understood the enthusiasm of our teacher who wanted to get in at any price.

My adolescence was dominated by the idea of becoming a conductor. As a result I never went in for teenage rebellion on the grand scale; I was far too busy for that, and I didn't feel that a great deal was missing from my life. I put all my energy into music: the piano and the viola, the scores that I was studying, visits to concerts and performances of opera. To this day I can't feel that meant I was neglecting 'real' life. It is usual to say that adolescence must express itself in contradiction, in trying to upset the established order, revolt for the sake of revolt. I can't confirm that from my own experience. Or at least my contradiction was always of a different kind; I am not a stormer of barricades. I didn't feel impelled to occupy empty buildings or hang around the streets in ragged garments; I didn't play football or listen to The Beatles. The kind of music to which I devoted myself to excess seemed to be very far from reality, yet it opened up worlds to me, its own worlds. That was as much as I needed in the way of resistance to social norms and distancing myself from them.

Looking back, I see something definitely schizophrenic in the situation. Half of Berlin was calling for revolution at the end of the 1960s, but I myself, a child from the attractive suburb of Zehlendorf, went on going to piano lessons like a good little boy, as if nothing had happened. In the golden age of the Extra-Parliamentary Opposition in West Germany, the emergency laws and attacks on Theodor Adorno in the universities (for instance, the women students ostentatiously baring their breasts as a protest), I was still a child, and my parents certainly didn't discuss such events at the supper table. Similarly, I am one of a generation that learned, or was supposed to learn, to hate German music and above all the music of Richard Wagner. I defended myself first intuitively and then deliberately against this kind of political correctness. Here, as in much else, I am on the same side as Daniel Barenboim, who says that the politically correct don't like thinking for themselves. I was allergic to having such things imposed on me, not so much because my parental home was politically conservative (as it was), or because I had different political opinions (which I would have had to formulate first); I defended myself against political correctness because it would have meant tearing something out of my heart that I wasn't ready to give up for anything. And so I was thrown back on my idols.

My social life at school was bound to suffer. I realized that I was different from the others and my talent was something unusual, which easily inclines one to arrogance. I was regarded partly as some kind of weird and wonderful creature, partly as an outsider, and the worst of it was that neither of those opinions bothered me much. I had to get used to hearing such remarks as, 'You and your silly old Bach'. Was I supposed to strike back with, 'You and your silly old football'? I never really stopped to think seriously about what other boys did or what they thought of me. And I wasn't entirely alone. Some of the others at my school also played instruments, the cello, the violin, the trumpet; and we could laugh when the pop music fans asked what kind of 'song' we were playing. There were also opera fans, five or six of us committed to the genre who went to performances together, to Charlottenburg to hear works at the German Opera House there, of course, and also to East Berlin, to the State Opera House on Unter den Linden. That meant going to bed very late, when we had to get up early in the morning because we had French first thing, and in the afternoon I had to do homework and practise both my instruments – but none of that was any problem. I knew why I was doing it. However, I was not a very good student at school.

Bayreuth was always a mythical name to me. That was because of what I heard at home – my parents had been to the Festival I don't know how many times – and because of the names of the conductors who were beginning to haunt my mind: Furtwängler and Knappertsbusch, of course, as well as Hermann Abendroth, Heinz Tietjen and Joseph Keilberth. In 1980 I went to Bayreuth myself for the first time, as holder of a stipend awarded by the Berlin Wagner Association. Curiously enough, I can hardly remember *Twilight of the Gods* in the legendary production directed by Patrice Chéreau, which is still regarded as groundbreaking. But I was all the more impressed by *Parsifal* (conducted by Horst Stein, with Wolfgang Wagner responsible for the direction and the stage set); the sense of music welling up from the auditorium itself fascinated me immensely. The lights go out, the

Prelude begins – and the strings are playing not somewhere out in front but below me, above me, to the right and the left, in heaven and in hell, in the entire theatre. The sound has no source and is going in no direction, it is everywhere. The sound *is* the auditorium, the music *is* the world – and I am in the middle of it. As I sat there burning with enthusiasm, I felt confirmed in my belief: this was exactly what I had always expected. Fundamentally, I had never heard Wagner in any other way, either on the record player or at the piano as I was trying to study a score.

Events came thick and fast in those years; my life was like a game of dominoes. At the age of 18 I took my concert examination in piano (with Helmut Roloff), and at the same time entered the Orchestral Academy of the Berlin Philharmonic as a viola player, and studied playing from a score and conducting with Hans Hilsdorf. I took my school-leaving examination, the *Abitur*, at the age of 19, and in the same year, the season of 1978/9, I was given a contract at the German Opera House in Berlin. No one would have thought it possible, I myself least of all. I had been away that summer, and was just coming through the door at home when the telephone rang. Hilsdorf was on the line: a co-répétiteur wanted to get out of his contract at the beginning of the season, and would I like to go and audition for the post and play to Heinrich Hollreiser? Naturally I would, and tackled the first scene of *The Mastersingers* and a piece from *Elektra*, whereupon old Hollreiser said that they could 'take the lad on'; as a beginner, he'd fit in somehow or other. So on 1 November 1978 I had a contract for employment at 900 marks a month in my pocket, and was in bliss! I practised and played for all I was worth, more than any of my colleagues, for work in the theatre was exactly what I wanted. At Easter 1980 I assisted Herbert von Karajan in Salzburg on his own production of *Parsifal* – and a year later I was an assistant in Bayreuth. I can still see myself in a tiny room on the top floor of the Festival Theatre arranging the orchestral material, marking up directions for the bowing, adjusting the dynamics and so forth, for Daniel Barenboim's debut on the Green Hill with *Tristan and Isolde* (in the production directed by the great Jean-Pierre Ponnelle). I was in a state of great excitement, my ears red with pride. At least for the first few days.

In retrospect, the path I was taking may seem quite uncannily consistent. And it was inevitable so far as my own feelings were concerned, since after all I was sure that I wanted to be a conductor. Outwardly, however, by no means everything ran smoothly. At the age of 16, for instance, I had a conducting audition with Herbert Ahlendorf, who taught at the Berlin Conservatory (formerly the Stern Conservatory). Ahlendorf put on a record of the Prelude to *The Mastersingers*, and took me to stand in front of a tall mirror. I don't know which confused me more: the recording, which I didn't like, or my own extremely clumsy reflection. Whichever it was, the audition was a dismal failure; Ahlendorf thought that the will to do well was not enough in itself, and that I had no talent at all. I was devastated; after all, no less than Herbert von Karajan had advised me to audition. I had only recently had a chance to talk to him, and there was just one thing I wanted him to tell me: how do you become a conductor? Well, obviously not like this anyway, I thought after auditioning with Ahlendorf.

And then there was the Karajan conducting competition of 1985 at the Berlin College of Arts, with Wolfgang Stresemann, artistic director of the Philharmonic, chairing a jury panel consisting of Kurt Masur and Peter Ruzicka as well as Karajan himself. The work to be tackled was the Prelude to *Tristan*, and each entrant had 20 minutes. I was 21st out of 26 candidates. I took it as a challenge, worked on the vibrato of the cellos at the beginning and the clean intonation of the woodwind, trying to get the orchestra to breathe and make a good impression with my ideas of the sound and tempo of the piece – and got no further than bar 19 or 20. In the end I was disqualified and felt stunned. Tears shot to my eyes. I hadn't succeeded in getting through the score, that was the reason given by the jury. Luckily for me, the decision was not unanimous: both Karajan and Ruzicka, as it turned out later, were on my side.

So how do you become a conductor? It is right to ask the question, since after all the conductor is the only musician to make no sound of his own. He is and always will be 'a musician who dissects the air', as my friend the composer Hans Werner Henze put it so well. That is to say, the conductor needs an orchestra, and there isn't always an orchestra ready to hand. So how is he to rehearse, develop his own technique, gather experience? Karajan's answer to me was always the same: pass your final school exam and then get practical experience. He said it with such authority, indeed with the full weight of his own life history behind it, that I understood what he meant at once: no more studying, I must come up the hard way as co-répétiteur, répétiteur with duties as conductor, assistant to well-known conductors, second conductor, first conductor, general music director at a provincial or medium-ranking opera house, general music director at one of the top opera houses. And engagements as guest conductor and conductor of recordings as and when the opportunity arose. If possible, you should reach that point by the age of 40, or it is not only difficult to get the top contracts (you are simply no longer such an attractive prospect on the market), but you have difficulty in mastering the entire repertory. If you take a short cut to conducting, as it were, you will hardly be able to conjure up a *Lohengrin* or *Tristan* after just a couple of years in the business, without the necessary experience and mastery of the trade. On the other hand, even very early success as a conductor, diving into ice-cold water just because of an extraordinary talent or an enormous amount of backing, can turn out to be disastrous.

In short, I am a fervent champion of learning how to be a conductor the hard way, and would still recommend it to any young colleague. My own stages along that path were Berlin, Gelsenkirchen, Karlsruhe, Hanover, Düsseldorf and Nuremberg. I had to sight-read a great deal, and abandon my own first music written for the stage; I learned to breathe with the chorus and had to conduct performances of operettas without any rehearsal. Above all, however, I acquired a huge repertory, a knowledge of opera that I live on to this day: in the three years when I was co-répétiteur at the German Opera House in Berlin alone, I was involved in 70 works. And I learned so much from conductors of the stature of Horst Stein and Heinrich Hollreiser. Stein, with his short arms and short baton – I know no one who kept so clear and precise a beat going without making any fuss about it. Hollreiser, on the other hand, used a long baton, wielding it like a whip; you could positively hear the crack of the whiplash. I admired them both enormously, and would sit in on rehearsals watching like a lynx for fear of missing anything.

After a while, sooner or later, you do then get an idea of the profession. But it takes time, and you have to be patient. Patient with yourself, too, with the development of your own personality, particularly if, as in my own case, you don't easily fit into a collective or an ensemble. I am afraid that Thielemann the beginner was inclined to talk big, and often covered up for his insecurity by impudence. And of course, as an assistant you sit in on so many rehearsals that it is easy to think: I could do better than that! Then one day you are about to conduct the first *Parsifal* of your life (mine was at the German Opera House, Berlin, in 1998, directed by Götz Friedrich), and you realize how difficult it is and find that the music you love so much is either congealing into something slow-moving or crumbling to pieces – just because you love it so much, and because you think that Wagner's 'festival work for the consecration of a stage' should be solemn and very, very slow. Only when working at Bayreuth did I realize what a misapprehension that is.

You can't learn conducting in itself. The only teaching that I ever really had was, as I said above, from Hans Hilfsdorf, director of the Berlin Academy of Singing. This is how to indicate four-four time, said Hilsdorf, this is three-four time, this is a pause, this is a beat of five, this is a beat of six – fundamentally, that was it. Your two hands have to operate as independently of each other as possible, he also explained, the right hand is responsible for beating time, the left hand for everything else. Why? Because, for instance, it can happen that you have to use your left hand to help a singer who has lost his way and keep signalling, 'wrong, wrong, wrong' to him until you can bring him back into the ensemble again. As you do so, of course you must not lose your own way, and so the right hand must keep the beat going as regular as clockwork. I never really learned more than that.

Richard Wagner constantly dominated my years of apprenticeship and travelling. He was always knocking at the door, and then not quite coming in: there was the episode with Ahlendorf and the Prelude to *The Mastersingers*, there was the Karajan competition, my audition with Hollreiser, my first time as assistant to Karajan with *Parsifal*, my first time as assistant to Barenboim with *Tristan*. Even George Alexander Albrecht tested me in Hanover with a passage from the third act of *Tristan* (*Noch losch das Licht nicht aus*; 'Extinguish not the light'), which

I performed for him from memory. And it was to go on in much the same way: Wagner, always Wagner. Although a beginner has no business with that subject, since Wagner was and is a matter of prime importance in all opera houses. My ambition was spurred on all the more.

I don't hold esoteric opinions, but all the same I ask myself why I was so preoccupied with Wagner. A sense of being a kindred spirit? Fate? A particularly subtle set of circumstances? I have now been conducting Wagner for 30 years, and the wish to plunge head first into his scores may have become purified and refined, but it has never gone away. I do things differently today (that is to say, in organizing my time in general); I know how to husband my physical and emotional powers better. As I grow older, my tempi have become more fluid, and musically I am much more concerned than I used to be with transparency, in order to achieve the clarity so tellingly conjured up by Wagner. Some works, like *Tristan*, I have to put aside from time to time in order to recover from them – they take too much out of me. It is like a trip on drugs: you don't know whether you will ever find your way back again (an experience that I have spared myself). It is as if the membrane between art and life, between this world and the next, were getting thinner and thinner. An addictive element is part of the music of Richard Wagner, which is what makes him so much like a dangerous drug to me.

My official Wagnerian debut was in Italy in 1983, at a concert on the hundredth anniversary of Wagner's death at the Teatro La Fenice in Venice. The evening was attractively entitled *A Love Potion For Ever*, and I was to conduct the *Siegfried Idyll* and the Symphony in C major before the Swiss conductor Peter Maag took over on the podium for the *Wesendonck Lieder* and *Isolde's Liebestod*, with Katia Ricciarelli. Venice evokes many emotions in Wagnerians; after all, the Master died here in the Palazzo Vendramin-Calergi, and he conducted his last concert at La Fenice two months earlier for his wife Cosima's 45th birthday (with the same C major Symphony, a work of his youth). I had met Maag at the German Opera House in Berlin, and we understood each other at once: he as Furtwängler's former assistant, and I as a novice but with all sorts of ideas in my head. It was also Maag who soon after this, in 1981, brought me from Venice to be his assistant in a new production of

Tristan. He sometimes left me in charge of the rehearsals; for instance, I conducted Brangäne's song as she keeps watch, and the Prelude. That morning at La Fenice I had the Prelude played three times running, and after that I was in a state of such agitation, drenched with sweat, that I had to break off and take refuge in the hotel. As I couldn't stand it there either, I spent the rest of the day staggering through the city as if in delirium, under the steely blue winter sky of Venice, entirely enraptured and blissfully happy because I had conducted the Prelude to *Tristan*.

My full Wagnerian debut was in 1985, with a concert performance of *Rienzi* at the Lower Saxony State Theatre in Hanover. Then it was more or less one thing after another. In the 1988/9 season, when I was 29, I was appointed general music director at Nuremberg, where I conducted *Lohengrin* and *Tannhäuser* for the first time, as well as Pfitzner's *Palestrina*, Schumann's *Genoveva* and Weber's *Euryanthe*; I was to return to La Fenice in 1990 to conduct *Lohengrin* there. Inwardly, however, I could hardly wait to conduct *Tristan* for the first time. My opportunity came unexpectedly; in the autumn of 1988 Peter Ruzicka got in touch with me. He had just taken over from Rolf Liebermann as artistic director at the Hamburg State Opera House. He had obviously remembered the Karajan competition, and was calling to ask if I would like to take on some of the performances of *Tristan* in Ruth Berghaus's production, which had been something of a scandal. Would I! I knew that I could, scandal or not, but I also knew, of course, that it was a great risk. If I failed in Hamburg I could say goodbye to my career as a conductor of Wagner, and the danger of failing as a beginner with only two rehearsals behind me seemed high. Two rehearsals at the State Opera House of North Rhine-Westphalia on the Rothenbaum in Hamburg were to decide my fate.

I don't know what I would have done if it had gone wrong. Would I have gone on conducting, but not the works of Wagner? Would I have admitted that I was not yet mature enough to tackle *Tristan*? Would I have embarked on a different career with the Prussian Foundation for Castles and Gardens? A flop would certainly have left me in a state of deep crisis. Conducting for the sake of conducting has never interested me. Many have accused me of not being a musician who seeks his fortune in diversity, conducting works from early music to Stockhausen. It is true that I am more inclined to move in concentric circles. I have to proceed from a central point, my own central point, which means that I have never thought of my career, only and always of Wagner. If I had been woken at four in the morning and asked: what do you want to conduct? I would have cried: Wagner! And *Tristan*. So in a way I have staked everything on a single card, because of my obsession.

How did the Hamburg *Tristan* turn out? Today I would rather not hear it again. To be honest, I have only vague memories of it. Somehow or other it was all right. In spite of my nerves and hysteria, I gained confidence from somewhere, and in the end it was a success. Afterwards I couldn't sleep all night, I was in such a state of excitement and relief. At the time I didn't really notice the images of Berghaus's production: the notorious turbine in the first act, the stranded planet in the third act. But I was to return to Hamburg in 1993 for a revival of the production, when Berghaus herself was in charge of the set rehearsals, and they were a real revelation, my idea, so to speak, of an operatic Big Bang. She was a director who thought only of the music and nothing but the music in the design of the sets, addressing the score, not extraneous ideas or coincidences or dramatic whims. Of the other directors with whom I have worked so far, only Jean-Pierre Ponnelle and Götz Friedrich could do that.

In Hamburg I noticed how much the musicians in the pit depend on what is happening on stage. As long as the dramatic tension holds, the aesthetics of the set do not mean much to me, and I can conduct a performance of *Tristan* featuring deckchairs, or a turbine, or the Daedalus crater on the Moon. But there must be alchemy in the relationship between the stage and the pit, and Ruth Berghaus was able to conjure that up. She also said the musicians must light a fire down below in the pit, while the ice age reigns on the stage above. I think we made a good team – just because the difference between us could not have been greater: the critical East German and the epicurean West German, the convinced adherent of the Social Unity Party of the GDR and the apolitical Wessi, she a functionary, I probably boorish, she a Brechtian and I a pupil of Karajan – the list of labels and clichés could go on and on. For the rest, Ruth Berghaus could have been my mother.

She had me asking not only *how* Wagner was doing what he did, but also *why*. What does it mean when he makes the sun in the last act of *Tristan* flicker, so that you think he is still composing the black dots that you see when you have looked into the light for too long? What does it mean that love, every love, is an impossibility, magnificent excess, pure anarchy? That Tristan must die if Utopia is to live? In Heiner Müller's 1994 production of *Tristan* at Bayreuth, the set designer Erich Wonder made a tiny golden square appear behind Isolde, growing larger and brighter until the light filled the entire auditorium and only her outline could be seen. What a fabulous image! The consuming emotion of this conclusion, of all conclusions, the extinction of the individual, the power of music, the consolation of beauty, timelessness – it is all expressed in that image. I would have liked to express it like that myself.

The Hamburg *Tristan* gave a powerful impetus to my career as a Wagnerian conductor, and indeed my career as a whole. It was followed by engagements in Geneva, Rome, Bologna and the United States, and I accompanied the German Opera House in Berlin, which I had joined in 1991 with my *Lohengrin*, on tour to Japan. But I never heard anything from one small town in Upper Franconia, and it irritated me. I left my post as general music director at Nuremberg amidst some bad feeling, after a production of *Tristan* that won recognition beyond the local area; I was said to have been dancing at too many other weddings, which anyone could see was not the case. But Bayreuth lies at the gates of Nuremberg (or rather, to Wagnerians, Nuremberg lies at the gates of Bayreuth) – shouldn't Wolfgang Wagner, director of the Festival, and his wife Gudrun have come to one or other of the performances I conducted?

This question is one of the few blind spots in my relationship with the Wagner family. I have never found out whether they came to hear me or not, and I always felt embarrassed to ask. One way or another, I had to wait a long time for an invitation to Bayreuth. Nothing changed even when I became general music director at the German Opera House in Berlin in 1997, and Wagner was on the programme again, as he should be in such a great theatre. Had I lost my chance during my time as an assistant on the Green Hill? I was very precise and rigorous in my work, and I am sure not always as ingratiating as I might have been. Was there no call for any conductors other than Daniel Barenboim, James Levine and Giuseppe Sinopoli? Did I lack influential friends to back me? In retrospect, I will say that in the years when I was waiting for a sign from Bayreuth, I learned a useful lesson: never wait for anything, never want anything too much. Whether in the case of the Bayreuth Festival, or the Vienna Philharmonic, or the Semper Opera House in Dresden, such things always happen when you are not thinking of them. However, that assumes that when they do happen you will be well prepared.

And it happened exactly like that. In 1999 I was conducting a new production of *The Mastersingers* at the Lyric Opera in Chicago (with Jan-Hendrik Rootering as Hans Sachs, René Pape as Pogner, Nancy Gustafson as Eva and Gösta Winbergh as Stolzing). I was staying in a skyscraper on the 78th or 88th floor, or that was what it felt like, and could look out of the windows at Lake Michigan and down at the Magnificent Mile. It was snowing outside, the place was very comfortable, and I was just coming through my door with a plastic bottle of Coca-Cola and nachos or tacos of some kind, anyway something very unhealthy, when the phone rang. It was Reiner Barchmann, the double bass player from Dresden, who was orchestral director at Bayreuth at the time. 'Hello, I'm calling on behalf of Wolfgang Wagner – he'd like to talk to you. But I might as well say straight away that Herr Wagner will ask whether you'd like to conduct *The Mastersingers* for us.' I almost fell off my chair, nachos or tacos and all. Somehow or other I managed to stammer yes, and then hung up.

Next day Wolfgang Wagner called in person. He and Gudrun happened to be in the States, and we agreed to meet over a meal in Chicago. That first evening was entertaining and entirely uncomplicated, with stories about Knappertsbusch and Tietjen, and Wolfgang's brother Wieland. Once again I said yes to *The Mastersingers*, but meanwhile I had worked out that that was not enough for me. Naturally I was happy to step in as a replacement for Daniel Barenboim, who had other commitments, but a new production... And because the mood of the gathering was so good, and so was the wine, a moment came when I ventured to suggest it. Old Wagner just looked at me and said: '*Tann-häuser*, 2002, hmm,' (there was hardly a sentence that he didn't end with a little throwaway sound like that), 'yes, that would be the thing for you.' I was astonished. He had only been waiting for me to ask.

At one of the next *Mastersingers* performances in Chicago the Wagners were ensconced in the front row, right behind me. That is to say, the monitors (set up for the benefit of the singers and the stage manager) always showed Gudrun and Wolfgang as well. The backstage staff at the theatre were beside themselves: 'He looks *exactly* like his grandfather!' And they were right. Sometimes, when he was making his way through the front rows of the Festival Theatre during a rehearsal in Bayreuth, so that you saw him in profile, with his rippling white hair and that nose, you instinctively thought: there goes Richard Wagner himself, listening to his own music.

So from 2000 to 2002 I conducted *The Mastersingers* in Bayreuth, as well as *Parsifal* in 2001 (stepping in for Christoph Eschenbach) and Beethoven's Ninth Symphony; from 2005 *Tannhäuser*; and after 2006, as it soon turned out, also the new *Ring*. I had achieved my aim. Or had I? Does one ever?

In a certain way, yes, there is a Wagnerian aim to be achieved. For all who sense the aura of the opera house in Bayreuth and accept, even love its acoustic idiosyncrasies, conducting Wagner in his own theatre is the apex. There is nowhere higher to aim, and so far as my own need for expression and for beauty is concerned there is nothing more satisfying (although the individual works take effect in very different ways in the Bayreuth Festival Theatre). With success, however, my doubts have also grown. The more you know and can do, the more you find how much more there still is to know and to do. Then I think of the great figures of the past, Knappertsbusch in his white shirt and braces with his long baton, old Karajan, old Günter Wand, conductors who had no more to achieve on the podium, and I know that I am still light years away from that point. Music had become second nature to them, as my teacher Helmut Roloff always used to say. Richard Wagner confronts his conductors with such complex problems of technique and skill, such musical, mental, emotional, physical and intellectual difficulties, that any form of self-satisfaction or pride is misplaced. However high you climb on the Wagnerian ladder, there will still always be air above you.

Perhaps I don't show it these days, but in the last minutes before a performance I often feel, and not only in Bayreuth, that I would like to run away or drop dead. Say: goodbye, sorry, I can't do it, I've just this moment died. My stomach churns, my whole body rebels, and there is not just one weaker self protesting inside me but a whole troop of them. There are many stories about Carlos Kleiber, who suffered from this kind of stage fright. Apparently he once had to be brought from Munich to Bayreuth in a police car, because Wolfgang Wagner managed to persuade him to conduct a performance of *Tristan* after all when he had already declined to do it. Or there was the legendary note that Kleiber left for the Vienna Philharmonic after a bungled rehearsal of Beethoven's Fourth: 'Gone off into the wide blue yonder.' These are amusing anecdotes; we laugh at them, particularly as they are typical of Kleiber's other quirks. But I ask myself what state his mind was in. How great must his fear have been, and how enormously high his standards.

I couldn't react in that way; I am too down-to-earth, too aware of my obligations, and then again too frightened. At the moments when my weaker self protests, I say: all the same, I will do it. I will overcome myself. It's not a good idea to stand on the ten-metre diving board and refuse to jump.

Or as the late Beethoven implies in a late canon of 1825, with a text that runs: *Doktor sperrt das Tor dem Tod, Note hilft auch aus den Not.* * Yes, music helps us in our need. It always does.

---

* Translator's footnote: the German translates as: 'The doctor won't let death through the door, music helps us in our need.' There is a pun on *Note* (musical note) and *Not* (need).

II

Wagner's Cosmos

I WOULDN'T WANT TO MEET Richard Wagner in person. I think I would be afraid of him. If he were to come through the doorway, all 1.66 metres of him, maybe with unwashed hair under that velvet cap, talking away in his Saxon accent about the weather, his night's sleep, his dogs Russ and Putz and Molly, about satin trousers, dental ulcers, methods of administering enemas, his favourite women singers – it would be too much for me. I would be disillusioned. Not because I have such a strictly romantic image of him, but because I would have to face the ease with which the Wagnerian world disintegrates into the real and the possible. I would have to distinguish between the court Kapellmeister (the position as conductor that he achieved in Dresden), and the amateurish musician as which he liked to describe himself, and much more as well.

I suppose a conductor is assumed to know everything, but it can always be forgotten again. The older I grow, the less interest I take in the biographies of composers. After all, I have the scores, and it's all in there. Including, indeed in particular, the ambivalent and contradictory aspects of a composer.

How do I think of Wagner the man? As domineering, irascible, foolish and intensely aware of his mission. As a driven, crazed demagogue. Hans Neuenfels once wrote, when he felt that he had met him in Bayreuth (he was fantasizing, of course), that at the sight of the Master, it was 'as if he were pinned down like a moth in a collection'. I can well imagine it: eyes like daggers, seeing everything only too clearly! On the other hand, Wagner did indeed see a great many things very clearly, and his longing for totality in art, a kind of art that signifies everything, is quite familiar to me. Perhaps we are not so very different in our passions after all, although I myself find it easier to keep my feet on the ground. Wagner, on the other hand, liked to conjure up another Neuschwanstein in his imagination. In 1865, the year of *Tristan* and after his first meeting with King Ludwig II in Munich, he notes: 'I can and must live only in a kind of cloud. As I am entirely an artist, I can lead only an artificial life. That means hardly mingling with other people, not talking to them, or only in jest, never seriously, for then what I have to say always becomes passionate and useless. [...] I set up a complete court for myself. [...] At once I have not a care in the world. [...] and then it is like being in Versailles at the court of Louis XIV, living amidst the most rigid etiquette, like a puppet on a string.'

No doubt reality looked different. Wagner was in fact down-to-earth and practical, and at the same time 'amazingly hot-headed' – it is in the family to this day. He did not really float on clouds (or he would not have had to dream of it), but was to be found crawling around on the Bayreuth stage down below, furious because all was not exactly as he wanted it. 'The architect of the Festival Theatre, that man Brückwald from Leipzig, is an idiot! The wood creaks at every step! And where's the neck of my dragon that was made in London? Why has the machinery for the Rhine maidens gone wrong again? And who the devil ordered those tasteless provincial Red Indian costumes?' Ultimately Wagner's struggles are not so far from the everyday life of the theatre as it still is. True, these days Siegfried no longer wears a bearskin on stage, but if the director doesn't envisage a cliché-ridden version of the Rhine maidens, they are still apt to present problems.

That is another reason why, as a conductor, I don't feel that I have to know everything about Wagner's life, although what I really would ask him if he unexpectedly walked in through the door is: my dear Wagner, how can a man of your character and your skill have been so wrong in his judgement of Felix Mendelssohn-Bartholdy? And there's another thing, too: why, as a gifted practitioner of music, do you have so much *forte* in the orchestra in the first scene of *The Mastersingers*? Who can ever hope to sing against it?

I

Wagalaweia and *Hojotoho*!
A First Approach to Wagner's Music Drama

Wagner was, as the French Impressionists in general have been accused of being, unashamedly over the top. A Pied Piper, the ultimate master presiding over his witches' kitchen. Much in his music seems to have been positively thrown in at random – and yet it is precisely, pitilessly calculated. Wagner sat in front of his music paper like a man in a laboratory, with hissing and bubbling and vapours all over the place, and no one knew whether the study where he composed might not be blown sky-high at any moment. A little more strychnine here, a touch of orange zest there to disguise the bitter almond flavour, and finally a dash of sweet-smelling bergamot oil – and the poison, the drug, is ready. The third act of *Tristan* is finished, radically manic-depressive, and so is the second act of *Parsifal*, with its wild, unruly mixtures of sound.

Performing musicians are by definition practitioners; that is their salvation and sometimes their curse, and they approach Wagner and his magic spells in a practical way. They will argue for hours on end about the third horn from the left, where the chorus *has* to stand in this or that scene, where it *must not* on any account stand, and at first sight there are no preconditions, there is no particular artistic concept, no musical aesthetic or anything else in the background. That is of course deceptive, for without an overall perspective and a background, opera won't work, particularly not in Wagner's case. Anyone who doesn't wonder what his witches' kitchen actually consists of is lost. Where do the ingredients of his concoctions come from, where do the pots and pans hang, is he still cooking over an open flame or on gas? In other words, the conductor must start out with a precise understanding of the Wagnerian orchestra, he should study the language of Wagner's

libretti, and know why Wagner chose those particular subjects and
not others. Wagner was entering virgin territory in all three fields –
the orchestra, the libretto, the subject – and in all three fields he is
constantly disconcerting us. The orchestra: enormous and noisy; the
libretti incomprehensible and long. The subjects: old-fashioned and
convoluted! I think it's time to start casting some light on the darkness
of these prejudices.

The Wagnerian orchestra

The Wagnerian orchestra is a paradox. The larger it is, the more refined
and quiet and the more like chamber music it sounds, while the smaller
it is, the louder is its effect. Loudest of all are the more youthful of the
composer's works, *Das Liebesverbot* (*The Ban on Love*) and *Der fliegende
Holländer* (*The Flying Dutchman*). But the Wagnerian orchestra is not
always the same; the instrumentation can differ widely. In *The Flying
Dutchman*, for instance, there are only four horns and two trumpets
in the pit, and the sound can be deafening. In *Twilight of the Gods*, on
the other hand, there are eight horns (two of which can be tenor tubas
and two bass tubas), three bassoons (the second being a contrabassoon),
a contrabass tuba, three trumpets and a bass trumpet as well as three
trombones and a bass trombone – and the sound is nothing like as loud.
True, there are passages here played with a triple *forte*, but they are
very specific, or the effect would be lost. Wagner differentiates more
and more subtly in the composition of his orchestra. To express what
he wants to express, he employs a constantly increasing, ever richer and
more diverse range of instruments. The orchestra becomes larger and
larger, but at the same time the musicians seldom play all at once now.

So far as the strings are concerned (first and second violins, violas,
cellos and double basses), Wagner likes to write for 'an excellent and
strong' body of instruments. In principle, he wanted as many musicians
in the pit as it could hold. In Bayreuth, that is to say after 1876, that
means an ensemble of 16, 16, 12, 12 and 8 – 16 first and 16 second
violins, 12 violas, 12 cellos and 8 double basses. There are two remarkable features here. For one thing, Wagner wants two equally large
groups of violins. That may be on account of the covered orchestra

pit at Bayreuth, the 'mystic abyss', in which the second violins – sitting on the conductor's left – have to play under the ceiling. To make up for this 'disadvantage', Wagner's orchestra, unlike those used by Mozart, Weber, Verdi and Strauss, has as many second as first violins. For another, we can see how sparingly Wagner's music employs bass instruments. Eight double basses out of 32 stringed instruments are not very many. The impression of deep, dark sound pouring out like volcanic lava may therefore derive from entirely different harmonic, synaesthetic or other such subjective factors.

Among the wind instruments, the Wagner tuba (also called the horn tuba, the *Ring* tuba or the Rheingold tuba) is a special case. Wagner had it built especially for the *Ring*. The name is misleading, since this tuba is not a tuba at all but one of the French horn family. Its shape is reminiscent of the tenor horn, slender and elegantly elongated. The instrument comes in two sizes and pitches, in B flat (in the tenor register, when it is smaller) and in F (in the bass register, when it is correspondingly larger). The Wagner tuba sounds like a tuba without losing the characteristically rounded, noble impression of a horn. It has a natural, slightly shadowed, almost mystical timbre, and it shows how meticulously Richard Wagner tried to put his own ideas of sound into practice. Ever since he had begun thinking of an opera on the subject of *The Ring of the Nibelung*, that is to say since the 1850s, he had been in search of this instrument. The famous Belgian wind specialist Adolphe Sax (to whom we owe the saxophone) could not produce one to satisfy him, and the hybrid that Wagner wanted was developed only with the help of the Mainz firm of Alexander in the early 1860s. The Wagner tuba is also used in the late symphonies of the Wagnerian Anton Bruckner, and in Richard Strauss's *Die Frau ohne Schatten* (*The Woman without a Shadow*) and his Alpine Symphony.

Wagner's orchestra also contains another special instrument: the Beckmesser harp, as it is known, in *The Mastersingers*. This is another of Wagner's own creations: a small harp with 20 steel strings and two pedals, imitating the sound of the lute with which the town clerk Sixtus Beckmesser tries to make an impression as a suitor for Eva's hand in the second act. By comparison, a concert harp has 47 strings, usually made of gut, seven pedals, and a much suppler sound. Why didn't Wagner use a real lute for Beckmesser's performance? Because it would hardly have held its own against the opulent scoring of the *Mastersingers* orchestra (four horns, three trumpets, three trombones, bass tuba and a large number of instruments being played on stage). In addition, we have here the principle of parody, which involves a certain artificiality. In terms of composition, Beckmesser may have been given the most progressive and unconventional music in the entire opera – but he never has a genuine chance of winning Eva's heart, and the harp says so clearly.

A layman will probably imagine that it is much more difficult to conduct a large orchestra than one of small or medium size, but that is not so. Indeed, it is often easier to stand on the podium and conduct Wagner than to conduct Beethoven or Mozart. For a large orchestra is not just more anonymous, it usually offers more opportunities to give the music structure. In addition, it is not common for all the musicians to be playing at the same time.

Incidentally, Wagner's chorus does not always sing at full strength either. Sometimes the music is composed in that way, but sometimes it obeys the practical demands of performance. Wilhelm Furtwängler is considered the first to have pruned the chorus in the notorious brawl scene at the end of Act 2 of *The Mastersingers*. In this scene the good citizens of Nuremberg, whose sleep Beckmesser has disturbed, gradually come to blows with each other. Musically, the score here is based on a *fugato*, a fugue-like structure, which is to say that Wagner gives the utmost chaos an appearance of mathematical precision – perhaps because ultimately the good folk of Nuremberg cannot change their own nature. In any event, it is not easy to adapt this 'fugue' for a chorus 130 singers strong, particularly as there is a certain amount of action in progress on stage. Furtwängler regretted these problems of co-ordination and hit upon the useful idea of splitting the chorus into a main body, which does not move about much during the scene and keeps the musical scaffolding in place, and separate groups that sometimes sing, sometimes act, and alternate with each other as much as possible. The spectators hardly notice this distinction, so it is generally adopted today. Quite apart from that, the music would be much too loud anyway if all the masters, journeymen, apprentices and neighbours of both sexes were letting fly in a full *tutti* effect at the same time.

With time, as I have said above, Wagner's orchestra became ever richer and larger. In practical performance, this development led to the transfer of the strong string section of the *Ring* to the earlier works as well. In a production at Bayreuth of *Tannhäuser* or *Lohengrin* today, there are also 16 first and 16 second violins in the pit, regardless of whether there would ever have been room for them all at the premières of *Tannhäuser* in Dresden in 1845, and *Lohengrin* in the small Weimar Opera House in 1850. At that time Richard Wagner was probably content with eight first and eight second violins, and they will have served his purpose well. But what is correct for a historically faithful performance? To stick to the presumed original composition of the orchestra, thus showing why he was not content to let it rest at that? Or to defend him from himself by assuming that even in his younger days he would rather have had an 'excellent' and 'strong' number of musicians performing? To me, a historically authentic performance entails reading the music with the eyes of the composer's time and hearing it with today's ears: to understand what is written, see it in relation to the opportunities then available – and transfer the effect to present circumstances. Myself, I would like to hear the difference between early and late Wagnerian operas in the orchestral settings as well as other respects. Even such a great master did not fall fully formed from heaven.

Words and music

Richard Wagner was his own librettist from the first. There may be pragmatic reasons for that – his life, full of vicissitudes as it was, would hardly have allowed for tranquil co-operation with a writer. But the main reason must be that his Utopian concept of the *Gesamtkunstwerk*, the total work of art, never envisaged anything else. It was Wagner's aim to synchronize all the disciplines of the theatre with each other: text, music, dance, décor and lighting. At the time of his central writings *Die Kunst und die Revolution* (*Art and Revolution*), 1849; *Das Kunstwerk der Zukunft* (*The Work of Art of the Future*), 1850; and *Oper und Drama* (*Opera and Drama*), 1851, this idea may not have been entirely new; it was known in classical antiquity, in the Florentine origins of opera in the late sixteenth century and in the Romantic period. But no one formulated it as consistently and comprehensively as Richard Wagner, or on such a grand scale. By extending his concept to include architecture, the artistic circumstances of production and the manner of the audience's reception, he develops no less than a theory of society. It runs like this: 'Drama is imaginable only as the fullest expression of a joint desire for an artistic statement; that desire, however, will in turn manifest itself only as joint participation.' In other words: the operatic audience constitutes the public of the future. 'To remove the population from their common everyday interests, to bring them to devotion and to understand the highest and most ardent feelings of which the human mind is capable' – that is the task of art. Wagner's idea can be seen lived out in practice from 1876 onwards, particularly in Bayreuth.

Here *what* is concerned is as important as *why* it is concerned, and vice versa. To Wagner the text, the written word, is the 'procreating seed' (that is to say masculine), and the music is the 'element that brings forth' (that is to say feminine). Music, he says elsewhere, is the breath that gives language 'the power to move'. One is unthinkable without the other, and Wagner accordingly constructs the relation between speech and sound as symbiotic, often onomatopoeic. Sometimes the text is merely conversation, sometimes it accelerates the course of the action, sometimes it serves as material, as sound to pad out the music. Lines like those of Tristan and Isolde, *gib Vergessen / dass ich lebe; / nimm mich auf / in deinem Schoss, / löse von / der Welt mich los!*, for instance ('give oblivion / that I may live, / raise me up into thy lap, / ah, release me/ from the world') could perhaps be replaced by others; they are more like amorous babbling than language that makes any literal sense. What matters here is for the singers to perform first *legato*, then quietly, and thirdly very slowly – 'very softly', Wagner writes on the score.

I could cite any number of passages that we may laugh at now. Wagner is thought particularly rewarding in that respect. The Saxon dialect seems to play a part in his texts. And then there is the huge obstacle of inevitably incomprehensible passages to be overcome (something from which opera in general suffers, not only in Wagner). I don't think that he always intended it or even decided to accept it. He can't have thought that Tristan's laments in the third act could be heard distinctly – the tenor has to make too much of an effort for that, since the orchestra is permanently playing *forte* and *fortissimo*. Nor can he have supposed that in the first scene of the first act anyone would ever understand Isolde's *Entartet Geschlecht, / unwert der Ahnen! / Wohin, Mutter, / vergabst du die Macht, / über Meer und Sturm zu gebieten?* ('Degenerate race, / unworthy of our ancestors! / Why, O mother, / did you give up power / to command sea and storm?'). Indeed, why else did he write in the stage directions that she is 'raving wildly'? Is the point here her turbulent emotion in itself?

Richard Wagner is one of those who rediscovered the alliterative verse form in the nineteenth century. This variety of alliteration complied with his requirements in several ways: it helped his libretti to appear in what looked, although artificial, authentically medieval, and in addition their language could be made musical in itself, so to speak, through the onomatopoeia of alliterative initials, as if the text were at an early stage of composition. It is easy to laugh at Wagner's alliterative lines, and there is often good reason to do so. Phonetic creations of his own such as the Rhine maidens' *Wagalaweia* and the Valkyries' *Hojotoho* have passed into the collective vocabulary of German. There are also lines like Alberich's *garstig glattem / glitschrigem Glimmer* [roughly translated, 'sorrily smooth / slippery shimmer'] which invite a guffaw. Apart from the fact that Wagner could in fact handle irony and had enough humour to laugh at himself, these digs at him seem to me cheap. Are we to turn our backs on one of the best librettists in operatic history because of a single *Wallala weiala weia*?

First and foremost one must acknowledge Wagner's achievement. Think of the many large tomes of source material through which he made his way: the *Edda*, the different versions of the *Nibelungenlied*, Gottfried von Strassburg's *Tristan* and Wolfram von Eschenbach's *Parzival*, and many more. And how well, with what a wide command of the material, he musters all the strands, subjects and levels of the plot and arranges them in good order. Wagner also set standards as a dramatist, and can compete with professionals in that area – professionals such as Arrigo Boito, Giuseppe Verdi's librettist (who translated *Rienzi*, *Tristan und Isolde* and the *Wesendonck Lieder* into Italian). Boito and Verdi's *Simon Boccanegra* and *Otello* are undoubtedly operatic masterpieces, demonic and full of tension. But the relationship between the words and the music is very different. Without wishing to go into detail and compare developmental impulses in both works, one could say that Boito and Verdi are setting the words to music – Wagner is setting sound itself. Boito and Verdi are cutting, distilling, dramatizing – Wagner is letting the sound flow. Much as I love Italian opera, a heart like mine, devoted to sound, will always beat more strongly for Wagner.

There are differences of level, however, in the sheer mass of textual material that Wagner wrote. Some phrases no one knows and no one ever hears, because they are simply lost in the tumult. And just as well. A line about the stallion having his way with a mare is no great loss. On the other hand, Wagner also writes very fine, poetic, well-thought-out lines. Brünnhilde's *War es so schmählich / was ich verbrach, / dass mein Verbrechen so schmählich du bestrafst?* ('Did I commit so shameful a crime that you so shamefully must punish it?') is a line with some weight to it. Lohengrin's *Das süsse Lied verhallt; wir sind allein, / zum ersten Mal allein* ('The sweet song dies away; we are alone / alone for the first time') has a breath of eroticism about it. Often the language concentrates on sound so much that the singers are not really aware of what they are singing, but not all in Wagner is babble or aural padding. I see precise interaction with the libretti as essential. It was the idea of Walter Felsenstein, founder of the so-called realistic music theatre and for many years director of the Comic Opera House of Berlin, to get his singers to read aloud the libretto of every new production (not just of works by Wagner). I sometimes suggest doing the same in rehearsal: if there are any problems of declamation, it can be extremely useful to read aloud a line or a passage exactly as the German language naturally has it, disregarding the musical rhythm. For in general, Wagner composed just as one would speak the libretto.

When for once he does not, he usually has a good reason. Before the quintet in the third act of *The Mastersingers*, for instance, he deliberately does not set the words as the rhythm of speech would have them. Hans Sachs speaks of the '*seligen Morgentraum-Deutweise*', putting this very remarkable compound word in inverted commas.* Wagner, skilful

---

* Translator's note: it refers to the method of interpretation of Walther's Prize Song, which begins with mention of the singer's morning dream. The element *Deut* indicates interpretation, so the compound means 'morning-dream interpretation'.

as he is, places the emphasis neither on *Morgen* nor on *Weise*, but on *Deut* – *Morgentraum* – *Deutweise*. Why? To show that it is all about the correct interpretation of what has happened: Eva's love for Stolzing, Sachs's own renunciation of his love for her (*Mein Kind: / von Tristan und Isolde / kenn'ich ein traurig Stück: / Hans Sachs war klug, und wollte / nichts von Herrn Markes Glück*),* and above all Stolzing's Prize Song, a new kind of Mastersong that appears to break all the rules but at the end of the singing competition carries off the prize. We must get used to it, Wagner is saying with a single shift of emphasis, as if pointing it out with a wink, we must get used to new music.

Neither the conductor nor the singers will be able to bring off that effect unless they have mastered the German language. We are living in a globalized musical world, and if a conductor does not know German it is usual for his assistants to do part of the work for him by familiarizing the singers with the pronunciation and articulation of the libretto, pointing out instances of wit and irony, indeed all the more important questions of content. I think this is wrong, indeed fatal. The fact that Wagner sets what is happening on stage to music, or rather expresses it musically in the way I have just described, does not mean that we can rely solely on the music. I learned Italian in order to understand Verdi and Puccini better. To this day, however, I do not speak Russian or Czech – and I would not want to conduct Janáček and Tchaikovsky in the original languages of their operas, but would rather, in the old-fashioned way, conduct them in German translation. Aesthetically and politically that is not particularly correct, but if I do not know exactly what the libretto is saying I deprive myself of a vital dimension. The conductor must know *what* he is conducting.

Wagner seduces and tempts us with his perfumes, his orgies of sound, his idiosyncratic essence. If we are not to be lost in the psychedelic state of intoxication that he evokes, we have only one chance: we must take him at his word, literally, we must understand what can be understood, and cast light into the furthest corner of his box of tricks. What still remains of the riddle is quite large enough.

---

* Translator's note: 'My child, of Tristan and Isolde / a sad tale I could tell. / Hans Sachs was wise, and did not want / the fate that Marke befell.'

The subjects

Today the subjects of Wagner's operas often do not appear to us very seductive, indeed they are more likely to put us off. Why these worlds of Germanic myth, full of dark rites and cults, with their Norns, elves, trolls and Valkyries? We like the bright light of the ancient legends of classical antiquity; we are not so much at ease with Wotan and Erda. However, Wagner must also be seen as a man of his time. The nineteenth century was a period of young, emergent nations and their symbols. After more than 600 years Cologne Cathedral was finally completed, Marienburg Castle and other historic buildings were restored, enthusiasm for Poland broke out in Prussia in 1830 – and the whole sense of self-assurance founded on the past peaked in 1871 in a project as visionary as it was speculative, the founding of the German Reich. That is the spirit into which Wagner was born in 1813, and he drew on it to the end of his life. Wagner saw himself as both a conservative and a revolutionary; from the first, the tension between those two aspects of his nature was essential to his art. It is also the driving force that we still feel in his work today.

Richard Wagner wanted to describe life as it is, all of life. For that he needed material that both underpinned this requirement and also allowed him enough freedom. He therefore needed myths, but fundamentally he was only making use of such sources as the *Edda*, the *Nibelungenlied*, the *Tristan* and *Parzival* epics, seeing them as instrumental for his own purposes. He wore these mythological writings like precious archaic robes, costumes in which he pursued very different, contemporary, subversive ends. Wagner's idea was not just to set either the *Edda* or the *Nibelungenlied* to music – that was far from his mind. He wanted to create an international form of drama describing, on a gigantic scale, what happens when modern man forgets himself in striving for wealth and possessions. First he conceived the idea, then he looked for the myth or other subject that would convey it, not vice versa. We may take that as a general Wagnerian principle. He could probably just as well have taken the story of Romeo and Juliet instead of the legend of Tristan and Isolde as his point of departure, but in the middle of the nineteenth century Shakespearean subjects had to some extent given way to an enthusiasm for the courtly Middle Ages, and that was probably the deciding factor.

Seen in that light, Wagner's path towards the myths he used makes sense. As a child of his time, he was attracted by the Middle Ages and did not have to make great efforts to justify his choice of this or that subject. A *Lohengrin* or *Tannhäuser* theme was easily understood in itself; after all, people identified with their forebears and liked to see them as examples. They were regarded as guarantors of the collective identity that had been more or less lost since the Middle Ages, and was now due for revival. Wagner provided the models. However, the detailed use that he made of the legendary characters and their stories in political, psychological and aesthetic terms is another matter. He was careful never to damage the historical disguise that he adopted.

To me, however, Wagner's modernity ultimately lies in the music rather than the subjects of his operas. I have always kept a certain distance from those, and will readily confess that I still do. I have nothing against his vision of the total work of art, and certainly not against Wagner as a librettist who made virtuoso use of language. Perhaps I see only the costume into which he slips, and distrust it because I am far more interested in what lies behind or within it. In writing opera, Richard Strauss too likes to work with mythological subjects, although on Greek rather than Germanic themes (think of Elektra, Ariadne and Daphne). Apart from the fact that, as I said above, this Hellenic world is more familiar to us, I feel much the same about Strauss. As a conductor, am I really expressing concern for the fate of Ariadne, the king's daughter, as she laments her lover's abandonment of her on Naxos, or am I wondering why Strauss set this subject as the opera within an opera, and what that element of artifice in his music is trying to tell me? Probably the latter interests me more, and this discrepancy was already present in Wagner – in his case with a strong tradition behind it. Handel, Mozart and Gluck all tried to break new ground in musical theatre, and succeeded. The difference in Wagner is just that there is a particularly wide gulf between the archaism of his subjects and the avant-garde nature of his music, as if one were deliberately pointing to the other. What a challenge. And what a stroke of good luck.

2

'If you weren't all such tedious fellows':
Wagner and his Conductors

Wagner's visions became architecture in Bayreuth. Nowhere else do we see his blueprint for another, freer, more just and more artistic world so closely as in the Festival Theatre there. And whether or not we know our way around the Wagnerian theory of the total work of art, what strikes us here more than anything is the way that every little cog-wheel in the whole is important; the end result depends on all the details. Only the conductor stands out a little from the Wagnerian collective. In the orchestra pit at Bayreuth he is enthroned higher above the musicians than in any other opera house in the world, like a preacher in the pulpit. The conductor is king of the evening, the composer's deputy and assistant; all the threads come together in his hands, both figuratively and in practice. So I would like to devote a chapter to him here, for if we are in search of a gauge to help us deal with the extreme demands of Wagner's art, we shall find it first and foremost in the honourable ranks of his conductors. And if we want to get to know them, we must begin with Wagner himself. After all, like most composers of his time he was also his own interpreter, and he made a name for himself as a conductor.

Wagner on the conductor's podium

With Mendelssohn and Hector Berlioz, Richard Wagner may be regarded as one of the first professional conductors. It shows, for instance, in his use of a baton. Not that the baton itself was new in the nineteenth century, but it gave the conductor new power and the music itself a new dimension. During the eighteenth century, proceedings were usually directed by the instrumental soloists, or by the leader of the orchestra sitting with the first violins, and if time was indicated at all it was *audibly*, conveyed to all the musicians by tapping or knocking on the floor with a stick. Remember the famous tale of the French composer Jean-Baptiste Lully, who drove a stick of that kind into his foot in the heat of the moment, refused medical treatment for the injury and died of blood poisoning. Then, at the beginning of the nineteenth century, the stick moves from a vertical to a horizontal position, emancipating itself, as it were, from the force of gravity by becoming an extension of the human arm rather than an old-fashioned percussion instrument – thereby making the conductor the centre and focal point of the performance.

Apart from the fact that Lully's misfortune could never have happened to Wagner (who would have gone to a doctor at once anyway), it is not easy to form an image of his conducting. Mendelssohn, writes his sister Fanny, used 'a nice, lightweight whalebone baton covered with white leather', while Berlioz, also according to Fanny, had a 'huge baton made of linden-wood, with the bark still on it'. Similarly, Wagner's baton was obviously not one of the slender, more modern kind, and in the older manner he held it a little way from the lower end. That does not suggest a particularly flexible beat and fine musical brushstrokes. Rather, Willi Bithorn's silhouette of Wagner conducting conveys his sheer energy, and the characteristic position adopted – arms ecstatically raised aloft, coat-tails flying, his whole figure rearing up as he stands on tiptoe, passing the wind he raises straight on to the musical notes. But for the unmistakable Wagnerian profile – that nose and chin – we might think we were looking at one of those silhouettes that Otto Böhler did of Gustav Mahler a little later.

I will turn, then, to Gustav Adolf Kietz's *Memories of Richard Wagner.* Kietz tells us that: 'Head raised, torso motionless, his left hand resting by his side and his right hand holding the baton, conducting not with his whole arm but from his wrist – that is how Wagner stands before the orchestra in performance. Outwardly his passionate nature seems to be under control, but it vents itself in the play of his facial expression and, in particular, the look in his eyes, which he describes as his most important means of conveying what he wants.' To me, that sounds credible. But Kietz was a sculptor; perhaps his account owes more to the physical appearance of his subject than to the musical facts?

It is even more difficult to form an idea of Wagner's style as a conductor. There is no shortage of witnesses, with plenty of statements by
Wagner himself and by critics, close friends and arch-enemies alike.
From these, we might conclude that Wagner's conducting was notable
mainly for 'changes of tempo', a '*rubato* technique' that was always
breaking its bounds, and great 'expressivity'. But did those terms mean
the same in 1855 as they do today? The career of the conductor as a
solo performer was still something of an innovation, and the idea of any
musician conducting others from the podium was suspect in itself – was
it just sensationalism? Today, of course, it is just what the audience
expects. In addition, we would probably despair of the technical standards of orchestral musicians at that time. The line between subjectivity
and carelessness, anarchy and dilettantism must have been very fluid. It
is also important to remember that all his life Wagner regarded himself
as a composer rather than a conductor. To him, conducting was more
of a crutch than a passion, more a means to an end than the end itself,
a strategy. He wanted fame at any price – so that he could promote the
fame of his music dramas to better effect.

To be honest, I have no idea how he managed it. Not only was he
self-taught (which did not mean much at the time), he was a poor
pianist and a hopeless violinist. He even had difficulty in reading a
score, and transposing his *own* compositions for the piano was hard
work for him. What was someone with such poor qualifications doing
in front of an orchestra? And how could he dismiss the normal operatic
and concert practice of the time as 'a travesty' and 'useless'? Where did
his hubris come from?

But upon a single glance at the score of *Tristan* or *Parsifal*, that argument dissolves into thin air. We are left facing a huge discrepancy. The
man who, among all his contemporaries, was least like a virtuoso in
practice – not a youthful prodigy like Mendelssohn, not a musician
of demonic energy like Paganini, not a free spirit like Franz Liszt
– ploughs the musical landscape more deeply than any of them, as a
creative artist himself rather than a creative interpreter of the work of
others, as composer and conductor alike. We often read that Wagner
liked to describe himself as a dilettante in order to make all the experts,
all the guardians of tradition, look foolish – and to appear, in the end,

surrounded by the aura of a messiah. George Bernard Shaw puts it rather more neatly in saying that, with Wagner, 'it is the adept musician of the old school who has everything to unlearn'.

The Wagner School

From all that we know and that has been written about him, Wagner liked conducting works that he knew by heart (his favourites were Beethoven's symphonies, which naturally endears him to me). That also explains the particular 'look in his eyes' mentioned by Kietz, his emotional approach to the musicians. As a conductor, Wagner saw himself as a musician realizing musical works, a congenial re-creator of them. His aim was for the audience to experience a piece as if it were being created there and then, for their own ears. Wagner wanted to bring art into the present moment, and the world with it (for what else would be the nature of a successful performance?). Many of his ideas, in particular the practical ones, are still effective today. Without Richard Wagner, theatrical revolutionary that he was, the modern theatre would be a very different place. Dimming the house lights during a performance, new-fangled gas lighting on stage, an auditorium allowing the whole audience good visibility – we owe all that and more to Wagner.

However, a messiah needs disciples – and Richard Wagner had the Wagner School. It is interesting to do a little archaeological digging at this point. We begin with the four first-generation representatives: Hans Richter (who conducted the première of the *Ring*); Arthur Nikisch (conductor of the Leipzig Gewandhaus Orchestra and the Berlin Philharmonic); Felix Mottl (who was assistant at the première of the *Ring*, and is said to have lent a hand in propelling the legendary vehicle of the Rhine maidens); as well as Hans von Bülow (Cosima's first husband, an ancestor of the humorist Loriot).* Von Bülow later took the young Richard Strauss under his wing; Richter and Mottl taught, among others, Alfred Cortot and Hans Knappertsbusch; while Nikisch in turn influenced Wilhelm Furtwängler and Gustav Mahler. Bruno Walter was among the latter's pupils.

* Translator's note: Vicco von Bülow, 1923–2011, German graphic artist, actor and humorist.

It reads like the perfect family tree of the modern conductor, but it
is not, if only because there is more than one such family tree. Even
Wagner had to accept the existence of Mendelssohn (with his whalebone
baton) and Berlioz, before him and in his own time; Furtwängler always
had his opposite, Arturo Toscanini. After the early 1960s, Karajan had
Nikolaus Harnoncourt and other early music specialists close on his
heels – and even in my own generation people divide conductors into
two schools: adherents of the German sound (whatever that may mean)
versus adherents of the non-German sound, the emotional versus the
rhetorical, the instinctive versus the intellectual. With the best will in
the world I don't see how anyone can conduct 'instinctively' or 'intellectually'. All I know is that we should be on our guard against the
distinctions drawn by ideologues.

If we look at conductors who have actually worked at Bayreuth we
come first, and inevitably, to the many members of the Wagner School.
Photographs of all the Bayreuth conductors hang in the famous Rogues'
Gallery, a corridor some 20 metres long, partly underground, linking
the stage and restaurant areas of the Festival House. In fact the place is
more of a tunnel – cold, low-ceilinged, oddly lit and perfunctorily plas-
tered. Here, on both sides, hang the portraits of all the conductors who
have ever worked on the Green Hill (at present 73 in all), from Hans
Richter in 1876 to Philippe Jordan, who made his debut here in 2012.
All of them, we may note, conductors, no singers or directors; such was
Wolfgang Wagner's edict in the 1970s. Great names like Furtwängler,
Toscanini and Knappertsbusch hang beside those not so well known,
such as Karl Elmendorff and Thomas Schippers; charismatic musicians beside honest craftsmen; the lucky and the luckless. In no other
opera house is the past so ever present, in its practical and aesthetic, its
mystic and its sensuous aspects alike. If you have chosen to eat pork
and dumplings rather than salad in the interval, you repent your choice
twice over on meeting the stern eye of Pierre Boulez on your way back
to *Twilight of the Gods* or the third act of *The Mastersingers*.

Many of my colleagues see this phalanx of grave young men (as
yet, I am sorry to say, there is not a young woman among them) as a
threat, a gauntlet that they must run. I think the tradition in Bayreuth
had many faces from the first. They all look at you, and in the thick

of rehearsals and the Festival you often don't have time to look back. However, now and then I stop in front of some of my colleagues and have little conversations with them in my head. It is fascinating to look more closely at some of their faces and their stories. As a Wagnerian, I have to know whose shoulders I am standing on. I have to know so that I can forget it again. For unless I forget, I can do nothing of my own.

The Bayreuth Rogues' Gallery

From the pit, you first turn right up a ramp, then go through double doors into a storage area containing cases and chests for the large stringed instruments, the double basses and cellos – and then you are looking at the face of the first conductor. It is not, as many would expect, the face of Richard Wagner. He did conduct his own works, but never in Bayreuth. At least, not officially; he did not have time (as director of the *Ring* and *Parsifal* himself) to concentrate enough on conducting. Only on 29 August 1882, at the last performance of *Parsifal* in the summer of its première, did he take over the baton from Hermann Levi after the transformation music in the third act, and conducted his 'festival opera for the dedication of a stage' to its end – unnoticed by the audience because of the covered pit. Talking to their children that night about 'what had happened', writes Cosima, they agreed that 'the orchestra had not sounded the same when he was conducting it, and H. Reichmann had sung *Sterben, einzige Gnade* ('Death, the only mercy') in an incomparably different way'. Did she take the words of Amfortas as an omen? Scarcely six months later, Wagner died of heart failure in Venice at the age of 69.

HANS RICHTER, born in 1843, conductor of the première of the *Ring*, was the first to conduct in Bayreuth and had been close to Wagner since the 1860s, when he prepared the score of *The Mastersingers* for printing. Richter enjoyed food and drink, his photo shows him with a big, bushy, professorial beard, and he was regarded as something of a character in the musical world. He could play almost all the instruments of the orchestra himself, and when musicians complained of insuperable technical difficulties he had a disconcerting ability to demonstrate that he knew better. He demanded – and got! – 46 orchestral rehearsals for the revival of the *Ring* at Bayreuth in 1896. Although Wagner regarded Richter as 'the best', he considered his tempi too slow. 'I really do think that in general you rely too much on crotchets, and that always impairs the verve of a tempo, for instance in long notes such as often occur in Wotan's angry scenes. So far as I am concerned you can even do away with quavers where that improves the precision; you will never keep the character of a lively *allegro* going by means of crotchets.' I can confirm Wagner's dictum from my own experience. Richter died in 1916 and is buried in Bayreuth.

Next to him hangs the picture of HERMANN LEVI, born in 1839, conductor of the première of *Parsifal*, and court Kapellmeister in Munich. He was the son of a rabbi. Levi too has a beard; there is a sad expression in his eyes. Wagner chose him for *Parsifal* because he was not satisfied with Richter, but promptly found himself unable to refrain from making anti-Semitic remarks. He wanted Levi either to convert, or 'to go about with his back always bent as a token of humility'. On another occasion Wagner read aloud a scurrilous anonymous letter to Levi, whereupon the conductor offered his resignation. And when, soon after the successful première of *Parsifal* at Bayreuth, Levi fell prey to depression, and the Wagner family were anxious on his behalf, it was soon too much for the Master himself; there was no bearing these 'Israelites', he complained in his Venetian palazzo. 'Either they fall mentally ill over your treatment of them, or they react with arrogance!' Levi conducted *Parsifal* in four hours four minutes, a length regarded as ideal (only Clemens Krauss was faster in 1953, at three hours 44 minutes). Wagner seems to have been satisfied with Levi professionally, merely criticizing him for conducting 'with the arm' too much, instead of from the wrist. Levi died in Partenkirchen in 1900.

It is difficult to find out much about the next in line, FRANZ FISCHER (1849–1918). But after him comes FELIX MOTTL, born near Vienna in 1856; the photo shows him with a neat side parting in his hair, a moustache, and a pair of pince-nez on his nose. He conducted the Bayreuth première of *Tristan* in 1886, and to this day is alone in having conducted all 10 music dramas in the Wagnerian canon on the Green Hill, that is to say all the works traditionally performed at the Bayreuth Festivals. In 1876, Mottl joined Levi, Heinrich Porges and Julius Kniese as one of the 'Nibelung Office', the group drawn from the talented younger generation who helped Wagner by making clean copies of orchestral scores, piano scores, and above all with preparations for the *Ring*. Mottl's diaries, like the memoirs of the Bayreuth Festival by Porges, are a fascinating source, giving us an idea of the demands that Wagner made. Two of the Master's comments during rehearsals are particularly illuminating. Once he is supposed to have said, 'If you weren't all such tedious fellows, *The Rhinegold* would be over within two hours.' A bold claim, indeed over-bold – impossible! I for one would want at least two and a half hours for its performance. But the comment shows that Wagner was always keen to keep the action moving forwards. The second remark is: 'Atmosphere counts for nothing. Knowledge is and always will be what matters most.' It is easier to understand the implications of that maxim in Bayreuth than anywhere else. Mottl, by then ennobled as Felix von Mottl, died in 1911 in Munich after collapsing while conducting his hundredth *Tristan*. The same fate awaited Joseph Keilberth half a century later. A good way to die? I don't know.

Another step to the left, and I am facing RICHARD STRAUSS, born in Munich in 1864. Strauss was assistant at the 1889 Festival, and in 1894 conducted five performances of *Tannhäuser*, with his future wife Pauline de Ahna singing Elisabeth. Cosima Wagner thought highly of the lanky Bavarian, and her liking was expressed in her attempt (which was unsuccessful) to marry him off to her daughter Eva. Family life was always important on the Green Hill. Like Wagner, Strauss was a typical composer-conductor, notorious for his unostentatious beating of time and his brisk tempi (still to be heard in some historic recordings, particularly when he was conducting his own works). 'It's not that I've speeded up in *Parsifal*,' he justified himself later, 'it's that the rest of you in Bayreuth are getting slower and slower. Believe me, that's the wrong approach.' This was in 1933/4, when Strauss took over from Toscanini and conducted not only *Parsifal* but also Beethoven's Ninth Symphony at the Festival Theatre in Bayreuth (marking the occasion on 22 May 1872 when Wagner himself had conducted Beethoven's Ninth at the Margrave's Opera House in the town, to celebrate the laying of the foundation stone of the Festival Theatre.) To say that after Hitler's 'seizure of power' a sentimental, emotionally febrile, 'Nazi' style took over performances of Wagner's work does scant justice to the situation. Ideological misuse of the music does not necessarily imply that its interpretation in performance was distorted. In 1949 Strauss died in Garmisch-Partenkirchen at a great age, as a very wealthy man.

At first he was a close friend of the successor to the Bayreuth throne, SIEGFRIED HELFERICH RICHARD WAGNER, Wagner's only son, born at Tribschen in 1869. Siegfried was composer, conductor, director, set designer and director of the Festival – like his father. An interesting figure but not a genius. He felt misunderstood, in particular as a composer, and thought he was 'ignored by the court theatres', for which he blamed Strauss among others. It saddened him, he said, to think that *Parsifal* should be performed on a stage that had been trodden 'by the repellent character of [Strauss's] Salome, and an Elektra who can only be called a mockery of Sophocles, a profanation of classical antiquity as a whole. My father would be turning in his grave if he knew about the decline expressed in the operas of Richard Strauss [...] When did art become identical with smut?' In 1894 Cosima got her son to take over, successfully, on the conductor's podium during a rehearsal of *Lohengrin*, and in 1896 Siegfried made his debut as a conductor at the Festival (plunging straight in at the deep end with the *Ring*). His merits, however, were evident in other areas. For one thing, despite his homosexuality he prevented the Wagner dynasty from dying out by marrying, in his mid-forties, the 18-year-old Winifred Williams Klindworth and having four children with her: Wieland, Friedelind, Wolfgang and Verena. For another, he gently introduced reforms both on stage and in questions of production. Most important of all, however, Siegfried placed the economic existence of the Festival on a sound footing from 1924 onwards. In 1913, 30 years after the composer's death, as was usual at the time, the main royalty on his works ran out – and that time was one of galloping inflation. Other sources of finance had to be found. Siegfried proposed to turn the family business into a 'Richard Wagner Foundation of the German People', collected donations, chased up royalties on his own works, travelled around giving lectures, and went on extensive tours as a guest conductor that took him as far as the United States (although his anti-Semitism lost him several potential sponsors there). Not until 1928 was he back in Bayreuth, standing in that 'mystic abyss', the orchestra pit of the Festival Theatre – for the last time. He died on 4 August 1930, in the same year as his mother Cosima, after suffering a heart attack during rehearsals for the Festival.

The next conductor is ANTON SEIDL, with his fine head of hair and remarkable side-whiskers. He was born in Pest in 1850, died in New York in 1898 – and conducted in Bayreuth for only a single summer, that of *Parsifal* in 1897. Seidl was sensational above all as a member of the legendary 'touring Wagner company'. It had its own chorus and orchestras, as well as complete stage sets and technicians. They toured all of Europe in the 1880s, and Seidl conducted the *Ring* 135 times – everyone wanted Wagner! DR KARL (CARL) MUCK could not boast of such impressive numbers, but with his wide-ranging, classic tempi he made his mark on the era from 1901 to 1930, principally as conductor of *Parsifal*. Muck, born in 1859, had a striking face and was the first in the Rogues' Gallery to be clean-shaven. His was a rather emotional credo: 'What matters in Bayreuth is for those appointed there to be in accord with the ideas of the place, for the artistic doctrines of the Master as laid down in his writings, and the scores of his works, to have taken intellectual possession of them; and for them to bring to their work in the Festival Theatre the modest humility and sacred fanaticism of true believers.' Muck died in 1940.

On his left is MICHAEL BALLING (1866–1925). A viola player, he was discovered by Felix Mottl, rendered good service to Wagner in Great Britain, and married Hermann Levi's widow. Not much more is known about him. The same applies to FRANZ BEIDLER (1872–1930), chiefly known as the husband of Isolde von Bülow, who in fact was Cosima's first daughter by Richard Wagner. But as Isolde was born while Cosima was still married to Hans von Bülow, she was not recognized as one of Wagner's heirs (her mother in person backed the court ruling keeping her out of the succession). Consequently Isolde's son Franz Wilhelm, Richard Wagner's first grandson, was also excluded from the succession. One wonders whether he might have guided the fortunes of the Green Hill in a different direction.

In 1924, the singer Emmy Krüger apparently said of the next candidate that 'the Wagners do not like him' (in spite of his blond German good looks). FRITZ BUSCH, born in 1890 in Siegen, and general music director at the Semper Opera House in Dresden until 1933, made heavy weather of the time he spent at Bayreuth, where he complained of the poor artistic standards and was at odds with both Muck and Siegfried Wagner. Those who have heard Busch's recordings can guess that his *Mastersingers* was outside the scope of a merely pious approach to Wagner; he conducted the opera with great sensitivity, meticulous attention to the libretto and vigorous tempi. When he suggested inviting Arturo Toscanini for the 1925 season, the idea was misinterpreted. Eight years later, however, after the Nazis had come to power and Toscanini withdrew from his contract at Bayreuth, Busch came to mind again. 'A hand was held out offering me all that I had wished for, and I knew that I would not take it,' he wrote sadly in his memoirs. He declined the offer, emigrated soon afterwards, and died in London in 1951.

While WILLIBALD KAEHLER (1866–1938), with his chic 1930s glasses, enjoyed only two appearances at Bayreuth, the brawny KARL ELMENDORFF (1891–1962) became a regular mainstay of the Wagners' opera house. He conducted at Bayreuth almost every year from 1927 to 1942. FRANZ VON HOESSLIN, however, born in 1885, and principal conductor at Breslau, had a Jewish wife and so increasingly found himself in difficulties after the mid-1930s. Winifred Wagner, who was now running the Festival, helped him by inviting him to Bayreuth in 1934, and again from 1938 to 1940. In the neighbouring European countries, especially France, von Hoesslin was regarded as 'one of the greatest living masters of the baton, together with Toscanini'. In 1946 he missed his flight to Geneva, where he was to have conducted *Così fan tutte* the same evening, and, anticipating the modern jet set, chartered a private plane. It came down over the Gulf of Lyons, and Franz von Hoesslin and his wife were killed.

And now I come to ARTURO TOSCANINI, the legendary leader of the NBC Symphony Orchestra in New York, father-in-law of Vladimir Horowitz, feared as a despot on the conductor's podium, an Apollonian rather than a Dionysian and the first 'foreigner' to conduct on the Green Hill. Toscanini first appeared there in 1930, conducting *Tristan* and *Tannhäuser*, and triumphed over the obviously humdrum Bayreuth approach of the time, his adversary

Muck, and the difficult economic conditions, winning over the orchestra as well. The same musicians over whose heads he had broken several batons during rehearsals would now happily have carried him aloft from the Festival Theatre. In 1931 Toscanini made a reputation for himself as the slowest Wagnerian conductor in the word, taking four hours 42 minutes to conduct *Parsifal* – 23 minutes longer than Muck and a whole 38 minutes longer than Levi at the première of the work. To this day his is still the slowest time recorded. And here is a paradox: in his tempi the fanatically precise Toscanini, guardian of the principle of musical objectivity, took the 'Bayreuth style' initiated by Cosima, which conceived of the operas as museum pieces, to extremes. Was he aiming to make fun of it? Or was language the problem? Siegfried Wagner, who spoke excellent Italian, was dead, Toscanini's assistant 'incapable' in general, according to Winifred – and who else could have helped the maestro, who knew the works themselves by heart, by translating the accounts of rehearsals, Wagner's own written comments, and directions for performance written in on the score? Furtwängler, as the newly appointed director of the Festival, complained that Toscanini lacked 'deeper insight, a more lively imagination, greater warmth and commitment to the work'. The outcome was jealousy and friction, and the summer ended with discord on all fronts. All the same, Winifred induced Toscanini to conduct at the next Festival in 1933; they agreed on five performances of *Parsifal* and eight of *The Mastersingers*. On 1 April, however, the Italian sent a telegram of protest from New York to the German government: the official boycotting of Jews threatened many of his artistic colleagues. His withdrawal from the Bayreuth Festival followed on 28 May, also by telegram, signed 'with feelings of unchanged friendship for the house of Wagner'. Instead, Toscanini agreed to conduct at the Salzburg Festival, and in 1937 he emigrated to the United States, where he died in 1957 at the age of nearly 90.

Next to him in the gallery is the declared 'anti-Pope', WILHELM FURTWÄNGLER. Born in 1886, he was chief conductor of the Berlin Philharmonic, succeeding Arthur Nikisch from 1922, and was also, from 1933, director of the Berlin State Opera – he was one of the most important and influential conductors of Wagner in the twentieth century. Toscanini dismissed the born charismatic as a buffoon, no doubt a dig at Furtwängler's rather unorthodox manner of gesturing. In 1930, after Karl Muck left in a huff, Heinz Tietjen (to whom I shall turn soon) and Winifred Wagner paid court to Furtwängler. He made the most of that; after all, he could afford to. He demanded to be musical director of the Bayreuth Festival, got what he wanted, and made his debut a year later with *Tristan and Isolde*. The *Ring*, *Parsifal* and *Lohengrin* followed in 1936/7, and *The Mastersingers* in 1943/4, as well as two performances of Beethoven's Ninth Symphony after the war. In all he made about 70 appearances. But Furtwängler's path to Wagner was a long one and beset by crises. Even in Bayreuth, indeed above all there, countless difficulties lay in wait for him. There were constant power struggles with Winifred and Tietjen, rows, and in addition Furtwängler's tactic of serving the Nazis only where they could be useful to his career did not always work. There is a legendary anecdote that says much, describing Furtwängler conducting in 1942 on the eve of Hitler's birthday, obliged to lean down from the podium and shake hands with Joseph Goebbels, and wiping his own hand afterwards. Wilhelm Furtwängler, his widow Elisabeth remembered many years later, simply could not bring himself to abandon so many of 'his people'. Other non-Jewish colleagues of his, like Erich Kleiber and Fritz Busch, emigrated early; Furtwängler stayed on.

It had all begun for him when he was a boy, and his father gave him tickets for the *Ring* at the Cuvilliés Theatre in Munich. Franz Fischer was conducting, and the cast featured well-known singers. Those four performances, Furtwängler remembered, writing in 1936, had destroyed his illusions about Wagner and his love of the composer's music for years. Why? Because he felt that they 'lacked all true emotion', it had all been 'theatrical, nothing but theatrical'. In fact, Furtwängler said three years later in 1939, when Wagner as a musician and librettist was denounced as a 'man of the theatre', it represented 'a deep misunderstanding', indeed 'a counterfeit'. In other words, Furtwängler distrusted the equal status granted to words, music and staging as specified in the Wagnerian total work of art. He put the music first. That attitude naturally affected his interpretations – and their reception. To this day

Furtwängler's Wagner is regarded as 'subjective, emotional, romantic, symphonic and Wilhelmine'.* Similarly, his tempi are considered irregular and 'arbitrary', his *rubati* excessive, and his handling of the singers often as of secondary importance. It irritates me that the critics do not discriminate more. Furtwängler is not always the same, as a simple comparison between periods will show: he conducted his first *Ring* cycle in 1936 in 14 hours 26 minutes (2 hours 36 minutes for *The Rhinegold*), making him three minutes faster than Hans Richter at the première. In his last *Ring*, on the other hand, a concert performance recorded by RAI in Rome, he took 15 hours 6 minutes, that is to say 40 minutes longer, even though stage productions fundamentally take longer, and the acoustics of the Bayreuth Festival Theatre traditionally slow performance down. That illustrates Furtwängler's development: his style became broader, slower, more comprehensive. However, we should not forget that the choice of tempo is always relative, and quite often there is a discrepancy between absolute and perceived time. Perhaps in his later performances Furtwängler felt much closer to Wagner than the statistics would have us think and as we perceive it. At least, he would have liked to know Wagner as a conductor, he says in 1918 in an essay on Beethoven, for Wagner was 'the first to indicate the slight but constant change in tempo that alone can make a piece of music not a rigid, classic example, played as if from the printed page but what it really is, growth and development, a living process'. I would like to put my own name to every word of that. Furtwängler, the Dionysian, the 'procrastinator' (as his opposite and successor Herbert von Karajan liked to call him), died in 1954.

A comment of his on a colleague, one that does neither party any favours, shows how conscious Furtwängler was of his position and his influence: the colleague, he complains in a letter to Goebbels in 1937, was 'not a conductor but an organizer, and at best a hypocrite'. It did him little good: despite Furtwängler's protests, the baton for the Bayreuth *Ring* in the years 1938, 1939 and 1941 went to Göring's protégé HEINZ TIETJEN (born 1881), the legendary artistic director of all the Prussian state theatres since 1927, artistic director of the Bayreuth

---

* Translator's note: Wilhelmine = of the period of Kaiser Wilhelm II up to his abdication in 1918.

Festival from 1931 to 1944 – and Winifred Wagner's lover. Even Adolf Hitler, who counted himself a friend of Furtwängler, bowed to Winifred's wishes here. As conductor, director and a talented puller of strings combined, Tietjen, good-looking and shy, must have cut an anachronistic figure. Together with the set designer Emil Preetorius, he was to the fore in the aesthetic modernization of the Festival in the 1930s, often in defiance of Nazi taste (something chalked up entirely to Wieland Wagner's credit after the war). Conflict with Furtwängler was bound to ensue, since Tietjen had his heart set wholly on the music. His relationship with the leaders of the Third Reich was a troubled one: they sensed his intellectual superiority, understood his tactical manoeuvres, and did not trust him. Wieland's attempt to oust Tietjen from the Green Hill at the beginning of the 1940s and take over power himself failed. Politically rehabilitated and widely recognized as an artist, Tietjen died in 1967.

I cannot say much about VICTOR DE SABATA (1892–1967), who looks a little like Yehudi Menuhin in his Bayreuth photograph, and was the second Italian to conduct on the Green Hill, or RICHARD KRAUS (1902–78). Both spent a single summer conducting at Bayreuth, while Mottl's pupil, HERMANN ABENDROTH (1883–1956), whose photograph hangs beside theirs, was there for two. As general music director of Cologne, and Kapellmeister of the Leipzig Gewandhaus Orchestra, Abendroth alternated on the podium at Bayreuth with Furtwängler in the 'wartime Festivals' of 1943 and 1944, conducting *The Master-singers* at a measured tempo and amidst the scent of lilac. The pacts that Abendroth was alleged to have made with the political powers both before and after 1945 were his downfall. The Federal Republic of Germany (in the person of Chancellor Konrad Adenauer) declared him *persona non grata* as a former member of the National Socialist Party and a citizen of the German Democratic Republic, and from then on Abendroth had no access to major Western orchestras. In the East he held leading posts 'only' in Weimar and with the radio symphony orchestras of Leipzig and East Berlin. It was the fate of a man caught between the two Germanys.

With Abendroth I haven't even reached halfway point, or gone right down one side of the ancestral gallery. However, I must pause for a short time. The wartime Festival of 1944 was the last for some time; the Festivals did not resume until seven years later, in 1951, and then with what was called the New Bayreuth. The Festival Theatre itself suffered almost no damage in the war, but the Villa Wahnfried, Richard Wagner's own residence and the family seat until 1966, was devastated by a bomb. And everything had to be reorganized after the war. Could there and should there be 'new' Wagner Festivals after the end of the Third Reich in Germany? How were they to be financed? Who was to run them? And for what audiences? Where were the artists to come from? All these questions had to be answered. Almost more fascinating, to my mind, is the fact that there had been a double break: the musical tradition that could claim almost direct descent from Richard Wagner also ended at Bayreuth in the middle of the twentieth century. Between 1940 and 1950 the first two generations of Bayreuth conductors finally died out. All who had known Wagner himself, or were pupils of his pupils, had suddenly gone, and with them knowledge of many practical details of performance at Bayreuth. Even though there had never been an authentic Bayreuth style (when would Wagner have forged it?), even though Cosima as priestess of his cult had if anything distorted and falsified it, yet in the first 70 years after Wagner's death there must have been a specific aura, a spirit, a spark from which music arose: something like a belief that even if music drama could not change the world, it could yet explain it. That spirit was now beginning to take flight.

Richard's son Siegfried Wagner had never made much of the 'Wagner School' of conductors – a considerable reason for the break with tradition. Increasingly, conductors now came from outside, and the search for suitable candidates who were as well known as possible was as laborious after the war as before it. One of the few still to build a bridge at this point was HANS KNAPPERTSBUSCH, who had been general music director of the Bavarian State Opera until 1935. Knappertsbusch, born in 1888, was assistant to Hans Richter and Siegfried Wagner from 1909 to 1912. The fact that he was not engaged as conductor earlier is due first to the traditional rivalry between Bayreuth and Munich, secondly to Winifred's original preference for Fritz Busch in 1924, and thirdly to what the Nazis saw as Knappertsbusch's political 'unreliability'. He did not make his debut at Bayreuth until 1951, when he was 63 – but then conducted *Parsifal*, the *Ring* and *The Mastersingers* all in the same year. Wieland Wagner was director of both the *Ring* and *Parsifal*, and was also responsible for the sets. Knappertsbusch mockingly described his characteristic disc on the stage as like a ring on a cooker, and he thought for a long time that the *Parsifal* sets were so bleak because Wagner's grandson simply hadn't finished working on them. Knappertsbusch conducted at Bayreuth almost every year until his death in 1965.

Knappertsbusch's dislike of rehearsals is proverbial, and the source of countless anecdotes. ('Gentlemen,' he is said to have told the orchestra, 'you know the piece, I know the piece, we'll see each other this evening.') When we *see* him conducting in old film clips, however, with his long baton and a wisp of hair over his high forehead, using sparse gestures that betray no vanity, I am sometimes reminded, for all the difference of temperament between them, of Richard Wagner as Kietz described him. To follow Knappertsbusch's aims as a conductor, concentrating hard on doing nothing or very little, and for the rest relying on his own personality, on suggestion, experience, nobility of heart – that seems to me a great achievement.

There was another reason, however, for the break with Wagnerian tradition in the middle of the twentieth century: the new media. Radio, film and recordings made technical reproduction of the transient art of music possible. There was no longer any absolute need to go to Bayreuth (although to this day one must and does go!) in order to hear what Wagner's *Parsifal* can and should sound like. Or to find out the difference between Abendroth's wartime *Mastersingers* and the same opera under the young HERBERT VON KARAJAN after the war. You could also turn to taped versions. Karajan, who bestrode the Green Hill and with it the stages of the world in 1951, was the figurehead of the modern age of the media. In Bayreuth, however, as Wolfgang Wagner's autobiography tells us, he was determined from the first to run his head against a brick wall. True, his demand for a personal toilet was met, if with some rolling of the eyes, but when he went on to record the rehearsals for *Tristan* on tape in 1952 (so that he could check up on the singers better), and altered the order of seating in the pit (strings to the right, wind to the left), co-operation came to an end.

According to Wolfgang Wagner, much of the blame was to be laid at the door of Walter Legge, Karajan's powerful right-hand man in matters of prestige and finance. Karajan ('the man K.' as Furtwängler acidly called him) would never set foot in Bayreuth again.

With Herbert von Karajan, my biographies of the conductors have reached a figure who failed in Bayreuth by Bayreuth's own standards. I would probably regret that were it not for other conductors – HORST STEIN, HEINRICH HOLLREISER and DANIEL BARENBOIM, who flourished on the Green Hill. However, Karajan, whom I admire unreservedly for the homogeneity and transparency of his Wagnerian sound, is not the only one to have had difficulties and rubbed people up the wrong way. Even LOVRO VON MATAČIĆ and JOSEF KRIPS came to the Green Hill for only a year, and the same is true of THOMAS SCHIPPERS, ROBERT HEGER, CARL MELLES (the father of actress Sunnyi Melles), ALBERTO EREDE, HANS ZENDER, EDO DE WAART and MARK ELDER. WOLFGANG SAWALLISCH fell out with Wolfgang Wagner after seven successful years because he would not accept Anja Silja as Eva in *The Mastersingers*. GEORG SOLTI wanted to remove the cover from the orchestra pit – and gave up conducting the *Ring* after only two years in 1984. Many and various as the detailed reasons for failure to succeed in Bayreuth are, I am convinced that ultimately you either have an affinity for the house or you do not. Wagner can be learned and practised in Bayreuth only on certain conditions.

There certainly have been and are several colleagues absent from the list of conductors. Arthur Nikisch, for instance (who had played the violin in Beethoven's Ninth under Richard Wagner in 1872), was a conductor of concerts rather than opera, and thus did not enter into the equation; Hans von Bülow of the goatee beard was damned if he would conduct at Bayreuth – after all, Wagner had cuckolded him and seduced his wife Cosima; Gustav Mahler was busy in Vienna and was also a Jew; the critical Felix von Weingartner did not get on with Cosima when he came to Bayreuth as assistant; Engelbert Humperdinck was probably suitable only in an assistant capacity; and Ernst von Schuch was unwilling. Names missing from the list later are those of Bruno Walter, Erich Kleiber and Otto Klemperer, or today Riccardo Muti and Mariss Jansons. But what has not been may yet be.

Anyway, the conductors of the Bayreuth Festival are an honourable company. I often wonder whether perhaps the famous dead are watching us all and think poorly of what we do. Or think it acceptable. Or even good. The idea that the opera house has eyes and ears is one that I find enormously inspiring.

3

Cobwebs, Solemnity, Sausage Salad:
Bayreuth and its Green Hill

The Green Hill in the small town of Bayreuth in Upper Franconia has been the epicentre of the international Wagnerian world since 1876. The composer built his legendary Festival Theatre here, creating the ideal geographical, architectural, acoustic and political conditions for his art. A Mecca in the provinces, in the heart of the young German Empire. A place for myths that itself soon became the greatest myth of everything to do with Wagner. To this day all that is best and most famous in connection with him belongs to Bayreuth and aims to be there. Battles for audiences have been fought here, ideologies have exploited the ritual of the Festivals, great moments of music and drama have set high standards. Richard Wagner without Bayreuth? I can't imagine it even in abstract terms.

The theatre

I always felt that the Festival Theatre is alive. It breathes, it listens, it looks at you. And it is on its guard. You must be wide awake when you set foot in it, and you must be able to abandon yourself to it. As long as you do that it will keep faith with you. However, it does not forgive any sense of alienation or indifference. Then it will be revenged, it will not adapt atmospherically and acoustically so smoothly, and it will not be so enjoyable to work here. The theatre is like a valuable instrument or a demanding lover. It wants to be taken seriously. Every time, you have to pay court to it again.

My first visit to the Green Hill in summer always feels rather like an initiation. The quickest and most practical way to the grounds of the Festival Theatre is along Tannhäuserstrasse, approaching it from the back. This is where you find the car parks, the rehearsal stages and the entrance to the main auditorium. Once I have arrived in Bayreuth, however, I take Siegfried-Wagner-Allee, the main driveway. It is as if I *must* pay my respects to the Festival Theatre, I actually feel it insisting on my doing so. And I like the way the old building seems defiantly enthroned up there, while I feel both small and exalted before its face. Sometimes I stop halfway up the road to it, open the car window and take a deep breath of Bayreuth air: this is where the most exciting music of all time is played! This is the scene of the greatest hysteria ever aroused by an opera house, here in the province of Franconia in, let us say, a family environment. The Festival Theatre was and is a temple, a workshop and a place of pilgrimage all at once. To this day its inimitable mixture of informality and sanctity, solemnity and daring sends shivers down my spine. Then, a few days after my arrival in Bayreuth, I see the rats in the production of *Lohengrin* directed by Hans Neuenfels tripping over the stage and ask myself: how does it all fit together?

Much research has been done into the way Richard Wagner fixed on Bayreuth, and there are many accounts of it. He was impelled by two things: his idea of a Festival – and a wish to get away from the vicinity of his great patron, backer and fervent admirer King Ludwig II without alienating him entirely (which would have meant losing his financial support). Against Wagner's will, Ludwig had had the premières of *The Rhinegold* and *The Valkyrie* given in Munich in 1869/70, and now he was making plans to do the same for *Siegfried*. Wagner had to act, and quickly. He read the entry on the Margrave's Opera House in Bayreuth in the Brockhaus Encyclopaedia, and paid a visit to the little town in April 1871, the year of the founding of the German Empire. The Baroque theatre proved unsuitable, the auditorium in particular was too small, but he liked the place itself. Early in 1872, Wagner packed up his things in the Swiss villa of Tribschen where he was living, and on 22 May, his 59th birthday, the foundation stone of the Festival Theatre was laid on the Green Hill. It was pouring with rain, but the Master was not going to miss his chance to build Ludwig's telegram of congratulations personally into the foundations.

Politically, Wagner could not have hoped for a better moment. The young German Empire craved new (meaning ancient) myths, and everything speculative and emphatic was welcome to the ethos of the time. However, there were major economic difficulties. The total budget for the Festival Theatre project, estimated at 300,000 thalers, was ultimately exceeded by about a third, sales of 'patronage certificates' at 1,000 thalers each were slow, and the management board that was appointed had soon exhausted its financial expertise. There were several breaks in the building work, paying for rehearsals in the year 1876 was a problem – and if Ludwig had not stepped in, making huge contributions, Wagner would have failed spectacularly. 'I will serve you as long as I live and breathe,' swore the king in a late letter to his favourite artist, despite the intermittent disagreements between them. And so something that the world enjoys to this day succeeded: an anarchic idea was institutionalized. What would Richard Wagner say if he knew that his Festival had now taken place over a hundred times?

Originally, a quarter of a century before Bayreuth, the idea of a Festival was entirely a provisional arrangement. It was to counter the 'sickness' of the prevailing 'economy of the theatre' as a 'fiery cure' in the cleansing and destructive sense. Wagner's letter of 22 September 1850 from Zürich to his like-minded revolutionary friend, the Dresden violinist Theodor Uhlig, is famous, and says it all (at this time he was busy with an early version of the *Ring*, the drama *Siegfried's Death*): he writes that he has had 'a rough stage of planks and beams constructed to my plan, on a beautiful meadow outside the town, and furnished only with the décor and machinery necessary for the performance of *Siegfried*'. He engaged the singers individually, the chorus and orchestra were recruited from 'volunteers', the advertising for his 'dramatic music festival' was a case of 'announcements in all the newspapers', and admission was to be free. 'Once everything is in proper order,' Wagner went on, 'then I will have three performances of *Siegfried* given in a week; after the third the theatre will be torn down and my score burnt. And I will tell those who liked it, go and do likewise!'

Apart from the lack of any economic dimension in these first ideas (for what revolution stops to wonder if it will be profitable?) and the fact that the Festival Theatre has not to this day been torn down, surprisingly little has changed since Wagner set out his vision. The singers are still hand-picked, the chorus and orchestra still volunteer, and often sacrifice their summer holidays to the Festival, like all the seasonal workers in the technical department. However, for decades Bayreuth has not needed to advertise for an audience, and if the ticket prices are modest by international standards they have to rise. German history, as it happens, has seen to the burning of the scores, at least figuratively. The manuscripts of the early operas *Die Feen* (*The Fairies*) and *The Ban on Love*, of *Rienzi*, *The Flying Dutchman*, *The Rhinegold* and *The Valkyrie*, and the third act of *Siegfried*, left the possession of the Wittelsbach family in 1939 for the Reich Chamber of Commerce, and from there, on his 50th birthday, passed into the hands of Adolf Hitler. We do not know if the dictator sank them in the depths of his Wolf's Lair, incorporated them into his private Führer Library in the Villa Castiglione on the Austrian border, or cast them into the hail of bombs over Berlin – but at any rate, since the end of the Second World War they have been regarded as lost. That did not affect the myth of the Festivals or the continuity of the ritual.

In 1874, after two years of building work, Wagner and his family moved into the Villa Wahnfried, his 'peaceful home' on the outskirts of the Bayreuth court garden. The house was another gift from Ludwig II, and with its hall, marble busts and gilded frieze showing the Nibelung story in the gallery above, its chief aim was to impress. In this case one of those citadels in which Wagner took refuge all his life became a festive place fit for the gods. His liking for luxury was proverbial: his preference for silk underwear, brocade curtains and pelmets, valuable instruments, expensive furniture and so on. The conductor Heinrich Esser wrote to the publisher Franz Schott that his friend not only didn't know how to manage money, he claimed that he couldn't work 'unless he lived like a grand seigneur'. It was as if all inspiration rose from exuberance and excess. In Wahnfried this inclination took permanent shape. 'Here, where my illusion [*Wähnen*] found peace [*Frieden*] – let me call the house Wahnfried,' runs the inscription over the entrance.

I have always marvelled at the worlds that separate the villa and the Festival Theatre. The former is his Valhalla, the latter the 'quickly erected wooden building', down below is splendour, up above

Protestantism. Even Wagner must have realized that he would not be able to offer a suitable standard of accommodation to the artists he wanted in Bayreuth: the court Kapellmeister of Vienna, Hans Richter, star singers of the time such as Franz Betz and Lilli Lehmann. No grand hotel, no hot springs, no comforts, let alone luxuries. And fundamentally matters stayed like that. Until well into the twentieth century, orchestral rehearsals were held in wooden structures of varying quality for lack of anything else. Musical personalities of the first rank came here, famous virtuoso professors of chamber music from Vienna, concert masters from Dresden and Berlin, to rehearse in a wooden shack and stay at the nearest farmhouse. A few grander hostelries are allowed in Bayreuth today, and the orchestra stays at the restaurant of the Festival Theatre during the time spent in rehearsal, but accommodation short of what might be expected and the renunciation of privilege is part of the Festival principle, and there is something relaxing about it for all concerned; the conductor of *The Flying Dutchman* earns as much or as little as the conductor of *Twilight of the Gods*, director's fees are halved each time a production is revived (100 per cent in the year of the première, 50 per cent for the first revival, 25 per cent for the second revival, and so on); Lohengrin X, a megastar, is paid the same as Lohengrin Y, who is just beginning his career and has a great voice. Beyond the red carpet of the annual opening on 25 July, the Bayreuth Festival is not a glamorous occasion, on principle – and even the red carpet is rolled up again on the night of the opening. All really are equals at Bayreuth, for to this day there has been only one star here, and he died in 1883.

The pit

On arriving in Bayreuth my first visit is always to the pit. I have to smell it, breathe in its air: the smell of wood, the pitch-darkness, the toil and trouble of so many brilliant (and not so brilliant) hours, as well as the pride of tradition, the euphoria when everything fits together one evening. Since the first Bayreuth Festival of 1876, about 9,700 hours of Wagner have been played down here in the 'mystic abyss', counting only performances, not rehearsals. Over 400 days of Wagner in all! All this music has settled deep in the pores, fibres and crevices of the pit; you feel that it has actually impregnated the old timbers.

As early as this in the season, at the beginning of June, the instrumentalists' chairs are still cleared to one side, stacked on each other; sheet music is lying around, and so are last year's rehearsal timetables. I enjoy that moment a great deal. To me, the air in the pit is a little like the dragon's blood in which Siegfried bathes. It gives you courage and strength, it can be extremely inspiring – but also extremely intimidating. It doesn't say: you're invulnerable for ever because you are conducting at Bayreuth today. Far from it; those who conduct at Bayreuth and have come to terms with the special features of the house know their own limits. Those who fail, fail because of their own shortcomings.

Here, in the underbelly of the theatre, you are also close to the truth structurally. You have only to stamp your foot hard once: everything sounds hollow. There is no firm ground, just sand, cobwebs, loose stones and small, dead creatures. And any amount of water (a new drainage system was laid only in 2010, to prevent the foyers from flooding quickly in thunderstorms or torrential rain). A look at the catacombs here shows you that the theatre is built on stilts, almost like Venice, and except for the masonry of the foundations it is all made of wood. That is excellent for the acoustics: the wood vibrates. And in 1872 of course timber was cheap and easily available as building material. In the 1960s parts of the structure were replaced by concrete or steel, although only above the ground. To this day, as a result, it has been impossible to build air conditioning into the Festival Theatre. If it is hot outside and cold indoors, if too much damp is drawn out of the rooms, the wood threatens to split, and everything warps. So the moderate duct cooling system installed in 1990 has to suffice for the auditorium, and we in the pit atone for all our sins at a temperature of what, in *Twilight of the Gods*, feels like 48 degrees. The conductor Karl Böhm is said to have ordered two basins of cold water on such days, one for each foot. And with Wolfgang Wagner's permission I arranged to have two ventilation tubes fitted to the conductor's podium. They do not look very attractive, but they keep the air circulating. In any case the podium, with its little lamps and lights, its cables and strip lighting, looks antediluvian, like an underground cockpit – not at all

like a pulpit or lectern. At least the seat of the conductor's chair gets a
new cover every summer, which is reassuring.

The famous pit is both monstrous and unique: a shaft driven steeply
down into the hill, a tunnel with two wooden tone-control devices. The
first is mounted above the brass instruments, the second, which is visible
to the audience, above the strings. Richard Wagner did not want the
chairs, the instruments or the faces of the musicians to be on show, and
certainly not the silhouette of a gesticulating conductor. He wanted an
'invisible orchestra', and he devised one in Bayreuth. Music as a mystic
event, a force of nature: nothing was to distract the audience from its
purely aural effect. A sound like the air we breathe, simply there. And
Wagner obviously knew how that ideal was to be acoustically achieved.
The pit at Bayreuth is laid out in the form of terraces, six stages leading
down from the conductor's podium. At the top are the violins, followed
by the other strings in order of their depth of tone, then the woodwind
and harps, then the lighter brass instruments and finally the tubas and
trombones. In arithmetical terms, that comes to 1.129 square metres
per instrumentalist with his or her instrument – that is to say, if the
orchestra comprises 124 people, there are 140 square metres in all, not
a great deal of space. The cellists and trombonists have to handle their
bows and slides, and of course the rather stouter string players, or those
blessed with more hair than their colleagues, have to sit at the back of
their groups.

The acoustics

Acoustically, this orchestra pit is a marvel. The sound traces an
S-shaped curve, rising from the brass over the woodwind and the
strings to the stage, and only then pouring out into the auditorium.
The idea, as I have said above, was Wagner's own and was highly
speculative. How could he have known that his dream of the perfect
mixed sound would work? Together with the Teatro Colón in Buenos
Aires, Bayreuth today offers the best operatic acoustics in the world.
Wagner risked a good deal for it; even when everything was almost
finished he had the pit enlarged again, this time sacrificing the two
front rows of seats in the auditorium. And when he could do no more

in terms of construction, he reworked the instrumentation of some passages in his scores, including the *Ring*. This shows the depth of his concept: for Wagner, the total work of art is the criterion, not the notes. Everyone and everything must work together, in the same way as the receptionist sits next to the star Heldentenor in the Bayreuth canteen, harmoniously eating together. One element in the Bayreuth team may be considered the heart of the Festival, another the brain, a third the eyes, a fourth the liver, lungs, the spleen or the stomach, and the heart is no more important than anything else, nor is it right for the eyes to claim that the rest of the organism is blind without them. It is a single being, and only together do the parts make up a whole, vital body. That was Wagner's vision.

Of course the pit can be temperamental. For debutantes, yes, but also for experienced musicians. Two examples: if I stand on the podium thinking that the chorus and orchestra are performing wonderfully well together, then they are sure to be doing the opposite out in the auditorium; the chorus is coming in too early. Not much too early, only a little, but still. Or when the singer of Brünnhilde in *Twilight of the Gods* embarks on her final passages, I have to read the words in which she calls for the building of a funeral pyre from her lips, because I really can't hear her; the orchestra drowns her out. In effect, the only place to be in the Bayreuth Festival Theatre is in the audience; only there are the individual elements ideally mingled. In a way we interpreters lose our function; the orchestra hears at most a piping or a distant cry from the singers. Apart from that, the musicians also find it very hard to hear each other, the singers feel that they can never prevail against the broadsides coming from the pit, and the conductor may see everyone and everything, but cannot trust his own ears. That is why there is a telephone beside the conductor's podium during rehearsals, an old-fashioned grey one, with a little red light on it that comes on as soon as the assistants checking up in the auditorium notice something too loud, too soft, too slow, too fast. During performances there is no telephone (I sometimes wish there was). At Bayreuth, Daniel Barenboim once said, the conductor is not allowed to hear the music.

What are we looking at, then? A schizophrenic and inhumane system? The megalomaniac fantasy of a single composer who dominates us to this day because we think so highly of his music? I would like to put it more positively. Bayreuth says we must all pull together. None of us can rely on ourselves alone. Everyone is important, as I have just said, including the orchestra, perhaps the orchestra most of all. The horn player with his solo, the leader of the orchestra who ensures homogeneity in his group, the harpist who plays harsh sounds so well on the Beckmesser harp, the chorus conductors who sit on the left and right of the proscenium arch in *Lohengrin* and *Tannhäuser* and beat time for the singers on stage, because at the back of the stage they have no chance of seeing the conductor, and depending on the set design there may be no monitors there either. And of course the conductor himself has a part to play if he goes along with this eccentric attempt to put things in order.

A conductor at Bayreuth must do a good many things that go against the grain. He must let his assistants tell him when the tempo is dragging or the sound is too loud, and take the chorus director's word for it that the entry is still coming in too soon. He can't simply follow what is happening on stage and rely on the intuition of his musicians (as is possible with very good orchestras playing in an open pit), but is obliged to anticipate the whole time. Above all, however, he must shake off any idea that he can aim only to achieve great art. The opera house easily takes offence at that. As a result, the conductors who succeed best on the Green Hill are the good, solid craftsmen who have a firm grasp of what is needed, not the adventurers and high-flyers. Not that I mean to say good craftsmanship and fine ideas are mutually exclusive.

With time, a conductor gets a sense of the major and minor imponderables, and comes to know that a *forte* in *The Flying Dutchman* is not the same as a *forte* in *Siegfried*. You can learn this house and its acoustics as you might learn a score, by taking advice. And also – this is very important – by going to your colleagues' rehearsals. If you have a few days free you don't leave Bayreuth, you stay and listen, draw comparisons, listen again and make your own analysis. Where else in the music business can you do a thing like that? The Green Hill draws on everyone's personal attitude – and on oral communication. It is all part of the family atmosphere and tradition. Anyone who doesn't go along with that, whether out of fear or arrogance, usually drops a brick.

I have known conductors who insisted on having the first violins on the left and the second violins on the right – as is the case everywhere else in the world. On the Green Hill it has always been the other way around, for a very good reason. When a violinist raises his instrument to his neck, the F-shaped holes through which the sound comes are pointing right. If the first violins, as usual, sat on the conductor's left in Bayreuth they would be playing to the cover of the pit all the time. That was not what Richard Wagner wanted because, to put it simply, it would have dulled the high notes and frequencies, and that is why the two groups have changed places. For those of us used to driving on the right of the road it is like driving on the left in England: at first it is disconcerting, but you get used to it.

Also confusing is the long time it takes for the echo to die away in the Festival Theatre. Unfortunately the numbers don't always agree; some assess it as 1.8 or 1.9 seconds, while others put it at a fabulous 2.25 seconds (only the Teatro Colón and the New York Met come anywhere close to such a long echo). Be that as it may, in the pit you feel that the sound goes on for ever, and that tempts you to adopt 'broad' tempi that don't sound so good out in the auditorium. If I linger too long on Wagner's music, the outcome is often that false sense of sacred celebration to which the composer himself, as a practical man of the theatre, must have been allergic. He told his singers on 13 August 1876, the day of the first performance of *The Rhinegold*, 'One last request: clarity! The large notes can look after themselves; the little notes and the text matter most!' I really understood what he meant only on the spot. Down in the 'abyss' I must not let mists rise, or try to create an aura. Instead, I must be meticulous in observing what is in the music itself.

And in relation to the total work of art, directors and set designers also have to struggle with the acoustics now and then. For instance, self-contained sets with too many wall surfaces, from which the sound echoes back too strongly, are a problem in every opera house. In Bayreuth they can be disastrous. That is because the sound traps itself, and does not move in an elegant S-shaped arc but gets dents and holes in it. It sounds almost over-modulated. Another tricky point is just where the singers are placed on stage. That has nothing to do with the usual arguments between the director and the conductor – one wants them on the forestage, the other behind the proscenium. At Bayreuth, if the singers are too far forwards, i.e. on the apron or forestage, many of their voices will sound shrill, even those that demonstrably are not. Here again the sound gets trapped, and suddenly the effect is of a badly worn tape recording. That seems to me significant, indicating that Wagner did not want a stage with an apron. Ever since his days in Dresden, the operatic conventions of the nineteenth century had been a thorn in his flesh, or rather his ear. In that respect, the nightmare of the fat singer hogging the forestage was settled early at Bayreuth, from 1876 onwards, for purely architectural reasons. Which doesn't mean that we have not had to defend Wagner against his own reputation again and again.

My only school of conducting

Bayreuth is the only school of conducting I have ever attended. It is where I learned to domesticate my heart. The Festival Theatre confronts you with yourself, which is not always pleasant, but is illuminating in the long run. I have always considered myself something of an intuitive musician, but in Bayreuth I was brought to realize that I must not on any account emphasize my emotional side. It was getting me nowhere, and the result, if I may say so, was only a sophisticated mushiness. Enjoying the foam bath of that orchestra pit, I had fallen into the trap of pleasure. I didn't know at first that the opium of the Bayreuth Festival Theatre should be taken in measured doses. I was shocked; I felt as if the ground were giving way beneath my feet. Then I was told it was the same for every novice. That was not much of a consolation, but I resolved that now I would simply listen to Wolfgang Wagner and the assistants. I would try to be good and obedient. When I made my debut on the Green Hill conducting *The Mastersingers* I was 41 years old, an age at which a conductor has to some extent established a reputation. I had in fact done so, and my artistic opinions often did not coincide with what I was advised and expected to do in Bayreuth. But then I faced Wolfgang Wagner, with all the weight of his personality and experience, and it inevitably struck me that he had heard all the great conductors here, from Furtwängler by way of Toscanini and Knappertsbusch to Böhm and Carlos Kleiber. If someone like that says he thinks this transitional passage rather lacking in tension, and that tempo too broad, you accept it and take it to heart, or at least you try to.

All the same, there were passages that went right against my own inclinations. I was doing something without being convinced it was right – and yet I felt it must be done. An inner voice told me: do it, grit your teeth. In retrospect, I think that I learned to adjust only in conflict with my stock of musical feelings. Suddenly I had to plan, think ahead, act with deliberation; I couldn't just leave it until the last minute. It could be said that I really grew up in Bayreuth.

The pit has its own language. Since both in the pit and on stage the music sounds so different from the way it is heard in the auditorium, I need a kind of translation aid while I am conducting. It is like learning verbs: what technicality must I master to achieve this or that effect 'outside' the pit? And the only common factor is that the translation for *The Mastersingers* is not entirely the same as the translation for *Parsifal*.

I spent a good deal of time in rehearsals by my colleagues: Giuseppe Sinopoli, Antonio Pappano and Adam Fischer, Pierre Boulez and Peter Schneider. As a general rule, a student conductor at Bayreuth profits most not from the good rehearsals, but from those when something doesn't work. Then the assistant may say: it sounds so dense because the violins should play these runs *staccato*, and they aren't doing that clearly enough – or the *forte* sounds forced, because while the direction *forte* is written on the score, the conductor is muting the sound too late. It isn't easy to achieve a really good *forte* or *fortissimo* at Bayreuth. The best efforts still fall short of the ideal by 5 per cent, and perhaps that is the right formula. Like that, you slowly add one little piece of mosaic to the next in practical performance.

One of the most intriguing and exciting discoveries I made was that you have to protect Richard Wagner from himself at Bayreuth. Often it says *fortissimo* on the score, and the most you can indicate is *piano* if the orchestra is not to drown everything else out. I believe that Wagner would have changed a great many of those directions if he had been given the chance, for one reason to make things easier for the conductor: is he to be faithful to what is written, or interpret the music from the aspect of its effect and then, if necessary, diverge from the written instruction?

At Bayreuth, *The Mastersingers* is regarded as the most difficult of all the operas to perform, closely followed, I would say from my experiences in the summer of 2012, by *The Flying Dutchman* – very closely followed. However, a distinction must be drawn: in the *Dutchman* the difficulties are mainly of a dynamic nature; its score is typical of the *Sturm und Drang* [storm and stress] style of a rather earlier period, and it is up to the conductor to de-stress it as far as possible if he is not to be overwhelmed even in the Overture. This score has an element of violence in it, and you have to pay great attention to voices in the modal register to compensate for the lack of refinement in the instrumentation. Even so, it is hardly possible to perform a number like the famous ghostly chorus at Bayreuth. We know what Wagner had in mind here – and we feel that he lacked the means to express it. The general public may find the *Dutchman* an ideal introduction to Wagnerian opera, but any production of *Lohengrin* or *The Valkyrie* is easier for conductors on the Green Hill. In this respect *The Flying Dutchman* tends to be underestimated.

A conductor also clearly realizes that *The Mastersingers* was not composed for the Festival Theatre, and if it were not such sacrilege the cover ought to be taken off the pit for it. Here we do not have such an alchemical mingling of musical colour as in *Parsifal*; we are concerned with the mechanism of comedy, which has to be as direct and precise as possible. To make your debut with *The Mastersingers* is like jumping in at the deep end of Wagnerian waters. Astonishingly, I managed it pretty well in 2002. I still remember that on 1 August that year, when the first note of the Prelude died away, I knew it was going to work, and that is something I have very rarely experienced in my life. At the time I was intrigued by the contradictions: doing justice to a score not intended for Bayreuth, in spite of the Bayreuth conditions, but indeed using them to give the work its due – could there be a better way to explore the qualities of the Festival Theatre?

And something else makes working at Bayreuth both easy and difficult for the conductor: the orchestra. This orchestra – about 200 musicians drawn mainly from German operatic, radio and symphony orchestras, who give up their summer and theatre holidays for the Bayreuth Festival – is one of the most hot-blooded and volcanic known to me. None of them is brought here by a sense of duty, they all want to come, and most of all they want to come back again. As a result, an orchestral musician in Bayreuth is having a much better time than usual, exactly what you often long for in other places. Normally, the conductor is kept busy inspiring and motivating the musicians, telling them to put a bit more heart into it. It is the opposite at Bayreuth, and that entails different problems. Here you have to be constantly urging the orchestral players to control themselves – not so much feeling, please, not so much temperament, let's have a bit of moderation! But if you do manage to apply the brakes without spoiling the musicians' pleasure, the outcome can be very satisfying for all concerned.

In 2006, my first year conducting the *Ring* at Bayreuth, the musicians gave me a T-shirt with the words *Nur Forte!* [Only *forte*!] on it in large letters. I must have been saying that at frequent intervals. To understand my point, you have to be aware that the musicians play at much greater volume at Bayreuth than in houses with open pits. Upbeats, for instance, necessarily have to be louder and more striking, or they would fall flat and go unnoticed out in the auditorium. That in turn can lead to the orchestra playing everything louder on principle, so that as a musician I am suddenly hearing instruments that I never hear at home. The sound level is considerable here anyway, over 100 decibels for the wind instruments (human pain tolerance goes no further than 110 decibels). Here a chain reaction threatens. To prevent it, the conductor must be very careful to keep the prescribed dynamic in the low area. So first and foremost, 'only *forte*' meant: please don't keep playing *fortissimo*!

I have always found it very instructive to listen to radio broadcasts from the Festival Theatre. They have often made me think: what did I do with this or that tempo in the pit? Because, heard over the radio, the music flowed very well, measured and exactly right. Such observations are unsettling, because normally I notice whether or not the tension is maintained. But in Bayreuth? So much hysteria expended on such an infinitesimal output?

Sometimes the 'mystic abyss' seems to me like a very thick hotplate on a cooker: I have to turn the heat up high from underneath to get a reasonable amount of warmth up above. And it is even more difficult to turn the heat down again.

The Wagners

The Wagners liked to eat sausage salad. At receptions in the intervals, at the famous parties given in their home, sausage salad always
featured. I don't like sausage salad, but fundamentally that is all that
stood between us.

When I think of Wolfgang Wagner I don't usually see him on
his folding chair to the left of the stage, where he still spent whole
acts during performances even into his old age; I do not see him on
his deathbed, certainly not, although I was one of the last to visit
him; nor do I see him leaning on his stick as he goes over the zebra
crossing between his villa and the Festival Theatre – usually for the
second time that day. He had often been to the office early, and would
then go home for breakfast and return to the theatre at the beginning
of rehearsals. No, I see Wolfgang Wagner standing in front of me in
his dinner jacket after a performance of *The Mastersingers*, talking.
People used to complain that he never said anything nice, and that
was true. At the most, I can remember seven or eight situations in all
those years when he growled something like 'a relaxed performance'
or 'nicely transparent'. But no more than that. Gudrun Wagner's face,
however, always showed whether or not she had liked something,
and she said what she thought, nor did she keep her criticism to
herself.

Normally I recognized Wolfgang Wagner by his step. He usually
paused for a moment at the top of the stairs before making his way
down the corridor to the conductor's cloakrooms. However, after the
Mastersingers performance mentioned above I couldn't hear him because
I was in the shower. So I came out of it (not for nothing were those
cloakrooms called rabbit hutches), holding only a small towel – and
there he was in front of me, beginning to talk. About the chorus and
the singers and this or that passage. It was terribly embarrassing, and
I tried to draw attention to myself. 'You know, Herr Wagner, I feel
somehow odd.' To which he replied, 'It's not the first time I've seen a
naked man,' and went on. There was no point in protesting. After he
had said what he wanted to say, he turned round, wished me a good
evening, and went away. By then I was dry.

This scene is typical of Wolfgang Wagner: he shrank from nothing when he wanted to make a point. He could be extremely irascible and inclined to flare up, and then his voice rose. Not for long, and never when talking to me, but the walls in the Festival Theatre are thin. We never discussed private matters; in spite of his jovial manner he was not a man to open up to others. Professionally I liked that; it was very much in the style of the old school. All the same, I related to him as I would to a father figure; he seemed to me kindly, stern and affectionate at the same time. I have not met many people who made so little fuss about themselves. He personified the Festival, he was the patriarch, the prince, the undisputed, unassailable ruler of the Green Hill and its artistic, social and economic fortunes. And, as is appropriate for a good ruler, he knew all about his vassals. The wife of an employee might need expensive medical treatment, someone else had children to be educated, donations were wanted for a Wagner Society somewhere – the Wagners helped many good causes and did not talk about it.

Wolfgang, born in 1919, was the third child of Siegfried Wagner and his wife Winifred, and their second son. Photographs show a pale, fair-haired little boy, apparently only a reasonably good pupil at school, and a poor eater. It was some time before anyone noticed that he had the Wagner nose (a feature typical of the dynasty ever since Richard Wagner married Franz Liszt's daughter Cosima), and no one could tell that it would be he who left his mark on the Festival until into the twenty-first century. The siblings, in their little winged helmets, equipped with bearskins and cardboard swords, acted out the stories of *The Valkyrie* in the garden of the Villa Wahnfried. For a long time Wolfgang was overshadowed by his brother Wieland, two years his senior; he was considered the less gifted of the two, and really wanted to be a conductor, but when the war prevented him from studying he became assistant director at the Berlin State Opera. In 1950 he and Wieland took over as joint directors of the Bayreuth Festival, with Wolfgang in charge of finance and organization. He also began to direct productions.

When Wieland surprisingly died at the age of 49 in 1966, his 'little brother' set his own standards. He made the Festival, along with what remained of the family archive and the Villa Wahnfried, into a foundation, engaged exciting artists (conductors like Pierre Boulez and Carlos

Kleiber, directors such as August Everding, Götz Friedrich and Patrice Chéreau), continued his own work as a director, married for the second time, moved into a house of his own on the Hill – and secured himself a lifetime contract as director of the Festival. For almost 60 years Wolfgang Wagner guarded and defended the Bayreuth Festival, and according to contemporaries ruled with a strong hand. His 'house rules' were notorious: covered in sellotape and fixed to doors and lifts, copies of them forbade entry to anyone not expressly allowed in, and banned photography and tape recordings. These messages always signed off with the words that Eva uses in Act 2 of *The Mastersingers* to beguile Hans Sachs the cobbler: 'Art reigns here'. They were also printed on the leaflets distributed by the brothers for the opening of New Bayreuth in 1951: 'In the interests of the smooth running of the Festival, we ask visitors to refrain from political conversation and debate on the Festival Hill. Art reigns here.' There was never to be any misuse of the music again, no more propaganda.

When we met in Chicago in 1999 Wolfgang Wagner was 80, an old man of incredible vitality. At the time I would have taken him for 50 at the most. But of course he was a walking history book; you could ask him anything – and thanks to his phenomenal memory he knew everything. How Knappertsbusch sat on the green meadow outside the Festival Theatre, handing out autographed postcards; the arguments with Karajan, naturally, and in detail; why Solti failed here; how people arrived to hear Chéreau's production of the *Ring* in 1976 armed with whistles, and came to blows in the auditorium; how the family could get about in public only under police protection, and a furious visitor tore Gudrun Wagner's evening dress. And there were many other stories too.

After the performance three or four of us, including Wolfgang's daughter Katharina, sometimes met in the old sitting room on the ground floor (where the offices of the half-sisters, Wolfgang's daughters Eva and Katharina, were to be later when they took over the Festival). The long table was laid, there was a huge bowl of the inevitable sausage salad, but pretzels and cheese as well, and Evi, Katharina's nanny, brought a few bottles of beer. Then shoes were taken off, shirt buttons undone, and the company often relaxed there together until late at night. However, I preferred to steer clear of the interval receptions. I don't know how a number of my colleagues manage to spend an hour in small talk and then go on to conduct, say, the second act of *The Valkyrie* or the third act of *Tristan*. But I did go to one such reception in 2003 when Joseph Ratzinger, still a cardinal at the time, came to a performance of *Tannhäuser*, because I really wanted to meet him. And I went to meet the then Chancellor Gerhard Schröder because I wanted to tell him about the situation of the Berlin opera houses.

I have often been asked whether Wolfgang Wagner was an artist. I don't know what I am expected to say. No, he was only pretending for dynastic reasons? No, but we had to bite the bullet and put up with his productions if we were to go on working at Bayreuth ourselves? I think the Old Man was much more of an artist than he could or would show, conscious as he was of his standing as the figurehead of the family. My former agent Ronald Wilford once said that Wolfgang Wagner was 'the best artistic director in the world', and I can only confirm that. The only other theatre I have known as perfectly run and organized as the Festival Theatre at Bayreuth is the New York Met.

There has been at least as much mockery of Wolfgang Wagner's down-to-earth Franconian manner as about his skill as a director. Not many people realize that the down-to-earth bluster was also a mask, a part he played to protect himself. As for his productions, I learned to value his profound knowledge of the scores and the house highly. Wolfgang Wagner could tell you in detail why he had staged certain scenes in *The Mastersingers* in one way rather than another: so that Stolzing wouldn't have to bellow in this or that passage, or so that the chorus could hear itself as well as possible in the notoriously difficult fugue accompanying the scuffle at the end of Act 2. He knew at once which sets would work and which would not. And he was an indispensable adviser on musical matters. Phone calls would come through to the pit: 'Herr Wagner says it's too slow,' 'Herr Wagner says it's too loud.' Sometimes he was on the line himself. The telephone in the pit doesn't ring, it blinks, and you hold the receiver in one hand while you go on conducting with the other. There are many passages where to this day I still hear the Old Man's rasping voice in my ear. You learn your trade first, then come your feelings – that, too, was something I learned from Wolfgang Wagner.

Of course he could be difficult; that's almost to be expected in such an outsize personality. There was the way he exiled his daughters and son from his first marriage from the Green Hill, not to mention his brother Wieland's children. And the arrangements for the succession were certainly among the most absurd cultural thrillers of Germany in the twentieth and twenty-first centuries, perhaps the last of their kind. Wolfgang Wagner held his lifetime position as director of the Festival, as mentioned above, from 1987 on, leading those politically responsible something of a dance. Several inquiries were set up and abandoned without coming to any conclusion. First Wolfgang wanted Gudrun to take over, then came the bid by Eva Wagner-Pasquier, Wolfgang's daughter from his first marriage. Neither idea came to anything; the politicians gritted their teeth, the Old Man resentfully insisted on staying where he was – stalemate. Finally, in 2008, there was an agreement; everyone gave way a little, no one lost face. Eva and Katharina were to take over the management jointly. 'Sisters' blood is thicker than cousins' water,' wrote the *Frankfurter Allgemeine Zeitung* at the time, referring to Wieland's daughter Nike, whose own bid together with Gerard Mortier had failed.

To those of us working on the Green Hill at that time, the situation often seemed schizophrenic. The press claimed that Wolfgang Wagner was senile, incapable of making any reasonable decision – and the next moment we would see him coming round the corner, as happy as a lark, and hear him arguing with the technical director. We read that the mood in the Festival Theatre was at rock bottom – and we were feeling perfectly cheerful. In 2002 we fell upon Brigitte Hamann's biography of Winifred Wagner, which really did contain some explosive material, relished some fruity comments – and yet had a feeling that the whole story was at a considerable remove from us and could not spoil our pleasure in the music. Ultimately the troublemakers overestimated their power: the shocked politicians, the investigative journalists, the family members consumed by envy and jealousy. They had thought they could shake the rock that was Wolfgang Wagner, but it was not shaken. And the more critical the outside voices were, the stronger our internal solidarity grew. The fortress mentality – those voices liked to accuse the Festival of such an attitude, and still do – really did manifest itself in these tense situations.

Many of the Festival staff revered Wolfgang Wagner as a father figure. And I am sure that the affection shown to him in the opera house was genuine, despite the criticism and the occasional grumbling about his unorthodox style of leadership. He was a popular man.

A number of people found it harder to get on with his second wife. Gudrun Wagner was very frank and direct, and did not mince her words. I was happy with that myself. A Berliner and an East Prussian, as she originally was, are likely to understand each other. Gudrun Wagner always told me she had been born on the day when the Tannenberg Monument* was blown up. Her mother, she said, had been in hospital in Allenstein (now Olsztyn), and as soon as the windows were opened they could hear the explosions in Hohenstein (now Olsztynek), 25 kilometres away. Engineers of the German army had been given orders to destroy the monument, latterly renamed the Reich Memorial, thus getting in ahead of the advancing Red Army. It was a dramatic story, particularly as little Gudrun and her family were said to have fled by way of the Vistula Lagoon on the Baltic coast shortly afterwards, and never saw her native land again. However, there is a problem: it can't have been like that. Gudrun Armann (her maiden name) was born on 15 June 1944, and the Tannenberg Monument was not blown up until the end of January 1945, at the very last minute. Obviously her mother was mixing real memories with inventions, history with the fears of the time. According to another source the family reached Langquaid in Lower Bavaria, where Gudrun was to grow up, in mid-July 1944, in which case they cannot possibly have escaped over the icy, brackish waters of the lagoon.

Leaving that story aside, you could depend on Gudrun Wagner 100 per cent. Once you had discussed something with her, it was settled. She was professional, highly committed, and really did understand the business of the Wagner industry to a high degree; she was at one with the Festival heart, body and soul. She had worked her way up in the

* Translator's note: the Monument had been set up to commemorate the Battle of Tannenberg in 1914.

firm from secretary in the press office, by way of office manager to Wolfgang Wagner, and so to being the 'secret director' of the Festival, as she was publicly regarded in the last years before her death. She was a very clever woman, with a gift for quick perception. In auditions, Gudrun Wagner was often the first to know whether something was or was not going to work.

And she was always there. I can't remember a time when Frau Wagner wasn't at the Festival Theatre. In my mind's eye I can still see her red crocodile-leather key ring, and the way she would lock the door of the west foyer at midday, saying she would be back in the office in an hour's time. She told me stories of my own younger days at Bayreuth that, with the best will in the world, I can't remember myself. For instance, that when I was Barenboim's assistant I always sat in the Bayreuth auditorium with my feet up on the back of the seat in front of me. She'd told me off for that a number of times, she said! Later she told me that story again and again, and it was part of our game that I would reply: I really can't remember any such thing, dear Frau Wagner; to which she would reply: but I remember perfectly!

Only once did we disagree, in 2004, over the première of Christoph Schlingensief's production of *Parsifal*. The Wagners were unhappy with his extremely unconventional staging; they felt it was more like an artist's installation than real opera, real music drama, and was also far too static. I think they simply didn't understand what Schlingensief was trying to do, and after a while they lost confidence in him. One day Christoph came over to me in the canteen and asked about the flower maidens in the second act: what kind of action did the music allow here, and what would be reasonable? I said, truthfully, that I wouldn't advise too much in the way of extreme activity; it would detract from co-ordination and would only annoy the conductor and the chorus master. Schlingensief promptly took that to heart. Whenever anyone complained that nothing much was happening on stage in his production, he parried by objecting, 'But Thielemann himself says...'. Gudrun Wagner was cross, because she felt I was meddling in what was none of my business. After a while I went to see her, taking a white rose. She was sitting in her office, and the atmosphere was not good. I said, 'Please would you stand up, Frau Wagner?' 'Why?' she asked.

'Just stand up,' I said, whereupon she muttered something and stood up. I gave her the rose and a hug – and all was well again.

What parties we had on the Green Hill! For instance, there was always a reception on Gudrun Wagner's birthday in June. Everyone was invited and wished her a happy birthday. There were platters of cold meat, and a glass or two of wine for anyone who wanted. Choral parties were held, orchestral parties, technicians' parties with a whole pig roasted on the spit – and the Wagners sat at a table at the inn where the party was given, cheerful and affable. In what other opera house would such a thing be imaginable? It was very difficult to judge, from the outside, how the two of them divided the work. He probably saw to all the technical arrangements, she concentrated more on what went on inside the theatre and looking after the artists. He had the ideas, thought up the casting; she put it all into practice, as his right hand and his conscience. A classic relationship, if you like, and one in which Gudrun Wagner's influence must not be underestimated.

What has established rather than impaired Wolfgang Wagner's reputation as director of the Festival, in retrospect, is the new structure of the Festival: since 2008 the dynastic approach of an absolutist one-man firm has given way to a democratically run, modern company. The Federal government, the free state of Bavaria, the city of Bayreuth and the 'Society of Friends of Bayreuth', an association of patrons, all hold shares in the Festival. That means more control and much more administrative expense. In times when communes are feeling the pinch, and interest in 'high culture' is less and less to be taken for granted, however, I see this as a safety precaution. Germany feels accountable to the myth of the Festival and its potential as a cultural lighthouse. It was in the first Grand Coalition between the CDU and the SPD, and it still is under the present coalition government. Even a man as little given to emotional sentiments as Bernd Neumann, Minister of Culture when I was writing this book, never tires of pointing that out.

All the same, I regard the dynastic principle as indispensable in Bayreuth. Many voices claim that it has exhausted itself and is outmoded. Certainly artistic quality is not a question of genes, yet why break with tradition as long as there are members of the Wagner family who want and are able to keep it going? Bayreuth has something that every festival longs and thirsts for, something on which much creative energy and money are expended all over the world: a truly exclusive element, an absolutely unique quality. The Festival means the Wagners – and the Wagners are the Festival. That identity is beyond price.

I never really said goodbye to Wolfgang Wagner. I would not let myself think of 'one last time'. But I visited him several times when he had stopped leaving his house, and I remember how tiny he seemed to me, transparent as glass. A man in the course of disappearing, extinguishing himself, a man through whom all reality was flowing away. Even in that condition, however, he had moments when he was wide awake, very much all there. He always knew who I was at once, and offered me his hand. He did not say much towards the end; instead, his daughter Katharina and I told him about this and that, while he listened. Not for long, maybe 20 minutes, but you could tell that he liked it. Particularly when he was told: Herr Wagner, you must get over to the Festival Theatre again, people are hoping to see you there!

Wolfgang Wagner died on 21 March 2010, a Sunday, at two in the morning. Three weeks later, on 11 April, there was a ceremony of remembrance in the Festival Theatre, in a very chilly temperature (the theatre has no heating). The chorus and orchestra played and sang, Wolfgang Wagner himself had chosen the musical programme, and I had the privilege of conducting. Only one photograph dominated the stage: Wolfgang aged around 80, wearing gold-rimmed glasses and a tie – as sturdy and invincible as if he would jump down from the screen any moment and dismiss the whole assembly with a single thump of his stick.

The myth

At Bayreuth I sometimes feel as if I were a character in *Parsifal*: year after year we unveil the Grail – yet we never know if it is the real Grail, if we have truly found it or ever will. So we always have to come back, all of us: pure fools and enchantresses, flower maidens, suffering kings, knights and squires. Wagner's characters, as everyone knows, are inclined to seek their counterparts in real life; it is one of the aspects of Bayreuth that make it such a special place.

It is wonderful when, as in Bayreuth, you can fit into a community of like-minded people. I enjoy being with those who are all on the same artistic wavelength. Loners have a more difficult time here, and bad behaviour is especially conspicuous. You need to be in tune with the place, not just musically but personally, and here again we come to the idea of a family: what use is an unpleasant bastard to me even if he plays the oboe divinely? As a conductor I find him useful, yes, but only in the short term. If he disturbs the harmony of the ensemble because he can't adapt to the orchestra in the pit, he may also do artistic damage. So there is discussion every summer about almost every instrumentalist and member of the chorus, and new decisions are made. None of the musicians have season tickets to Bayreuth in their pockets.

That doesn't mean that there have been no prickly characters on the Green Hill, or that all the members of the company are easy to handle. Neither Wilhelm Furtwängler nor Arturo Toscanini was the kind to knuckle under meekly, and those who remember Karajan's private toilet, or the uproar over certain productions in the history of the Festival (from Götz Friedrich's *Tannhäuser* to Christoph Schlingensief's *Parsifal*) will know that, if anything, the opposite is the case. Being among the like-minded does not mean forcing everyone to toe the line. Bayreuth is a paradox and lives that paradox, and we have to accept that. We see it as both the most sacred of places and the one where most freedom reigns. It means utter loyalty and desecration, cliché and anti-cliché, to be enlightened and to be overwhelmed, it means pragmatism and Utopia. Everything is possible here, and so is the opposite. It is possible to perform the same restricted range of operas for over a hundred years, yet feel that you are indulging lavishly. It is possible to abjure the world and conquer it, just as a summer in Bayreuth is of its very nature a strong vote against the globalization of the music business. We could do with so much more of what it represents. Six or eight weeks in the provinces, no long-haul flights and grand hotels, only a crisply roasted country duck now and then and a visit to the Lohengrin thermal baths – aren't such things the only true luxury?

Although Wagner offers us material of the greatest quality, his Festival has to be renewed over and over again. By directors and conductors who provide different readings of his operas, by successive generations of singers. We see the same in what goes on outside the Festival Theatre: the possibilities of today's media include public viewings, children's operas, opera shown in cinemas, live streaming on the Internet, all of these things part of the twenty-first century. That is as important as coming to terms with the political past, or the concept of the Villa Wahnfried as a museum for today. As I have said above, there is no single 'Bayreuth style' short-circuiting all our brains. I feel sure that old Richard himself could accept that. He puts up with us all, whether we revere him or rebel against him. He will accept even more, for he has survived other things. Wagner had a claim on the world that shows most of all in his indestructible quality. He saw himself as a creator; he wanted to explain life. Such a messianic approach, such hubris brings the envious on stage, exploiters, adversaries, plagiarists. Wagner has always been particularly susceptible where reactions to his music are concerned, and I shall be coming to that in a moment. But the more the Festival is profaned or condemned, the more significant it becomes; the more Wagner's operas are desecrated, the more sacred they appear, shining on in their magic.

When Nietzsche was still in harmony with Wagner he said, 'Some day we will all sit together in Bayreuth and wonder how we could bear to be anywhere else.' At the Margrave Bookshop's kiosk opposite the Festival Theatre, that saying can be bought today on a picture postcard.

4

A Very German Subject:
The Ideological Aspect

One of my assistants at Bayreuth once brought me back a T-shirt from Leipzig displaying a picture of Mendelssohn, caricatured with great verve in half-profile, with a wealth of hair and a hooked nose. I wore the T-shirt to one of the next rehearsals of the *Ring*, and the members of the orchestra were trying to puzzle out the figure's identity. Finally a pair of the musicians called out, 'Cosima!'. Cosima Wagner too had a great deal of hair and a prominent nose (inherited from her father Liszt). The ardent anti-Semite and Mendelssohn, a Protestant of Jewish descent – an innocent gift can lead you so quickly into the darkest depths of Bayreuth. Apart from that, Mendelssohn was a good idea to associate with *The Rhinegold* in particular, and we decided to play the music in as Mendelssohnian a style as possible: transparent, glittering, in a tone reminiscent of the *Midsummer Night's Dream* scherzo that is always light-footed but never fleeting.

Is C major still C major?

Comparing Cosima with Mendelssohn is certainly not politically correct, but we cannot think of the Green Hill without the shadow of its past. In principle I am not much interested in political correctness, which is often simply the way of least resistance. Nonetheless, the Bayreuth Festival does have a political past, and if we are honest it presents us with problems to this day. Can Wagner be blamed or can he not for the fact that *Rienzi* and *Lohengrin* were Hitler's favourite operas, and the dictator regularly had music from *The Mastersingers* played at Nazi Party rallies in Nuremberg? (We might just as well wonder whether it was Franz Lehár's fault that Hitler liked to pose as Count Danilo from *The Merry Widow* in front of a mirror, in a tailcoat, top hat and white silk scarf.) Was the calculated factor of the overpowering nature of Wagner's scores what first kindled megalomania in Hitler's mind? Can or must music and politics, politics and music, be considered in isolation from each other? Where does an interpretation end and misuse of it begin? What does that mean for the relationship of a work of art to its reception – and for me as a musician concerned first and foremost with the notes? Is C major still C major? Or is it an ideology? There is a great deal of Hitler in Wagner, Thomas Mann said, but could it just be that there is a great deal (indeed too much) of Wagner in Hitler?

For all the ideology that has been read or forced into interpretations of Wagner's works since 1933, and then again since 1945, the composer has chronology on his side. Wagner will always be a generation older than his most notorious admirer, for when Hitler was born in Braunau in Austria in 1889 Wagner, his 'prophet' (Joachim Köhler's term for it) had been dead for six years.

However, the political element on the Green Hill is not an invention of Adolf Hitler's, but is rooted in the story of Wagner's life. He stood beside Bakunin on the barricades in Dresden during the revolution of 1848/9. There was a warrant out for his arrest, and he spent two decades in flight alternately from his creditors and the police. That made little difference to his extravagant lifestyle; he had to leave Vienna too in 1864 to escape the threat of imprisonment for debt. A year later he went too far, politically and financially, even when he was under the wing of King Ludwig II; a public petition demanded his removal from the monarch's sphere of influence and Munich, where he was considered undesirable. And Wagner was not whiter than white in terms of bourgeois morality; after his marriage to the actress Minna Planer he indulged in many affairs: with the vintner's wife Jessie Laussot, with Mathilde Wesendonck, with Cosima von Bülow. He was not plagued by moral scruples; on the contrary, he seems to have needed erotic tension to stimulate his artistic work – just as he needed silk trousers and brocade wallpaper.

Politically, socially and morally, Richard Wagner was difficult to pin down. He was always in conflict, living at odds with his surroundings and indeed cultivating that discrepancy. Only in being different could he live out his need to be among the elite and his fantasies of redemption through art – which does not mean that he didn't crave fame, recognition, confirmation of his worth and love. The one was the necessary obverse of the other. Plenty of material there for analysis.

There is no doubt that Richard Wagner's thoughts and feelings were anti-Semitic, comprehensively and without exception. We can gather that from his writings and letters, and in this above all else Cosima fully supported her husband. Cosima's hatred of Jews, however, sprang more from ideas of 'good tone' and upper-class society, to which she claimed to belong by right of birth as the illegitimate daughter of a countess. Wagner's aversion, on the other hand, sprang from deep-rooted social envy. 'The Jews', who had been emancipated and then rose in social standing from the beginning of the nineteenth century onwards, represented a welcome object on which he could project that envy. Whenever something in his life went wrong he blamed it on the Jews: his attempt to get his first opera, *The Fairies*, put on in Leipzig; later in Paris, where he encountered such 'stinkingly terrible manifestations of operatic art' in the form of Giacomo Meyerbeer's work that he turned on his heel and left the city at once; and in the complex preparation of his project for the Bayreuth Festival. Wagner hated privilege unless it was given to him; he despised anyone who thought well of himself not for his achievements and his own work, but for his origins, his institution or his fortune. In his eyes, Mendelssohn matched this idea of his adversary perfectly: he came from a famous family of philosophers and bankers, he knew how to present himself to good advantage, he never had any financial worries in his life, and as if effortlessly he also stood sponsor to the rise of bourgeois music in Germany.

Excursus: Wagner and Mendelssohn

Richard Wagner, it has to be said, dug the grave in which the public opinion of Mendelssohn lay buried until well into the twentieth century. As a musician to whom Mendelssohn means almost as much as Wagner, I have always felt uneasy about that, and hurt by it. Wagner did lasting damage to Mendelssohn's reputation, not just in his inflammatory diatribe of 1850 on *Jewry in Music*, in which he claims that 'the Jew rules, and will rule as long as money is the power before which all our efforts are impotent'. What were Wagner's motives? Envy, resentment and jealousy. Jealousy of the privileged existence that Mendelssohn enjoyed all his life, of his success as a musician and a composer, of his popularity in Leipzig. Leipzig was Wagner's own native city, but it repeatedly cold-shouldered him, preferring Mendelssohn, only slightly his senior, a classicist and the representative, said Wagner, of 'a blind alley in the history of music'.

Yet the young Wagner, like many of his contemporaries, was well aware of the kind of music that Mendelssohn was writing. He himself several times used typically Mendelssohnian methods. In *The Fairies* he imitates Mendelssohn's choral style; his Overture *Columbus* makes no secret of the debt it owes to the spirit of the concert Overture *Calm Sea and Prosperous Voyage*; and to promote *The Fairies* he even tried to emulate Mendelssohn by exploiting his family network. In Wagner's case that network included his brother Albert, who in 1833 got Richard a steady job for a good year as chorus director at the Würzburg theatre; his brother-in-law Friedrich Brockhaus, who tried intimidating the manager of the Leipzig theatre by saying, 'Devil take him if he won't stage the opera!'; and finally there was his sister Rosalie, a much-admired actress in Leipzig, who also did her best to show her brother in a good light. But how do theatrical managers react to this kind of pressure? They look for ways and means of not staging the hoped-for production, and they let time go by. Richard Wagner, however, had no time; he felt he must have a hit now, in order, as he put it, to 'secure a position' in Leipzig. He must work fast – faster than anyone else, and that really meant faster than Mendelssohn, who was still music director in Düsseldorf, but an appointment as conductor of the Gewandhaus Orchestra was already a distinct possibility. No way led past Mendelssohn – that 'gadfly', as Cosima acidly calls him in her diaries. Richard Wagner himself felt it keenly. Leipzig brought him no luck; there was no production of *The Fairies*, and as a test of his talent it fell through.

Wagner took that failure very much to heart. He fled to the provinces as music director in Magdeburg, and from there tried to get in touch with Mendelssohn. On 11 April 1836 he sent him the score of a symphony in C major that he had written at the age of 18. It had been performed by Mendelssohn's predecessor at the Gewandhaus, Christian August Pohlenz. However, Mendelssohn did not react; in fact he did not even thank him for the music. Was he overtaxed by the business of the Gewandhaus Orchestra? Did he feel, subliminally, that no relationship with Wagner would turn out well for him? Or did he simply think that the symphony and its composer, a man unknown to him and struggling to make his way, were not worth his notice? Anyway, the score disappeared, and decades later Wagner claimed that Mendelssohn had destroyed it on purpose because it revealed 'aptitudes that were unwelcome to him'.

It was an insult for the conductor of the Leipzig Gewandhaus Orchestra to decline contact with the music director of Magdeburg – and it reinforced Wagner's nascent hostility. He came to a momentous decision that to a certain extent was caused by Mendelssohn. On 22 September 1836 Wagner announced, in a letter to his friend the writer Theodor Apel in Leipzig: 'For the time being I [...] am abandoning the concert hall entirely. I could do without your advice to send a carefully written Overture to Leipzig: I don't care to be regarded as a hanger-on, and your praise of Mendelssohn puts me off the idea very much indeed. So with respect to your distinguished magnificence, I am giving myself up to the glitter of the stage. From now on I am solely a composer of operas, and I shall throw myself into those operas body, soul, hope and all.' Significant and defiant words. To make his mark despite any disrespect for his person and his art, Wagner was bowing out as a musician practising in all genres. He was going to specialize. Creativity driven by an inferiority complex, confrontation as a capacitor – nothing could have been further from Mendelssohn. And in opting for drama, opera, music theatre Wagner, with a sure instinct, was choosing a field where his tiresome rival could not possibly be any danger to him.

So now all might have been well. Mendelssohn and Wagner, the two rivals, parted company, each devoting himself to his own artistic gifts – and the musical world could rejoice in having on the one hand an operatic revolutionary and passionate dilettante like Wagner, and on the other a versatile bourgeois virtuoso like Mendelssohn. But artists are not like that, and here we have a particularly extreme example.

There was still contact between the two composers, although they were not close; the number of times they met can be counted on the fingers of one hand, but they corresponded, and each conducted works by the other: Wagner conducted the *Calm Sea* Overture mentioned above, as well as Mendelssohn's setting of the 42nd Psalm and his Scottish Symphony, while Mendelssohn conducted the Overture to *Tannhäuser*. Mendelssohn hardly ever said anything about Wagner in public; his attitude was distant but civil. Wagner's tone in speaking of Mendelssohn, however, changed rapidly. Early letters still address him as 'Highly respected Sir' and are signed by 'your most ardent admirer'. Wagner was still courting the other man's favour. Later, the salutation ran 'My dear, dear Mendelssohn', or 'My most respected friend' – there had obviously been a certain rapprochement, they both committed themselves to the project for a memorial to Carl Maria von Weber in Dresden, they respected each other, at least as Wagner saw it. But upon the early death of Mendelssohn in 1847 all that changed entirely. Everything that Wagner had only hinted at before now burst out: envy, persecution mania, anti-Semitism. Wagner was fiercely determined to fill the vacuum left by Mendelssohn, and he hit upon the writing of music history as a proven method of exerting power. Whenever he had an opportunity, he ran Mendelssohn down as a superficial composer looking back at the past. 'Mendelssohn the foreigner, not in the least German,' wrote Cosima in her diary on 7 November 1872. It was character assassination, and it had consequences.

However, Jews were not all the same to Wagner. He distinguished, for instance, between Giacomo Meyerbeer and Mendelssohn, and he must therefore have been doubly hurt by Hans von Bülow's witticism to the effect that his own *Rienzi* was 'Meyerbeer's best opera'. He would never have ventured, he said in his memoirs, to compare his own abilities as a musician with those of Mendelssohn. But he remarks, in a letter to the Viennese critic Eduard Hanslick, that in his view all that he hated 'as internally meaningless and externally laborious in operatic music' was united in the name of Meyerbeer. Meyerbeer, the king of triviality and contrived stage effects, was not the same as the unimpeachable Mendelssohn.

However, Wagner had another arrow in his quiver to use against Mendelssohn, and it bore the name of Ludwig von Beethoven. With Beethoven, said Wagner, absolute music had reached its limits, and there could be no music of the future without 'poetic intent' (meaning without Wagner himself). Referring to Mendelssohn as 'affected by the classical style' and 'the representative of an outmoded aesthetic of art', Cosima wrote: 'Into what a shallow train of thought did Mendelssohn lead music back, after Beethoven had so magnificently struck notes of the true German folk tradition.' Wagner thus figures as the rightful heir of Beethoven, while Mendelssohn is only his pale imitator. Not a word about the lucidity with which Mendelssohn committed himself to Beethoven all his life as an interpreter and conductor, not a word about his intense concern, as a composer, with the Viennese master.

On the one hand, then, Mendelssohn was never able to show 'the deep effect on us, moving our hearts and souls, that we expect of the art of music, knowing that it is able to do so'. Both as a man and a musician, he always left a chilly impression on Wagner. On the other hand, Wagner was enthusiastic in his praise of the oratorio *St Paul* as 'evidence of the highest flowering of art', called Mendelssohn 'a fine musician' and described the *Hebrides* Overture as 'extremely beautiful'. Can all these views be reconciled? Yes, definitely, said Wagner, remarking in 1869 that an 'enormous talent' like Mendelssohn's was 'alarming' and at the same time 'cold', and therefore 'has nothing to do with our musical development'. Did he know how much he was deceiving himself?

Almost 60 years later, the National Socialists resorted to Wagner's strategy in Germany. I do not think that Wagner can be held directly responsible for the consequences. Certainly not without taking into account the spread of anti-Semitism and militant nationalism in the second half of the nineteenth century (in opera as well as in other respects: we need only think of Smetana's strongly nationalist *Libuša*, with which the National Theatre in Prague opened in 1881). But Wagner did have a strong influence on those consequences – in particular by giving the usual witch-hunting of Jews the outward appearance of an aesthetic argument.

None of this prevented him from continuing to help himself to Mendelssohn's musical ideas. The Prelude to *The Rhinegold* is strongly reminiscent of the waves motif in the concert Overture *The Fair*

Melusine; *Parsifal* quotes the Dresden amen from the Reformation Symphony. And at the beginning of the *Ring* cycle, Wagner's Wotan actually assumes the musical mantle of the introductory recitative from Mendelssohn's *Elijah*. Wagner's contemporaries must have been aware of these borrowings, and we should not forget them today.

Wagner had published his notorious pamphlet on *Jewry in Music* in the journal *Die Neue Zeitschrift für Musik* in 1850, under the pseudonym of K. Freigedank.* Almost 20 years later, in 1869, it appeared again in an even more outspoken new edition, now under his own name, and set off violent reactions. Mendelssohn and Meyerbeer were long dead, and Wagner merely felt that his ideas were confirmed by the new disagreement that was expressed. Very much the genius, he justified his 'sudden polemical excursus' as recreation from the 'ecstatic' work of composition, 'during which I am really to be considered an absolute eccentric'. Meanwhile, Mendelssohn's fame was fading, and the anniversaries of his birth and death passed without much public notice. Musical practice, however, obeys other laws; it loved and needed Mendelssohn, his lieder and choral songs were performed in private living rooms and salons alike, and the everyday life of German concert halls would have been unthinkable without his Violin Concerto and the *Midsummer Night's Dream* Overture. At the beginning of the twentieth century, the British lexicographer George Grove and the German musicologist Ernst Wolff were the first to plead for a more complete image of Mendelssohn than this kind of popularity covered. Alfred Einstein also deserves mention here for calling Mendelssohn's style masterly as early as 1920, when it had often been dismissed as merely polished.

Of course the Nazis put a stop to these developments in and after 1933. The years from then until 1945 wounded Mendelssohn's reputation, much as Amfortas is wounded in *Parsifal*. We may know all this today and think it as deplorable as it was mindless, but that does not really make much difference to the Mendelssohn problem. Mendelssohn is still the composer who, in Adorno's words, is *nicht ganz reçu*, not entirely accepted. The fact that the Mendelssohn memorial in Leipzig was torn down in 1936 and not replaced until 2008 speaks volumes.

---

* Translator's note: *Freigedank*, the pseudonym adopted, suggests 'free-thinking'.

It is easy to despise Wagner outright for his abuse of Mendelssohn, just as it is easy to see the terrible conclusion of his essay on Jewry relating to the Holocaust. In that conclusion he addresses the Jews as a whole: 'But remember that only one thing can release you from the curse on you: the release that Ahasuerus* knew – your *destruction*.' Did Hitler know this sentence? Very probably. As a conductor, however, I can only agree with Alban Berg, of whom Hans Mayer, the writer and musicologist, tells a wonderful story; it is to be found in an otherwise highly tendentious volume entitled 'Richard Wagner – How anti-Semitic may an artist be?' in the *Musik-Konzepte* (*Musical Concepts*) series. Mayer met Berg in the 1920s in Berlin, where his *Wozzeck* had been given its première under the baton of Erich Kleiber at the State Opera House. How was Mayer, the young Jewish Marxist and post-expressionist, to impress the famous composer? He roundly abused Richard Wagner. Mayer goes on: 'And Alban Berg – memorably – looked down at me from above and said, "Yes, it's all very well for you to talk like that, but then you're not a musician." '

Emotion and politics

Berg hit the nail on the head. A musician will always judge Richard Wagner by his music: his abilities as an artist and a craftsman. Since there is no doubt of those abilities, we soon find ourselves in a dilemma. What about the so-called ideological aspect? How do we deal with Wagner's anti-Semitism? There is no room for it in the music, where C major does indeed remain C major. Even Wagner's declared enemies have yet to offer the world conclusive proof that Beckmesser in *The Mastersingers*, Kundry in *Parsifal* and Alberich and Mime in the *Ring* are malicious caricatures of the Jewish character. If Wagner's music were really so uninspired as to present us with such clones, there would be no difficulty: we would be dealing not with art but with propaganda, and would have nothing to worry about. However, I can't play or conduct a six-four chord to make it sound either anti-Semitic or pro-Semitic, fascist or socialist or capitalist. I can be aware of its non-musical

* Translator's note: in German, the legendary figure known to the English-speaking world as the Wandering Jew is the Eternal Jew instead, and bears the name Ahasuerus.

connotations, and that knowledge may colour my interpretation. But when I am convinced that the score in front of me is a masterpiece, inexhaustible in its complexity, I can't look at it ideologically. I must comply with what the score itself demands, I must present it in musical terms.

It is a different thing to listen deliberately with capitalist, socialist or fascist attitudes in mind, or to have such attitudes imposed on one – and that is something I hold against those who have tried to 'explain' Wagner by citing Hitler after 1945 and especially after 1968. They aimed to prevent others listening to the music, and to some extent they succeeded. I have nothing against coming to terms with the reception of Wagner, far from it. After all, we are looking at one of the most instructive chapters in German intellectual history as a whole, with all its depths, heights and flaws. As a musician, however, I must not imagine that doing so helps me in my work. The literature from Adorno by way of Hartmut Zelinsky to Joachim Köhler gives me no information whatsoever about the strength of the chorus in the fugue accompanying the scene in *The Mastersingers*, or the correct dynamic in the Prelude to *Tristan*. That is both a fine and a terrible idea, simultaneously comforting and alarming. Once *Tristan* begins, nothing else matters. Music wins the day.

I was intrigued even at an early age by the ideological aspect of Wagner. As an adolescent I couldn't connect the music I loved with what I heard and read about Hitler's presence at Bayreuth, or the political entanglements of my heroes Furtwängler and Karajan. We were always discussing history at home. In addition, my mother was a friend of the daughter of the clarinettist Ernst Fischer, a former chairman of the board of the Berlin Philharmonic. Fischer's wife was Jewish, and he had had difficulties under the Nazi regime. At a very tender age I played to him on an enormous grand piano in his Wilmersdorf apartment, and I clearly remember the entertaining coffee parties at the Fischers' home. Frau Fischer, who seemed to me as old as the hills (she may have been around 60 at the time) used to invite her friends, all of them amusing older ladies who did not live in Berlin, had flowery names and read books backwards. One came from Paris to visit the Fischers, another from Belfast, a third from Jerusalem, and they all spoke German. The atmosphere was amazingly cheerful, warm and relaxed. I still remember feeling surprised to find these ladies having such fun together and laughing so much. Sometimes the conversation was more serious, and then they spoke of the time when they had had to leave Berlin. One now lived in Jerusalem, where it was very hot and you couldn't play Wagner. As a child I thought the idea of having to leave home was terrible, but I didn't see what that had to do with Wagner. It must have been too difficult for the grown-ups to explain it to me. At least no one said: don't touch his music, it's bad. Even when Wagner was mentioned in connection with Israel the ladies just nodded: oh yes, of course we have the records at home in a cupboard all the same. I am not sure whether a serious warning against Wagner would have cut any ice with me at that time. I was eight or nine, and once I was listening to *Lohengrin* in the opera house nothing else existed. So far as I was concerned, there was only the music.

Later I read widely, and I came upon much criticism of Wagner. It troubled me that his music seemed to be so controversial, particularly because I wasn't used to such observations in the opera house or my own environment. In 1976, on the centenary of the première of the *Ring*, Hartmut Zelinsky's book *Richard Wagner: Ein deutsches Thema (Richard Wagner: A German Theme)* was published. Reading it shocked and indeed infuriated me, for instance, when I came upon the following monstrous condemnation of the public: 'What kind of critical faculty can a society that considers itself Christian maintain if for decades, and even now in the year 1976, it allows, approves and actually welcomes the regularity with which *Parsifal* is performed on Good Friday in opera houses and on the radio? This work is described as the most refined and ingenious artistic product of modern European culture, and Wagner calculated its effect to give exactly that impression on the grounds that I have already mentioned. *Parsifal* [...] has nothing at all to do with Good Friday, but was conceived with the aim of destroying it, or at least the Christianity with which it is associated and the Biblical Christ himself. Their purification and redemption "from all Alexandrian, Judaic and Roman despotic disfigurement" [...] is what the key formula of the "redemption of the Redeemer" stands for. This constitutes the claim to redemption that Wagner announced in *Parsifal*, and to this day it is accepted by a public as susceptible as ever to myths and far from immune to calculated seduction.'

Art 'calculating' some kind of long-term political effect? A public unable to withstand 'calculated seduction' even in 1976? And a water-tight explanation of Wagner's mysterious formula about the redemption of the Redeemer? It seemed to me absurd. Here was a writer trying to take his ill will out on someone – young as I was at the time, I quickly suspected as much – and it only reinforced my opposition. Zelinsky himself does say that his book is not about Wagner's music but about the 'effects' of his work, his 'ideology', yet that hardly justifies such venom, so much bitter foaming at the mouth. In fact Zelinsky takes out his feelings on a wide selection of targets: Richard Wagner is described as 'Hitler's intellectual foster father'; Hans Jürgen Syberberg, who made a 'Hitler-fixated' film about Winifred Wagner, is suspected of throw-ing in his lot with the 'old National Socialists'; and even Wieland, co-founder of the New Bayreuth, is not absolved of the 'idealism of old Bayreuth'.

All this went too far for me. I saw Wagner's works reduced to stupid sentiment, a simple dogma of domination, and that couldn't be the truth. Zelinsky's Wagner and my Wagner were related in much the same way as the fanfare played before special announcements over the Reich Radio of the Nazi regime is related to the original score of Franz Liszt's *Les Préludes*: 150 wind instruments, played *fortissimo* and non-stop, simply have nothing to do with the music as it was composed.

It is here that I find the whole thing interesting. Aren't such critics as Zelinsky violating Wagner's work all over again? They tell the public what to think. They reduce the operas to ideology, and explain the political interpretation as the only satisfactory one, but reversing the circumstances. They rewrite the end of *Lohengrin*, turning the admonition: 'To fair Brabant's Duke make your vow / Taking him as your leader [*Führer*] now!' into 'Calling him your protector [*Schützer*] now!' And in the closing words of Hans Sachs in *The Mastersingers* they cannot stomach the line, 'Honour your German masters', but make it into 'Honour your noble masters'. They do not trouble about the way Wagner sets those words to music, they don't understand the emphasis or lack of it, the rising and falling rhythm that makes the accent lie clearly on 'masters' and not 'German'. We need to know these things, however, in order to see how clever, well-judged and witty Wagner's music can be.

I often heard *The Mastersingers* in the 1970s at the Berlin State Opera House, frequently with Theo Adam as Sachs. Adam was in the habit of eliding the 'd' in the word *deutsch* [German], singing not of what was *deutsch und echt* [German and true] but *'eutsch und echt*. In one performance the bass Siegfried Vogel sang the part instead of him, pronouncing every 'd' clearly, including the mention of what was *deutsch und echt*. The audience around me shifted in their seats; there was a definite reaction in the auditorium, and not one of protest.

As a singer I can emphasize or utter individual words so that his attitude to what is being said or sung is made clear. As a conductor I can do something comparable by injecting feeling into a passage or passing over it casually by adopting a certain tempo, or making it suddenly stand out from the rest by means of the dynamic. I can do that – but only if I know how. I need good musical and dramatic reasons to justify what I am doing to myself as well as others. Otherwise the interpretation will seem to be artificially imposed on the music and will lose credibility, making my aims appear either satirical rather than musical, or designed to obey the political taste of the time. I know that I must declare my support for the text that goes with the music, or no good will come of it.

The funeral march in *Twilight of the Gods* is one of those pieces that call for me, as a conductor, to nail my colours to the mast. Do I believe Wagner, who tells us that Siegfried, the saviour of the world, is being carried to his grave – or do I see this interlude of barely eight minutes as a pragmatic feature, necessary for changing the mood of the music, bringing the scene back from the banks of the Rhine to the hall of the Gibichungs and giving the stage hands time for it? Do I myself feel something like sadness, or am I conducting so as to nullify any such emotion? That sounds as if we had a free choice. But Richard Wagner would not be Richard Wagner if he did not rigorously deprive his interpreters of their freedom to decide, for he himself always combines emotion with pragmatism, Dionysius and Apollo going hand in hand, inspiration and calculation together. It all depends on the equilibrium, the right mixture. And on approaching the funeral march so that it does not sound like a self-contained musical number but a building block, a link in the context of the entire *Ring*. As the conductor, I have my work cut out for me in keeping the tension going for those eight minutes, just as I do over the 14 hours of the entire cycle. To be honest, I am considerably more interested in how to do that than in whether this or that is or is not a 'poor' passage in the text. I think that performing what is in the score to the best of my ability and my conscience, and leaving it to the audience to think about the meaning, is actually part of a historically correct approach to Wagner.

The political element seldom featured in my conversations with Wolfgang Wagner. He sometimes mentioned his mother Winifred, and told a few anecdotes about Hitler – when Hitler came to the Bayreuth Festival for the first time in 1923, Wolfgang was four years old and his brother Wieland six. The two of them grew up with the image of the dictator, like it or not. Those anecdotes, however, were confined to trivialities – for instance, Hitler poking the fire on the hearth in the Villa Wahnfried for hours on end while the boys were expected to entertain him, because he wanted to hear the news from America at three or four in the morning; how he came over from the Hotel Bube in Bad Berneck for tea or supper much more often than the public knew or was supposed to know; and the gossip about an alleged relationship between Hitler and Winifred.

I can't say much more than Wolfgang Wagner did in his auto-biography. Even in private there were no spectacular revelations about Hitler, no skeletons in the closets of the Festival Theatre, nothing off the record that the world did not know already. And Adolf Hitler was of no importance in our daily work. I do see that to this day the Bayreuth Festival has a certain amount of leeway to make up in the matter of 'coming to terms with the past', as the phrase goes in this particular German context (although that phrasing will always be a puzzle to me).* And the fact that Wolfgang Wagner cancelled the exhibition announced for the 100th anniversary of his mother's birth at short notice was not a clever move. Katharina Wagner and Eva

* Translator's note: the well-known and long-winded German term, with connotations of a cover-up, is *Vergangenheitsbewältigung*.

Wagner-Pasquier, however, have taken up the cause of investigating the Nazi period on the Green Hill. They commissioned two historians, and who knows, perhaps the correspondence between 'Wini' and 'Wolf' really will bring some startling details to light.

As a musician and a conductor, I often feel that too much is said about politics rather than too little. I can't hold Richard Wagner musically responsible for the misuse of his works by the Nazis. I can't conduct *The Mastersingers* fastidiously touching it only with my fingertips – I could only refrain from having anything to do with the work at all. Many of my colleagues do that, and the world must respect their attitude. But in the twenty-first century, are we to condemn all vegetarians and ostracize all German shepherd dogs just because Blondi existed and Hitler did not eat meat? Are our politicians to steer clear of the opening of the Festival because between 1933 and 1944 the drive up to the opera house was lined by swastika flags, and the Führer greeted visitors from the balcony of the Festival Theatre? No. Wagner is a universal artist because all kinds of different people have liked his music and still do. And today Bayreuth can still be an institution with which the whole country identifies. That is why the President of the Federal Republic, the Chancellor and other high-ranking politicians really should, as I see it, come to Bayreuth; that is why every prominent figure is welcome. And if the gutter press regularly reports on the most garish headgear and lowest necklines at the reception given for premières by the Prime Minister of Bavaria, people notice that too. A country cannot identify only with its economic strength; it must also protect and treasure its immaterial values, its culture and its spirit.

Goethe says, in *Faust: Was du ererbt von deinen Vätern hast, / Erwirb es, um es zu besitzen* ('That which your forefathers have left to you / Call it your own, to make it truly yours'). That is the challenge thrown down to us by Bayreuth year after year. Because Wagner wanted it to go on. Not for nothing do none of his music dramas end in a minor key. They all close in the major, even *Tristan*, even *Twilight of the Gods*. You may think that crazy, but it also represents a fine statement of defiance: in spite of everything life goes on. There is always a final remnant in Wagner, a last ember crying out to be rekindled.

5

'If we want Wagner, then Wagner is what we want', or:
What Makes a Good Performance?

I would not go so far as to say, with the comedian Loriot, otherwise known as Vicco von Bülow and descended from Hans von Bülow, that 'life without Bayreuth is possible but pointless'. Not quite so far. For today Wagner is performed all over the world, and it would probably be easier to count those opera houses that do not put on productions of his operas (because they are too small or cannot afford the necessary expense, which is considerable). At the moment there is a positive glut of Wagner. Because the prestigious glory of grand opera is consoling in times of crisis. Because Wagner should be suitably celebrated in view of the 200th anniversary of his birth. And because the globalization of the music market increases demand. Wagner for all? However, a few prerequisites should not be lost from sight, and certainly not from hearing. Among them are the architecture and acoustics of opera houses.

The architectonic element

The largest opera houses are not necessarily the best for productions of Wagner. The New York Met, with almost 4,000 seats, may sound fantastic, but anyone sitting at the very back soon loses touch with what is happening on stage. The architectural requirements for a good Wagnerian sound seem to me obvious: the Wagnerian orchestra, around 120 instrumentalists strong, should fit into the pit, which must not be too high up; the proportions of the auditorium should be right for it (and also right in its relation to the stage and the two sides of the stage); and where the shape of the auditorium is concerned a slightly elongated oval is always better than a shoebox. A good opera house for Wagner can be of medium size, and does not really need to have its walls covered with velvet. A good opera house for Wagner is one where the orchestra, large as it is, does not sound stuffy or muted, and the voices carry well.

Otto Brückwald, who built the Bayreuth Festival Theatre, was certainly an outstanding theatrical architect. Gottfried Semper, who stood on the barricades in Dresden with Wagner, had been another. But Georg Wenzeslaus von Knobelsdorff could hardly have been expected to build a theatre suitable for Wagner; after all, in building the Berlin State Opera on Unter den Linden he was planning for the eighteenth and not the nineteenth century. At the time of writing the Berlin State Opera was being renovated for the fifth time. Following a fire in 1844 in Knobelsdorff's original building, the first rebuilding was by Carl Ferdinand Langhans. The theatre was hit by bombs in air raids twice during the Second World War, and once, in 1941/2, had to be completely rebuilt. After the war Richard Paulick left his mark on what was then the leading opera house of the German Democratic Republic, and then, more than two decades after German reunification, the architectural firm of HG Merz set to work on it. It is interesting that the State Opera House on Unter den Linden is said never to have sounded better than in the two or three years when it was open during the war, as old opera-goers have told me. There was a fourth tier of seats then, and a middle tier of boxes, the cubic shape was changed to approximate more closely to a pear shape – and immediately the acoustics were not so dry. What this tells us is that a former Court Opera House will never be entirely suitable for the works of Wagner, but a few tactful changes will mean that it need not abstain entirely from including works later than Weber's *Der Freischütz* in its repertory.

These days opera houses organized on modern lines want to stage everything: Handel played on original instruments; flexible productions of Mozart; the great names of the nineteenth century as represented by Verdi, Wagner and Strauss; and also, ideally, Bernd Alois Zimmermann's *Die Soldaten* (*The Soldiers*) and Nono's *Prometeo* (*Prometheus*), as well as some recently commissioned twenty-first-century works with plenty of live electronics and some video effects. Architecturally and acoustically that is impossible. The repertory has never been as wide as it is today – but our opera houses are not so adaptable, or at least only to a very limited extent; they cannot meet all these requirements.

Musical cities like Munich are very well equipped in that respect: Munich has the Cuvilliés Theatre for Baroque opera, the National Theatre for Romantic and modern classical opera, the Gärtnerplatz Theatre for light opera and operetta, and the Prinzregent Theatre for much else. With its 1,000 seats it is, so to speak, the little brother of the Bayreuth Festival Theatre. It was designed in 1900 by Ernst von Possart and Max Littmann as a festival theatre for the works of Wagner, as if to make up for King Ludwig II's failure to build one in Munich in his own time. Like Bayreuth, it is laid out as an amphitheatre and has excellent acoustics. It also has a covered orchestra pit, but the cover can be taken off, and Lorin Maazel had it removed when, after thorough renovation, the theatre reopened in 1996 with Wagner's *Tristan and Isolde*. But while, with a little goodwill, 95 musicians will be enough for *Tristan* – and there is no room in the pit for more – it would be impossible to put on the *Ring* or *Parsifal* in the Prinzregent Theatre.

Wagner's own city of Dresden has only one opera house, and no real concert hall to supplement it. The Semper Opera House therefore has to do for everything, large and small, old and new, operas and concerts and, as if miraculously, it always manages. The house that we know today has been rebuilt three times. The first building, dating from 1841, fell victim to a fire – a frequent phenomenon at that time, when lighting was provided by candles or oil lamps (or in the case of Bayreuth by gaslights, then a pioneering innovation). The second Semper Opera House was built in the years 1871 to 1878, under the supervision of Semper's son Manfred. The architect himself had been forbidden to set foot on Saxon ground for life because of his former participation in the revolution, so he sent designs and plans from his exile in Zürich and Vienna. This second building was reduced to dust and ashes on the night of 13 February 1945 during Allied air raids. Finally, the third building was reopened in 1985, and is a great success. While Semper's proportions have been retained, the auditorium and stage are slightly enlarged, so that with 1,300 seats the house's acoustics suit both the singers and the orchestra very well.

I met the architect responsible, Wolfgang Hänsch, in Dresden in 2010. You can do a great deal of calculation and construction, he told me, you can try things out and draw comparisons and do your calculations all over again three times, but in the end the reason why an opera house or concert hall does or does not sound good is a mystery. A genius like Gottfried Semper or Richard Wagner (who is known to have done all he could to help with the building of the Bayreuth house) probably just had the right nose for it, the right kind of intuition.

Mastering the conducting of opera on the grand scale

As a rule there are no very young conductors of Wagner, and that was true of me. I had in fact begun young, but I was nearly 30 years old by the time I conducted my first *Lohengrin* on stage in Nuremberg. It had been preceded by a concert production of *Rienzi* in Hanover, and my first attempts at fully staged performances in Venice (incidentally, La Fenice, like La Scala in Milan, is a very good house for the works of Wagner). There are various reasons why it took so long: for one thing, it is more demanding to read and master the score of one of Wagner's major operas than the score of a Haydn symphony, purely from the aspect of craftsmanship, and of course you build up a repertory after initial difficulties. For another thing, until you yourself are chief conductor in a theatre you cannot really enjoy conducting Wagner properly. When I was assistant to Daniel Barenboim at his debut in Bayreuth with *Tristan* in 1981, I did stand on the podium now and then during rehearsals, so that he could sit up in the auditorium and hear the effect of what he had been working on, but he was usually back very soon, so the fact that I was conducting the music without the score, which I knew by heart, was not chalked up to my credit; after all, there is no point in it at Bayreuth, where no one will see you. I was also hopelessly nervous at the time.

During one performance of *Tristan* that summer, Barenboim had a high temperature, and I was asked to sit on the steps in the pit ready to take over if necessary. 'If I go off, you can carry on conducting,' he told me, but in the end it never came to that, and somehow or other I knew all along that it wouldn't. However, it reassured him to have me there, and it gave me the feeling of being closer to my aim than ever before.

How does a young conductor draw attention to himself? By hard work and industry, by acting as a répétiteur as often as possible and acquiring a good knowledge of a work. However, you also need to think strategically. It would be naïve not to do so. You have to prostitute yourself a little, accepting offers that may not be entirely what you want artistically but could open doors for you; you have to accept musical partners who have already made a reputation, and show yourself in all the important places. All the same, a time will come when you have to stop making these concessions, or you will forget yourself and be untrue to what you want. I recognized that quite early as a danger, indeed a threat. It was Georg Solti who said that it is terribly difficult to get into the music business – but even more difficult to get out of it again, and he was quite right.

That ambivalence is at the heart of the following story. London in the 1960s, the conductor Sergiu Celibidache is working with Daniel Barenboim (as pianist) and his wife the cellist Jacqueline du Pré. They were getting on very well, their recitals were successful. One day 'Celi' asked the two young musicians to his hotel and made them an offer: they were both so gifted, he said, they could really do great things – if they would turn down all other engagements for two years after this series of concerts and follow him to his island in the Mediterranean, where he was thinking of initiating them into the deeper mysteries of music. The young couple didn't know what to say. Next day Barenboim tried to explain to the maestro that what he was asking was impossible. Celibidache looked at Barenboim for a long time and finally sighed: 'Daniel, you're a tart.' Today Barenboim says that Celibidache was right, but all the same private instruction on a remote island was not an option. As so often, it was a case of maintaining an equilibrium between prostitution and refusal, esoteric vows of chastity and selling your own soul.

But what is the wonderful first time like? You step up on the podium, you raise your arms – Wagner's torrents of sound wash round you, and all the ideas you have had in your head for so long come true? Nothing of the kind. Every young conductor has a wealth of ideas for delightful details. You feel you are so talented! You can conduct such beautiful transitional passages! And how brilliantly you know how to solve this or that problem! None of this is entirely wrong, but much of it, when you hear it again later, simply does not make sense. You were too loud here, too slow there, you enjoyed that passage so much, but now it suddenly sounds stupid – in short, the relationships don't work, there is no internal equilibrium. That is exactly what you have to learn.

Basically, all young conductors should conduct Wagner as early as possible, because that is the way they will learn how to approach opera on a large scale. You can train on Beethoven, too, on Brahms or Bruckner, but it was to Wagner that I had to pledge myself first. Another factor involved, of course, is the sheer length of such a work as *Tristan* or *Twilight of the Gods*, and the necessary physical and psychological fitness for it. The conductor is like an extreme mountaineer tackling greater and greater heights: he must acclimatize himself, become familiar with the dimensions, or he will fail. And he must believe that he can conquer his peak, step by step, beat by beat of his baton. Then it will turn out that not every mountain is K2 or Nanga Parbat.

Above all, it is a case of your internal disposition, the flow of your powers. That takes thought, preferably thought in advance. At home alone with the score, in the cloakroom on the day of the performance, and then alone on the podium in the last few seconds before the music begins. That is why I like to be at the theatre early, so that I can run through it again in my head at my leisure: individual passages, certain transitions, or a swift review of the whole thing. I wouldn't call it a concept; that sounds too stiff and programmatic, perhaps the word 'plan' would be better. I need a plan. I have to think exactly how to build up the long conversation between Wotan and Brünnhilde in the third act of *The Valkyrie* while maintaining the tension, or how to approach the beginning of the first act without having a heart attack myself. That beginning is loud, a genuine thunderstorm, but it is not and must not seem to be the end of the world. I have to know that in advance. And I can know it in advance, because such things can be analyzed, explained, grasped. The same cannot necessarily be said of other aspects of conducting Wagner.

What is it that Bertolt Brecht says in the *Die Dreigroschenoper* (*Threepenny Opera*)? *Ja, mach nur einen Plan / sei nur ein grosses Licht / und mach dann noch 'nen zweiten Plan / gehn tun sie beide nicht* ('Yes, just make a plan / and cast a great light / and then make another / they can't both be right'). There is some truth in that (and Kurt Weill, the composer of the work, studied Wagner closely). First, not every plan works out for the young conductor, nor does every second plan. And secondly, plans change in the course of time, sometimes very markedly. Because we ourselves change, and are always finding something new and unsuspected in Wagner's scores.

The path to these great works can be very hard and tiring. You have to think about so much. I must have at least some idea about the works of Wagner's youth, before *The Flying Dutchman* (*The Fairies*, *The Ban on Love*, *Rienzi*). I must know his 10 central operas and music dramas inside out, from the *Dutchman* to *Parsifal*, for these works also all speak to each other and about each other. I must assess the size and acoustics of an opera house in relation to the music being performed there. I must be able to think in terms of musical colour and mood in tense conditions. I must know all the separate instruments and their technical implications. I must know that fast passages, if they are articulated more slowly, perhaps by semiquavers in the violins, often sound faster than if they are actually played fast. I cannot be autocratic in my modifications of tempo; every *ritardando* must be understood, and I must prepare for it meticulously. And if I should have the luxury of choice, I must be able to differentiate between an open or a covered pit. What flows so peacefully in one case may, in certain circumstances, seem deadly boring in another. And vice versa: what is too fast in Bayreuth, because everything that is not clearly articulated there soon becomes blurred, can sound brilliant in another house.

Above all, I must never feel satisfied with myself – Wagner's stature teaches one that, too. I must not indulge in enjoying myself; that would be fatal, the end. And I must not underestimate market pressures: a conductor who has early success will be indulged, particularly in Wagner. A baby-faced boy spurring 120 experienced musicians on to great achievements is more attractive than a man of 50 or 60 doing the same. As if you were still an infant prodigy in your late twenties. The audience acclaims you, the critics are enthusiastic, offers come flowing in: what more, you ask yourself, do I want? But you must not imagine that you can play this game with your career until you have reached the position you want – and only then turn back to what really matters, working on music and on yourself.

Only the will to expression can preserve you from such illusions, as I often see from the example of young colleagues. They want to do great things with Wagner and cannot (yet) put their ideas into practice. That is a good sign, because it means they will try to reconcile their craftsmanship and manual dexterity with their imagination and ideas. The will to expression, the pleasure in saying something, is not granted to everyone.

Excursus: The Kapellmeister

If you had to state your profession in a German passport or other ID, mine would say not *Dirigent*, the most usual German term for a conductor, but *Kapellmeister*. I would rather not have anything to do with the term *Dirigent* (from Latin *dirigere*, to arrange, to direct, to lead). It reduces my work to the mere claim of leadership and authority. It betrays the craftsmanship of art. I can equally well 'direct' cars into parking places or out of multi-storey garages. However, the word 'conductor' has made itself at home in musical language, so even I can't quite do without it. But I like the term Kapellmeister much better. To me, it embodies such virtues as knowledge of a work, great ability, and dedication to the cause of music. Moreover, it means just the same as the Italian *maestro*, who is the '*maestro di capella*', master of the chapel in the sense of orchestra. And why, while many German orchestras still go by the name of Kapelle (for instance the Dresden Staatskapelle, the Berlin Staatskapelle), should there not be a Kapellmeister?

Originally the Kapellmeister was not just the man who stood in front of the orchestra beating time, but also a composer and arranger, and in addition he had a number of wide-ranging tasks as an organizer, devising programmes and so forth. His profile was more like that of a general music director with an obligation to compose music; he provided his orchestra with all that it needed. An honourable and demanding profession. To this day the training of conductors at many music colleges in Germany is described as 'Kapellmeister studies', and that conveys something of the old all-round aspect of the conductor's job. On the other hand, I have never really found out why and when the term Kapellmeister was downgraded. In general, a Kapellmeister now describes a pale, meek figure beating time. A policeman on duty at the podium directing the musical traffic, no more.

I first realized what that downgrading meant in New York. I heard it said in English of someone (I don't remember the precise context), 'Oh, *he* is only a Kapellmeister'. I asked what the speaker meant, and was told that the conductor concerned had no charisma. There are certainly some boring characters in my line of work, no doubt of that, and charisma isn't something you can learn. But why pick on that particular German word to point up the difference? The idea, spoken or unspoken, is that the person dismissed as a Kapellmeister is below the maestro, the star conductor. The latter is supposed to be fizzing with inspiration and imagination, a man who makes a happening of every concert, as if he personally were throwing himself off the Castel Sant'Angelo after every other performance of Puccini's *Tosca*. Mere craftsmanship is beneath his dignity – and not because he is a master of his craft but because he doesn't need to be. You can manage without, it is supposed, you just have to combine the right charm with the right hair gel and wave your arms about with sufficient vanity, and you have outclassed the man who just beats time, grinding his teeth in frustration. How uncomfortable.

The world of music knew the term Kapellmeister long before 1933, when the National Socialists came to power, and as a Nazi usage it cannot easily be classed with other verbal exports from the Third Reich such as *Blitzkrieg*, but it can be taken to denote certain German stereotypes. 'The German' is, so to speak, a born Kapellmeister: thorough, reliable, tidy, punctual, industrious, modest and dutiful. After 1945 people wanted to do away with the aura of these virtues, and did it so thoroughly that even an innocent phenomenon like 'Kapellmeister' fell by the wayside. This tendency was reinforced in the years around 1968, accompanied by the progressive industrialization and popularization of classical music. And before you knew it music was, to put it bluntly, less and less about well-thought-out, authentic interpretations and more and more about perfect surfaces; suddenly only the event counted, not the craftsmanship. In such an atmosphere, the Kapellmeister did not have a good hand to play. I can imagine that our present crisis-ridden times would be inclined to turn that system of values upside down again.

The Kapellmeister may be allowed to fail as a conductor, but not the conductor as a Kapellmeister. In the first case he lacks a certain dimension: the urge to personal expression, original ideas. In the second case, however, the foundations themselves would be lacking: knowledge of a piece, theatrical experience and a certain routine drive that spares your own nerves. And then there is no room for *The Bartered Bride* in the subscription programme; repertory performances of Mozart's *Figaro* or Strauss's *Arabella* are floundering. The art of the Kapellmeister lays the professional foundations for everything else. Richard Wagner himself began as a theatrical Kapellmeister in Magdeburg.

I never found conducting any problem when I had worked thoroughly on an opera as co-répétiteur. Then I knew all the singing parts, the difficult passages were clear to me, and I had a good idea of what I wanted to achieve in terms of sound. Whether I could or can achieve that in practice used to be a question of manual dexterity and is now more of a mental one. I am not interested in what I look like on the podium. Many of my colleagues – and not only the vain ones – 'practise' at home in front of the mirror to find out what works, and how. That would only annoy me. At first I was often told that I conducted inelegantly and awkwardly, but I never really thought about it: I conduct first and foremost to be heard, not seen (which doesn't mean that I dislike appearing in front of the audience).

I know of none of the great figures in my profession who did not combine craftsmanship with imagination, technique and a certain aura, the Kapellmeister's approach and the eccentric aspect. I shall never forget my teacher Helmut Roloff telling me, after a piano lesson where everything technical worked well but not much else happened, 'Go on, surprise me!' He spoke gently in his usual way. I still remember sitting on the Zoo Station in Berlin waiting for the S-Bahn in despair. I was 15 and felt I couldn't do anything, never had done anything and never would. 'Play more slowly, faster, louder or softer,' said Roloff, 'play however you like. Only it must have a face.'

Much later, a time came when I understood what Roloff meant about the face, and wanting to be surprised. He wanted the music to set my mind on fire. He wanted me to trust my inner voice. Everything I had learned was just the vehicle; I had to pick up speed and fly by myself.

Reading Wagner

Richard Wagner taught me how to read scores. Very early on I wanted to know: how does he do that, how does it work, how are these extraordinary tonal mixtures achieved? Music is first and foremost sound. The sound, the tone, the colour come first, then the structure. Contemporary composers like Wolfgang Rihm and Aribert Reimann, if you ask them, say the same: what they hear first is musical colour, a timbre, a certain set of circumstances – and only then do they begin thinking about form. With that in mind, I would never call rhythm all-important. I would always put sound first.

Take Brangäne's watch song in the second act of Wagner's *Tristan*. Isolde's maid and confidante, writes the composer, sings 'unseen, from the battlements', while the lovers in the foreground 'sink as if entirely into reverie'. To me, bar 1210, just before Brangäne begins to sing, in dotted minims, *Einsam wachend* ('Watching alone'), seems to conjure up the birth of sound from silence as the world stands still, or the reflection of a distant ray of light in the depths of darkness. Two clarinet parts plus a bass clarinet, as specified in the score, three bassoons, four horns playing different parts, no other brass, but instead long chords, great *legato* curves of sound, breathing in, breathing out, *crescendo*, *decrescendo*, in addition a harp *glissando* and half the stringed instruments playing *con sordino*, with mutes, the dynamic marked as double and triple *piano*: that is the recipe. You can tell even from the look of the notes what Wagner has in mind: he wants to evoke an oscillation, a sense of hovering, musical air moving as if of itself. Genius that he is, however, Wagner goes a crucial step further. The extremely complex chords played by the wind instruments already contain all the harmonies of the scene; that is to say, all that is yet to come flows from them as if from a spring: Brangäne, her voice successively rising to a *forte*, thus comes closer to the action, as if in an optical projection, although she is invisible for most of the scene; the strings move more and more, blossoming to their full strength (without mutes now); then we have the three trombones that Wagner brings in for Brangäne's cries of *Habet acht!* ('Ah, take care!'), and the separate violin solos with their idyllically Arcadian ornamentation.

The way that Wagner closed this dramatic window again is equally interesting. For Tristan and Isolde's night of love is yet to come, and the quality of a scene must also be assessed by what happens next. *Bald entweicht die Nacht* ('Night will soon be gone'), Brangäne warns the lovers, and the word *verhallend* [dying away] stands over her last C sharp. The marking is *morendo*, also meaning dying away, as the wind and strings intone the conclusion; one last harp *glissando*, *ppp*, then a change of perspective and of key, from the melancholy and tragic F sharp minor to the mystic A flat major. 'Keep it very calm', runs the stage direction, as if Wagner feared an abrupt break where none should be. What does change is the musical length of focus, from far away to very close, from large to small. For the length of two note systems, until Isolde's *Lausch, Geliebter!* ('Hear, beloved!') the strings alone reign tenderly, feeling their way, as if the wind were rustling through the garden by night. Only at Tristan's programmatic *Lass mich sterben!* ('Oh, let me die!') is the woodwind heard again with erupting force in a *crescendo*.

I could go on like this at length – unfortunately, however, no descriptive analysis has ever made music. But what those 50 or so bars show, 11 pages of the score, is how clearly Wagner writes, and how logically, at heart, he can be read. Yes, there are more compact, complex and 'darker' passages in *Siegfried*, and passages even more harmonically complicated in *Parsifal*; in *The Flying Dutchman* the volume is the problem, in *The Mastersingers* it is the German *parlando* style – to sum up: you have to watch and listen extremely attentively if you are really to do justice to Wagner's finesse and diversity, intelligence and wit. At home, with the music on your lap, it is easy to learn how to read and practise scores. But in the pit I need a lion's heart, because everything – well, almost everything – depends on me. The larger the form – and that also applies to Richard Strauss's major operas, *Elektra* and *The Woman without a Shadow*, to the symphonies of Bruckner and Mahler's Eighth – the more responsibility the conductor must take.

He, or the Kapellmeister, whichever term you like, has to see himself as the composer's representative or interpreter, it is he who gets the composer the recognition due to him. In a Mozart opera the musicians in the pit can, if necessary, accompany the singers on stage themselves; they hear them, indeed the singers and musicians can hear each other. In Wagner that is just about impossible; his dimensions sabotage any idea of supremacy.

How does one memorize a Wagnerian score? Many of my colleagues have photographic memories, and when they conduct from scores that they know by heart they are constantly leafing through them in their minds. I do that too sometimes, but my memory is not photographic. When everyone suddenly sings *piano* in the second act of *Siegfried*, I know that the basses will be told to sing *sforzato pizzicato* on the next page. A conductor ought to know these things without highlighting them conspicuously on the sheet music. By the time I go over it all again and recollect what this red exclamation mark or that green squiggle is telling me, it is usually too late anyway. So the scores I use are usually in an absolutely virginal condition. I don't even write on them in pencil. I want my wits to stay sharp: who knows whether some entirely new detail may not leap to my eye at the next performance but one? I learned this from Herbert von Karajan. I need that freedom and tension if I am to make music.

But how do you imprint a Wagner score on your mind if you don't have a photographic memory? In exactly the same way as you would learn by heart Schiller's poem *Der Taucher* (*The Diver*), which is 27 verses long: you think of mnemonics to help you, build a rhythmical framework, concentrate on individual words. In fact it is much easier with music. Myself, I don't memorize notes but sounds, moods, colours – and thus the course of what follows. I lay out an emotional thread like Ariadne's clew through the labyrinth of the work. It leads me on, and I follow it.

Directing Wagner's operas

For some time I had few really satisfactory encounters with directors. These days I often feel insufficiently stretched. Sometimes my director colleagues have not mastered the material and would happily cut this or that passage, but don't read music – in which case it is pointless to discuss anything with them. This attitude (which the arts supplements are inclined to indulge) usually conceals inadequate craftsmanship: I have known newcomers to operatic direction who turn up for the first rehearsal with headphones on and equipped with a libretto from the Reclam series. Or novices who look at you in surprise when you explain that *The Flying Dutchman* is an opera where the chorus plays a large part – I have known them, too. Or then again there are directors who do know something about music, but are so awestruck that they forget their own real job and just say yes to everything. Then I meet with no resistance, there is no friction, no sparks fly. But the opposite case, too much resistance, can be crippling, too. If the director won't listen to anyone else there is usually trouble – with me, at any rate – and the work is no fun any more. I often had difficulty with Götz Friedrich at the Berlin State Opera House.

To my mind, Ruth Berghaus and Jean-Pierre Ponnelle were ideal directors. They could read a score, on principle they took the ideas for their productions from the music; on the one hand they knew what they wanted, and on the other they were independent enough to change their minds now and then. Götz Friedrich, however, could be very obstinate as he grew older. Then he would insist on action on stage that detracted from either the music, the general co-ordination of the production or its sound, and the success or failure of his production could depend on the casting of a single part when there could have been better vocal alternatives. As a young general music director I felt great respect for the artistic director of my theatre; after all, Friedrich was nearly 30 years my senior. These days, if I encounter a director with rigid opinions, and I sense that they will present difficulties for the musical atmosphere that I want to create or even destroy it, I am pragmatic. I try to salvage as much of what I want as possible. But that is not how a satisfying artistic dialogue or argument develops.

I would like to work, some day, with Hans Neuenfels, Peter Stein and Luc Bondy, and would also have liked to work with the late Patrice Chéreau, all of them directors with a strong feeling for art and good craftsmen. I was very happy with Philippe Arlaud's *The Woman without a Shadow* in Berlin, and my meeting with Christoph Loy in 2011 in Salzburg, when he was directing the same opera, was also a good experience. Questions of personal chemistry and working methods certainly play their part, and where Wagner is concerned you should work out whether you are more interested in the overall design of his work (as I am) or in the discontinuities, breaks and inconsistencies in it. Ruth Berghaus taught me how exciting it can be to show one thing on stage and conduct another in the pit – as long as the sense of erotic tension, mutual sensitivity and respect are right. I am certainly not a conductor to make a director's aesthetic possible for its own sake, as Michael Gielen did in the early 1980s in Frankfurt and Ingo Metzmacher in the late 1990s at the Hamburg State Opera House. I don't want people saying of me, later, that I helped this or that director to make his name; I want them to say whether I conducted the *Ring* well or badly.

That happened with our Bayreuth *Ring* in 2006 – although a high price was paid. I wish that Tankred Dorst and his co-director Ursula Ehler would have taken the concept of the Bayreuth 'workshop' more seriously, the unique chance, in all the years since the work's première, to revise its staging. Unfortunately, the chance was not taken, with the result that nothing like enough goes on between the characters in this production of the *Ring*. Incidentally, that seems to me one of the essential desiderata of modern opera production. Whether the singers on stage are wearing Chairman Mao suits, or Siegfried sports the proverbial bearskin as specified by Wagner, is of secondary importance when we realize that relationships are being explored; we are looking at what goes on between people. Today it is often the other way around: all the energy and careful attention can be drained from a production by cast-iron aesthetics involving gigantic theoretical superstructures, extremely complicated stage sets and much chatter in the media, because few directors know how to manage the interaction between the characters intelligently.

Originally, the Danish film-maker Lars von Trier of the Dogme 95 movement was to have directed the *Ring*, not Tankred Dorst. That would undoubtedly have been a coup, and would have pointed the twenty-first-century reception of the *Ring* in an entirely different direction, far from worn-out interpretations with their psychologizing and deconstruction. In retrospect, the Wagners have been accused of not taking enough trouble over the success of this project, or giving way early in fear of their own courage. I was there at the time, and can say two things: the Wagners don't know the meaning of fear, and they went to an extraordinary amount of trouble. Lars von Trier was allowed to pass a whole night alone in the Festival Theatre to sense and soak up the magic of the place, he spent months thinking the project over at home surrounded by walls densely covered with scenes from the *Ring* on pinboards, and he could have discussed it with all concerned at any time. I liked his extreme devotion to the idea and his undisguised, almost naïve commitment to the production. He kept emphasizing that he wanted Wagner to be experienced 'emotionally'. I felt that he understood and confirmed my own musical instincts.

But he was also difficult and eccentric. I remember a visit to Copenhagen in the spring of 2004, with Wolfgang and Gudrun Wagner. The north lived up to its poor reputation: it was cold, damp and uncomfortable, and we had been talking ourselves blue in the face about von Trier's concept when he suddenly stood up, practically tore off his clothes and said he was going for a swim, did anyone want to join him? Our jaws dropped – and he really did jump into the icy pool out in the garden. I don't think that Wolfgang Wagner had much time for such flights of fancy.

But there was something extremely enticing about his idea of understanding the *Ring* as a great theatre of illusion and playing it in an atmosphere of 'enriched darkness'. Lars von Trier had a striking explanation for what he meant by that: if A leads to C by way of B in one of the operas, then we would show only A and C on stage, and leave B to the audience's imagination. Having the action completed in the heads of the spectators, with the audience a necessary component of the total work of art – Richard Wagner would have been delighted! However, the technique of staging this 'black theatre' or 'magical theatre' in practice proved horrendously complicated, and would have ended up breaking all personal, financial and temporal bounds. Singers needing stand-ins as their doubles, a system of gauzy veils that would have made it difficult for everyone, including the conductor, to see what was going on, a dizzying choreography of 'patches of light' and video projections in order to identify A and C – the more concrete the preparations became, the more questions and doubts mounted up. Finally Lars von Trier backed out at a late stage and wrote an 'announcement of cession' by way of explanation. A production such as he envisaged, he said, would not have tolerated the tiniest mistake, and he had taken too little account of the theatrical realities in practice: 'I don't claim that it would have been impossible, but my pathological perfectionism would have made it hell.'

Much as I still regret the failure of this project, Lars von Trier was probably right about himself. However, I would warmly recommend the text of his 'announcement of cession' to all directors of the composer's operas. It puts forward a remarkable attitude to Wagner. Von Trier writes: 'Siegfried and Wotan and Fafner and Brünnhilde, and all the others, are real and live in a real world. They are not first and foremost symbols or illustrations, or decoration, or abstractions. They all have psyches, thus engendering conflicts and therefore emotional experiences and feelings in the audience. It can be strikingly effective to set Wagner's very human gods in the British Industrial Revolution or the Third Reich, but it doesn't improve the operas. We don't need parallels; in fact they are downright distracting. Let us leave parallels and interpretations to the audience. If Fafner is meant to give the audience gooseflesh, then it is damn well the director's duty to do his utmost to give them gooseflesh. If Siegfried was a hero, then he must be presented as a hero, however outdated, unrewarding and politically incorrect that may be. If we want Wagner, then Wagner is what we want. So let us stand by that idea; anything else would be cowardly. If Wagner drew his inspiration from the period of tribal migration at the end of classical antiquity and the beginning of the Middle Ages, then a director must approach his work with that principle in mind. If Wagner's artistic point of departure is a human image that we find it difficult to accept today, then the performance must go along with his views: forcing Wagner's *Ring* into the narrow confines of modern humanism would be as wrong and misleading as wallowing in the classics by making fun of them. Wagner made a myth out of the old myths, and anyone who is afraid of it had better leave his work alone.'

In my view we have to observe exactly that principle, whatever a production is like and wherever a director comes from, the world of the cinema or Honolulu. *If we want Wagner, then Wagner is what we want.* It is not a matter of subordination or restrictions or being 'faithful to the works', but of certain causes of friction that will kindle the imagination. We should not bend ourselves to Wagner's œuvre but confront it.

What I would like from a director is an atmospherically intellectual exchange of opinions, what we might call brainstorming. I think that would be very interesting. You read the libretto, you study the score, you listen to the music – and you ask: what mood does that evoke in us? What images come to mind? What conclusions do we draw? But the professional opera business hardly allows any such free co-operation between the director and the music at an early stage (unless those involved know each other and arrange it that way). If the conductor is present at the set rehearsal – the first, provisional construction of the stage set – and takes part in discussion of it before the first rehearsal, he is considered pushy. The normal thing is for the conductor to show up briefly at the beginning of rehearsals, then leave the work to his assistants, and reappear for the main rehearsals about a week before the première. Bayreuth has other laws, but internationally that is the everyday norm, which is really grotesque.

I won't conceal that we musicians profit by the decadence of the opera business. We sit comfortably protected from attention, fending off any ideas of the director's that might cause difficulty, and our careers are made. In fact I have profited by that myself. The only question is whether, and when, we shall return to other methods of working. The conductor doesn't have to be sitting in at every rehearsal on stage, but he should be mentally and emotionally present. I am afraid that, in that respect, too little has been heard from the musical side of productions in the last few decades, for lack of interest and imagination. If a director suggests something to me, I have to be able to imagine it. So I should have a certain amount of practice in visualizing the action on stage, just as the director must learn to think and feel musically.

However, the reality is usually different, and it has led to conductors leaving the field free for directors. Many notorious specimens of what is called 'director's theatre' would not exist if musicians would act more like partners. But I can't really talk; I wasn't especially keen at an early point to understand a director's ideas. Now, however, I feel ready for dialogue of that kind. I would like to have demands made of me, be challenged, be inspired. Why shouldn't my attempts at musical interpretation change, for once, in the light of ideas that a production has given me?

In principle there isn't much that I wouldn't go along with, as long as the director could convince me. I will make exceptions of pornography and political agitprop theatre, and my natural taste is certainly more at home with a decorative, extravagant approach to productions than with the adherents of aesthetic frugality. But I rebel most of all when the production goes against the spirit of the music. The Overture is a much-cited example: the director wants images from the very first bar on, the conductor protests – and soon finds that he has drawn the short straw, is regarded as narrow-minded and vain, old-fashioned and difficult. The argument that Overtures and preludes are traditionally meant to get the audience into the right mood for the evening's music, drawing them into the action of the opera, is often ignored. Of course there are borderline cases, some subtle, some less so. In Götz Friedrich's 1995 production of *The Mastersingers* in Berlin, an apparently conventional view of medieval Nuremberg was shown first during the Prelude, changing as the music rose to its climax before the end, and suddenly becoming transparent to reveal an image of Nuremberg in ruins in the year 1945. That point could be discussed, but in principle I am rather sceptical of such ideas in Wagner, for acoustic reasons among others. It makes a difference whether the music is played with the curtain up or down, and that is why Wagner always composed with the effect of the curtain in mind. The close of the *Mastersingers* Prelude, for instance, transplants the final chord to the first scene of the opera: first we get the whole rousing sound of kettledrum, triangle and organ, and then suddenly, from one bar to the next, as if in a film clip, the hymn *Da zu dir der Heiland kam* ('When the Saviour came to you') is heard. If I get the curtain to rise too soon here I shall spoil the dramatic effect. Something much the same happens in *Tristan* where it says on the score, 'The curtain rises'. This is bar 106, cellos and double basses alone and *pianissimo*. Then, six sombre bars later, follow two

quavers *pizzicato* – and you think the Prelude is over. A general rest.
But what does Wagner do then? He lets the young sailor's voice go on,
a capella: *Westwärts / schweift der Blick* ('Westward / goes my gaze').
He is singing 'from a height, as if in the crow's nest of the mast'. And
this extraordinary effect, too, will be lost if the curtain does not rise at
the right moment. One final example is *Lohengrin*. The Prelude proper
ends with a string quartet, delicately silvery, suggesting the ether, with
long rests. Then 'go on without a pause' Wagner says acutely, before in
the fourth bar of the first scene the king's men and their wind instruments positively sweep the curtain aside as they approach. In short, it is
not easy for conductors to go against the dramatic effects that Wagner
wanted, and they need the director to come up with extremely good
arguments before they will do it.

I conducted *Tristan and Isolde* in Bayreuth in 2015, with Katharina
Wagner directing. The cast of singers was decided long before I knew
much about the production. We live in uneasy times – but very stir-
ring times for this particular opera. So much is always going on, from
Fukushima to the financial crisis, and every time something like that
happens you feel as if the world has come within an inch of the final
disaster. But a remnant is left to make us go on living, a *nonetheless*
– such as one finds in *Tristan*. Its music represents meltdown; no one
can say exactly when the nuclear reaction began or how far advanced
it is inside the reactor. So I must go very carefully with those passages
where the score brings the music to white heat, paying great attention
to giving the right dose. If everything is equally intense, from the first
bar to the last, then nothing is intense. If you look straight into the
blazing sun you will be blinded.

But what will it be like in a few years in the future, how will the
staging of *Tristan* be able to engender such degrees of intensity then? It
has largely freed itself from the fetters of actualization (as I recognize
with relief). We no longer have to cite Auschwitz today, or wear Kim
Jong-il masks, to make Wagner's works of art meet the realities of life.
If I associate *Tristan* with musical meltdown, the stage will not need
any nuclear reactor for it.

Singing Wagner

I don't have much to say about the notorious crisis in the singing of Wagner today. My own diagnosis is that singers turn to Wagner too early, too much and too often, and also combine him with too many other difficult works in the operatic repertory. It is their own fault; I don't blame anonymous market forces, corrupt theatre administrators or greedy agents. Or us, the conductors, for playing too loudly. It's too simple to say that this or that conductor wants to make a big hit with Wagner, so the orchestra inconsiderately steals the show from the singers. Such things do happen, I won't deny it, and the trend for playing *piano* in Wagner is certainly a tricky subject; too little attention is paid to it.

But hasn't it always been like that? Between the wars, from 1919 to 1939, there were remarkably few complaints about the singing of Wagner, but before and after that time they proliferated. Some even came from Wagner himself: 'No branch of musical training is more neglected and practised worse than singing, by which I mean dramatic song. Irrefutable proof of that exists in the extraordinary rarity of outstanding singers who can be called on for higher purposes,' he said in 1878, according to the monthly *Bayreuther Blätter* journal. And the memoirs of Heinrich Porges, writing about the Bayreuth Festival and the 1876 première of the *Ring*, tell us that 'in many passages the dynamic markings indicating volume' had been changed, and often there was 'a *forte* instead of a *fortissimo*, a *mezzoforte* instead of a *forte*'. This, Porges continues, 'was done to make a singer's words and music clearly audible'. In addition, he says, the strength of the tonal quality must never reach its utmost degree, but the orchestra must carry the singer, in the Master's own words, 'as the moving sea carries a skiff', never 'putting it in danger of capsizing'.

Today there is a good deal of shouting on stage in Wagner. There are a number of reasons for that, including the fact that the Wagnerian orchestra plays louder than before, with more strength and brilliance. All the same, I stand by my thesis: singers who let its influence ruin their voices have only themselves to blame. Many extremely talented and famous musicians do not know their own limits. Everything is

so quick and easy today, you can fly from Vienna to Tokyo by way
of Chicago and back to London, globe-trotting non-stop, and if the
scheduled flights don't suit you then you can charter a private plane.
Young singers who are always overtaxing themselves, physically and
mentally, may profit by the endomorphin system and the adrenalin
rush that they get from success, but sooner or later they will ruin their
instrument, the human voice. I have often warned young people of that,
and I still do. Even when I was working in Nuremberg, I was accused
of standing in the way of the international careers of two or three singers because I advised them not to move on to more difficult material,
or to exceed their own vocal abilities at that time. Such Cassandra-like
warnings are usually ignored, but those who will not listen will feel the
force of them all the same.

But when such loud complaints are heard, I do wonder: is there
really a crisis? Is singing so much worse than it was in the 1920s, 1950s
or 1970s of the last century? I would hesitate to say so. I often discussed
this subject with Wolfgang Wagner; after all, he had heard almost all
the great singers live. We would be surprised today, he said, to hear
what the famous voices of those years were like: much smaller than
we think from recordings, much more lyrical. If we were to listen to a
singer such as Frida Leider on stage at the Bayreuth Festival Theatre
today, we would be straining our ears: we would hear not only her
characteristic vibrato and the emotion that she could bring to the part
of Brünnhilde or Isolde, not only her natural, radiant heights, but also
a vocal softness and a cultivation of the *piano* moments that we do not
readily associate with Wagner. Frida Leider was aware of that. 'To
achieve and maintain the necessary stamina for Wagner, I studied all
the *piano* passages very closely,' she writes in her autobiography. 'Then
I could sing his music without any danger. And the melodious sound
of singing *piano* gives listeners much more pleasure than if they were
hearing nothing but *forte* all through the evening.' I can wholeheartedly agree with that. Nor is it only voices that have changed (a high
dramatic soprano voice certainly had more leisure to develop in the
1920s); performance practice and taste have done so, too, immensely
increasing the demands made on singers. The same is true of visual
effects: it was once acceptable for Wagnerian singers to be rather stouter

than now, sturdy rather than slender. Today we laugh at old theatrical photographs from the 1920s and 1930s, showing Wagner's characters complete with mead horns and halberds – while we expect singers to have the figures of fashion models. That does nothing to take pressure off them.

Certain technical factors have also played a part. Once, the orchestra was in general tuned lower; the standardization of concert pitch as 440 Hz dates only from the year 1939. In German and Austrian symphony orchestras, even 442 or 443 Hz are sometimes heard. For the orchestra, this rise in the frequency meant a clear gain in brilliance. The high notes shone and sparkled, the volume as a whole was greater. The instruments themselves developed in the same direction: stringed instruments changed from gut to steel strings, the construction of wind instruments became stronger and more stable. And the more load an instrument can bear, the more its players can ask of it and themselves technically. That, in turn, influenced musical training: given much better and better-developed instruments, today's musicians can play much better and much louder music.

But of course that option is not open to the human voice. Operatic singing is often described as a high-performance sport, which is certainly accurate so far as its complex demands are concerned. In contrast to sport, however, there are limits to the voice's spectrum of achievement. The first official world record for the 100-metre sprint was 10.6 seconds in 1912, the present holder of the world record, Usain Bolt, runs it in only 9.58 seconds. The music market has become much more professional, particularly in the second half of the twentieth century; more funding goes into training, there are more opportunities to specialize, and what the physiotherapist is to the top footballer today, the laryngologist is to the star singer. In singing, however, we are not concerned with measurable records, victories or defeats, but with changing abilities and technical virtuosity of expression. Vocal cords, as a rule, can usually be trained or have their capacity enlarged only at the cost of flexibility and colour, and you cannot explore the intellectual horizon of a singer's part in an opera by Wagner or Strauss by means of ultra-fitness alone. The modern orchestra has armed itself heavily in terms of sound, instrumental technique and dynamics – not least because modern audiences, living as they do in a loud, noisy world, need increasingly strong stimulation. The modern singer cannot really satisfy such trends. That is the dilemma, and ultimately only the conductor can resolve it.

Our admiration for the great singers of the past is based on gramophone records. But what do we know about the precise circumstances in which they were made? Undoubtedly performances by tenors like Max Lorenz and Lauritz Melchior were stellar events: Lorenz made his mark with his blazing, slightly old-fashioned *espressivo* style, and the 'ejaculatory single notes' typical of him, as Jürgen Kesting writes, not without malice; and Melchior, the Dane, with his perfectly judged register and sensuously dazzling, incredibly virile timbre. His cries of *Wälse!* in the first act of *The Valkyrie*, lasting up to 15 seconds, are legendary, although I am inclined to doubt whether both these singers had such tremendous voices as is claimed for them today. I think it more likely that what counted was carrying power and strength, particularly as the great depth of the main stage at Bayreuth traditionally presents problems. Wolfgang Windgassen is the classic example of our ambivalent perception of a singer's voice. In the 1950s and 1960s he was considered unique on the Green Hill; few had ever known his equal for musical and dramatic intensity. In Berlin or New York, however, people often said, 'Is that the famous Windgassen? It's not how we remember him.'

Generally it is unfair and unproductive to compare historic and contemporary singers. Astrid Varnay, Martha Mödl and Birgit Nilsson had great voices and larger-than-life personalities. But they also lived with their portrayals of Brünnhilde and Isolde for almost a quarter of a century, and had time to grow into the parts. A singer like Gwyneth Jones was 37 when she sang her first Brünnhilde and 61 when she sang the part for the last time. Today, singers go on singing the part, on average, for seven to ten years, and that again is a result of increased demand: Wagner's operas have never been performed as much all over the world as now. Everyone wants Wagner, every festival, every little opera house – and they all have the same expectations, because they listen to the same CDs. When any municipal theatre used to stage *Lohengrin*, audiences were happy with lesser and not quite so dramatic voices, for lack of comparisons. Today, the Met's production of *Lohengrin* is distributed in cinemas all over the world, and in Weimar or any little local theatre alike no one really wants to accept any less a singer than Jonas Kaufmann in the title role.

But behind every Lohengrin, Siegfried or Wotan, behind every Isolde today there are 10 others who want to try the parts. And if their voices are not quite up to it, they force them: Wagner's high, loud, long notes are not sung with a clean introduction and natural vibrato, they are shouted, thrust, pressed out. The notorious habit of 'spitting out consonants' reigns. It may destroy the musical flow and line, but it calls for much less effort than working to perfect an individual sound with unique colours and nuances.

And with all this jet-setting, no time is usually left for the rest of the repertory. That was different in the past: singers like Lilli Lehmann naturally sang Mozart's Queen of the Night and Verdi's Violetta as well as Wagner's Brünnhilde and Isolde. Frida Leider always emphasized the importance in singing Wagner of having mastered Mozart's roles. And when René Kollo sang operetta and Christmas carols from time to time, it was not an aberration of taste: he knew that these allegedly sentimental genres were good for the voice. Some singers today do not concentrate solely on Wagner, but keep Italian bel canto, Verdi and Puccini in their repertory as well. In principle, I am convinced, specialization costs more than we get from it.

Fundamentally, nothing will prevail against the wish for all that is higher, faster and more expansive – the curse of our time – but the good old practice of working as part of an ensemble, even in a moderate, pared-down form: more work at home, fewer guest appearances. It helps to have people around who will tell you the truth, and not butter you up because they have their eye on the next suicidal venture: two days in Dubai, the next night flight back to Europe in order to take in the next rehearsal after glancing at the music on the plane, ignoring the change of climate. In such circumstances it is not surprising if the standards of conductors also leave something to be desired.

Unless singers have the constitution of an ox (which can happen) they will not be immune to such an artificial pace. If you go on too many long-haul flights in too short a time, you notice your vocal cords drying out, and you realize how much trouble it is to get back to your old form. Here the body itself is a good, healthy indicator. A conductor, however, may think that as his baton will not produce wrong notes, he can easily put up with a bit of jetlag or back pain.

I know many sad stories of singers, many great voices, many interesting, intelligent artists who have driven themselves mercilessly. It is easy to misuse their talent, when the emphasis is on youth. The market in singers has been compared to a shark pool, and those who do not obey the law of eating or being eaten soon find themselves pushed to the edge of that pool. Those who show weakness, who lower the mask of unconditional availability, who back out of a role or decline to sing are running great risks. Rumours of illness or crisis spread quickly in the Internet age – and it is very difficult to refute them. Then you lose work, you are thought of as demanding or 'difficult'. I know very well what that means.

Those who want to succeed in Wagner, all the same, should go carefully and slowly, particularly when lucrative offers come in from many quarters. To resist the temptations of the business you need a life, or that is my opinion. A life outside the theatre, the opera house and hotel rooms; roots, a home, friends. Otherwise you find, one day, that you have nothing left to say.

It was Richard Wagner himself who once said, 'The human voice is the foundation of all music.' His music drama acts like a magnifying glass turned on all the symptoms of today's disorder: market trends and mistakes in such an exposed field not only show up more quickly but make more of a difference. Wagnerian opera is the Geiger counter in this field. We still have it under control, I think, whatever way the counter points. It is said that every age has the performances of Wagner that it deserves. We don't have to be satisfied with that.

Interpretation

I have always greatly admired the conductor Otmar Suitner. A Tyrolean in Dresden, Bayreuth and Berlin. A man with two families, one in East Berlin, the other in the western part of the city (in 2007 his son Igor Heitzmann made a moving film about the situation). But what interested me most about Suitner was that he was a Kapellmeister of the late romantic 'German' style, a conductor of the old school. I remember a performance of *The Mastersingers* at the Berlin State Opera on Unter den Linden in the 1970s, when Suitner must have been about the same age as I am today. In the auditorium, the audience were already standing on their seats as he made his way to the podium. The atmosphere was electric. And as soon as he reached the podium he sat down, brought out a handkerchief with great ceremony, took off his glasses, breathed on them, and began cleaning them very much at his leisure, taking his time in front of the audience and the assembled orchestra. It took everyone's breath away. After a while he put his glasses on again, looked round as much as to say: ah, yes, there's my baton – and began on the Prelude. Madness in C major! The whole thing seemed to last for ever; the tension really got to you.

I wish I had nerves as strong as that. The power to clean a pair of glasses while thinking of the long, difficult musical work ahead of me. In the seconds just before an opera begins I always imagine the end of it. I sit on the podium, close my eyes and concentrate on the last two, three or four bars of the evening. Only then do I begin. Only then do I know where I want to go, where I must go. Perhaps that is my equivalent of cleaning a pair of glasses.

Those who describe Otmar Suitner as a Kapellmeister, and a German Kapellmeister at that, do not necessarily mean to praise him. They think of the conductor as a policeman directing the traffic, regulating what has to be regulated but going no further artistically. Apart from the fact that such clichés don't mean much to me (certainly not in the case of Suitner and his robust, highly lucid *Meistersinger*), that brings me to the question of musical interpretation. What is an interpretation? Where does it begin and where does it end? What may an interpreter do, or not do, and who is the judge of it? Interpretation, today's usage suggests, aims for extremes. Interpretation means being different at almost any price. In short, interpretation is the absolute opposite of the work of a Kapellmeister. Performing a Beethoven symphony without any vibrato is automatically regarded as a 'strong' interpretation – after all, no one has ever heard it played like that before – regardless of whether or not the ideology of the 'pure tone' behind the interpretation is appropriate to Beethoven. Spinning out the first act of *Parsifal* to over two hours, as Arturo Toscanini did at Bayreuth in 1931, also shows a 'strong' touch (although I would rather not imagine the crippling length of that reading of it). Put baldly, an interpretation is often what someone without a good ear takes it to be.

To me, an interpretation expresses itself in the artistic will. Making music so much your own that it becomes second nature is the interpreter's work. First of all, I am not asking for a spectacular effect; I want to lay the foundations like a Kapellmeister, doing justice to all the parameters: the libretto, the acoustics of the house, the various bodies of sound in the orchestra. Wondering who will be impressed by the outcome and why is something else. But I have to respect the 'face' of a work that a conductor shows me, as long as it is soundly based on the music. In many passages of Mozart's Jupiter Symphony conducted by René Jacobs, for instance, the hairs stand up on the back of my neck. His interpretation takes Mozart's testamentary symphonic work so literally that in the end little of its testamentary character is left. Jacobs is conducting not the emotion of a last work, but the wealth of Mozart's rhetorical experience. The idea is very interesting – and although it is certainly not mine, I acknowledge the will to create a form that it shows.

The term *interpretation* is from the Latin, and means to elucidate, translate or explain something, whether relating to a Biblical passage or a legal clause. Using the term for a musical interpretation, on the other hand, usually refers first and foremost to the performance. It begins at the moment when the conductor opens the score (and cleans his glasses or closes his eyes). Every entry, prelude, rest, change of tempo, passage in three-four time and *fortissimo* is being interpreted as it is played: elucidated, translated, explained, and thus placed in a context of its own. It begins with your own body structure.

Composers who were also conductors, like Wagner, Mahler and Strauss, wrote directions for playing or performance all over their scores. They knew exactly who they were dealing with. But does that make a score clearer and easier to read? And do we really have more difficulty in understanding Bach because there is nothing of the kind to be found in his music? In the details, yes. The conductor is more or less on his own with the question of the right tempo for a chorale such as *Ich steh an deiner Krippen hier* ('Here I stand beside the manger') from the Christmas Cantata. The tempo must flow both out of the recitative before it and into the recitative after it. Ideally, it grows from the rhetorical curve of tension of the entire cantata. There is nothing easier and nothing more difficult. In cases where one has to decide, I always think of *The Mastersingers*. Where is the border between what is free and what is arbitrary, between fidelity to the spirit of the libretto and following it to the letter? Stolzing asks Hans Sachs where to begin singing according to the Mastersingers' rules. Sachs replies, almost laconically, that he must make the rules himself and then obey them. In saying that the interpreter is his own master, Wagner puts his finger on the problem of interpretation. He is not giving everyone licence to do as he pleases.

Naturally analysis comes before every interpretation: you think hard about the work. The conductor should try to be honest with himself before the first rehearsal. What is close to my heart in this or that piece of music, what matters to me? Do images come before my mind's eye to guide me, do I sense any particular associations? Am I aware of the musical and emotional high points? The obstacles? How will I manage the transitions, and in what relation do the first tempo and the second stand to each other? All these questions cry out for answers, and in the end the result is a mixture. In this situation I often feel as if I were in a dream where things rush towards me and disappear again, sometimes looking very sharp and clear, sometimes blurred. Understanding the vegetative nervous system of a score, grasping it with the senses, is one aspect, the naïve aspect, if you like. Confronting it with analysis, your own knowledge of music, is another, is the reflective aspect. The combination of both is the beginning of your interpretation.

Ideas often come to me in rehearsal. It is a question of preparation and of daring to put an idea into practice. I often have an inkling in advance that something will happen at this or that point, I just don't yet know exactly what. In the duet *Lippen schweigen, 's flüstern Geigen* ('Lips are silent, violins whisper') from Franz Lehár's *Merry Widow*, for instance, the first verse belongs to Count Danilo, Hanna Glawari sings the second, and the couple come together in the third. *Valse moderato*, writes Lehár at the beginning, later *più moto* (with more movement), and finally *più lento* (more slowly). So the tempo is not the same throughout, but varies. The pulse quickens and then slows down again. Perhaps time even stands still at the end of the third verse, perhaps the world stops turning amidst all the billing and cooing: *Er sagt klar / 's ist wahr, 's ist wahr / Du hast mich lieb!* ('He says loud and clear / it's true, it's true / you love me too').

But how to vary the pace? I always felt I wanted to convey a glimpse, at the beginning of this duet, of the slow effect as it comes to a standstill. That is not easily done with singers, whose breath soon begins to run out, in the long phrases anyway. However, Lehár wrote an orchestral introduction to the third verse which serves the purpose very well. After it, I accelerate again as I conduct and slow down only just before the end, abruptly, as if someone were interfering with the spokes of the musical wheel. And now I have three variants that seem absolutely spontaneous, although I have thought hard about them.

What does this have to do with Wagner? A great deal. First, operetta (like German comic opera, a shamefully neglected genre) is an excellent teacher of the Kapellmeister's craft. And secondly, it helps us to study what it means to change tempo, in the sense of classic agogics,* in such a way that the effect is perceived as a change not of tempo but of expression. I am greatly in favour of *tempo rubato* (from the Italian *rubare*, to rob, to steal), that clever and at its best imperceptible shift of musical time that, put schematically, has the main voice sometimes hurrying ahead of the accompaniment, sometimes lagging behind it – and evens out this 'robbed time' at the end. The *rubato* technique did not enjoy a good reputation in the nineteenth century. Ignaz Moscheles dismissed it as 'playing *ad libitum*' and said it would quickly degenerate into loss of any sense of time; Hector Berlioz denounced its 'rhythmical independence', and even Franz Liszt spoke of 'time interrupted not according to any rule, flexible, abrupt and soulful all at once'. It does not sound very reputable, and such interpretations were soon accepted, like Frédéric Chopin's dismissal of it as sentimental and tasteless, affected and pretentious. At the beginning of the twentieth century it fell out of fashion entirely, and a certain taint is associated with it to this day. For

---

* Translator's footnote: the idea that you can vary the stress of a musical note by changing its duration rather than its volume.

interpreters, the line between fidelity and freedom, poetry and pathos, mind and feeling is a narrow one. But why not learn to walk it?

In my work on Wagner a free approach to tempi has been very useful; after all, we are not concerned with metronome numbers. A Wagnerian *rubato* can be thought out and planned ahead, or it can arise spontaneously – if you know how to deal with it. But you have to reject scruples. Is this allowed or isn't it? By the time you have thought that through, it is usually too late. The great musicians of the old days would just have laughed at all the musical traffic signs we put up today: they often simply went ahead and did as they wanted. And it was often the right thing to do. We must recover that certainty of feeling.

The same is true, indeed particularly true, of the great culminating points in Wagner's work. The announcement of death in the second act of *The Valkyrie*, for instance, Brünnhilde's *Siegmund! / Sieh auf mich!* ('Siegmund! / Look at me!') is extremely difficult because the music almost stops and freezes here. There are oblique chords from the low brass instruments, the distant roll of the kettledrum, but not much more in the way of meat to clothe the musical bones. It is as if the hero Siegmund's blood were congealing in his veins. The audience up in the auditorium, the musicians down in the pit all feel a lump in their throats. The music expresses what has been borne, and it is heavy with foreboding, indeed in the truest sense it expresses pathos (from Greek *pathein*, to suffer, to feel emotion), and there is a great temptation to take it too slowly and emotionally. One must not succumb to it, one must not interpret the feeling twice over and overload it, or the thread of tension will break. So what is the solution? To conduct with a fluid forward movement, slightly *rubato*, deepening the effect rather than piling it high. As we know, Richard Wagner often thought his conductors took the tempi too slowly. His grandson Wolfgang always said that you must keep the music flowing, always go just a little faster than your feelings tell you at first. Getting a sense of that is an important part of the interpretation of Wagner, and not just at Bayreuth.

To create your own image, as an interpreter, of Wagner's work you have to study it like a language: vocabulary, grammar, syntax, etymology, the choice of words, expression, idiom – they are all involved. Of course the tools you use to interpret *The Flying Dutchman* are not the

same as those you need for *The Rhinegold*, and those to which you turn
for *Twilight of the Gods* will not do for *The Mastersingers*. But certain
relationships and points of reference can be established. The famous,
or infamous leitmotif technique (Wagner himself preferred to speak of
'memory motifs') runs through almost his entire œuvre. While it is still
rough and ready in the *Dutchman*, we meet with it in almost narcotic
refinement in *The Rhinegold*. The net of motifs that Wagner casts out
here is rich and glitters – glitters like the scales that clothe the daughters
of the Rhine who open the *Ring* cycle in *The Rhinegold*, and close it in
Twilight of the Gods. Everything is connected to everything else here,
often only as nuances acting like individual 'signposts' (another of
Wagner's own expressions) and differing from one another in terms
of composition: the Valhalla motif differs from the fate motif, which in
turn differs from the sword motif, and again from the emphatic love
motif identifying the heroically sensitive Brünnhilde.

Like nature, Schiller says, art is inexhaustible. When I compare all
that I see and hear in the four scores of the *Ring* today with the little
that I heard and saw at my *Ring* debut of 1998 at the German Opera
House in Berlin, I can only say I would put my own signature to that
maxim in my heart's blood. With increasing craftsmanlike and musical
maturity, however, conductors develop their personal musical style. You
discover preferences, you develop your language, your repertory and
establish them. Just as one day Coco Chanel invented the little black
dress, the conductor, if he is lucky, finds his own means of expression
and makes decisions affecting his interpretation permanently. A certain
idea of sound, of homogeneity, an inner music – and ultimately you
find the image of Wagner or Bach or Mahler that is close to your heart.

People like to suggest that there is something indulgent and extravagant in my interpretations of Wagner, something that brims over.
They are not wrong, and of course I feel flattered. Who ventures to
serve a really satisfying meal today, with plenty of sauce to go with the
main dish? In the early twenty-first century we are good at finding
substitutes for food, and unfortunately it is much the same in music.
As for my image of Wagner, the luxuriant and opulent style is only half
the truth. To use a metaphor from archery, the largest bow is no good
if it cannot be bent. Only convincing details will add up to a convincing

whole. Wagnerian music drama that is only emotional or full-blooded, as clichés would have it, does not exist. Wagner was a master of magical effects: he knew that a permanent orgasm is not a proper orgasm at all. Passages like the announcement of Siegmund's forthcoming death, or the funeral march in *Twilight of the Gods*, can grip and overwhelm us emotionally if – and because – they are meticulously worked out in terms of drama as well as music.

This is the great contradiction that all interpreters of Wagner face: narcosis or calculation? Frenzy or analysis? A Wagnerian conductor needs the proverbial cool head and warm heart. In my view nothing will come of the opposite equation (a warm head and a cold heart). Those who think that they can undermine the Wagnerian mechanism of effects intellectually, disposing of all its dangers and potential chasms by analysis alone, draining all its structures, underestimate the dialectic element. Then we hear only analysis, bar lines, the tails of notes, chords, all of it as if measured on a slide rule. However, those who think it is all about putting the audience into a trance, a resonant state of intoxication, with the conductor out in front as a voodoo priest and medium, will be shipwrecked, too. Because then there will be none of the clarity, the stringency and the form without which there is no art.

Richard Wagner let himself be guided by that dialectical principle both as a composer and as the builder of Bayreuth, where the audience sits on seats that might be hard pews in a church – then *Tristan* suddenly starts and you feel that everything is flowing away. The musicians play as if they had one foot in the Hohe Warte hospital above the Festival Hill. The spartan and the psychedelic elements combine, the analytic and the atmospheric, mists and a clear view. We can't think of one without the other, that is Wagner's message. However different his interpreters may be as musicians and conductors – born analysts who understand how to leave the mists alone, enthusiasts who learn to discipline themselves emotionally, or practical theatrical people who, contrary to their convictions, taste the magic of the music – as long as they, we, are all prepared to go a little way in the opposite direction we shall come upon unforeseen pleasures in Wagner and ourselves. And we will have new, sparkling ideas pointing to the future.

6

Money or Love:
Wagner for Beginners

Don't be afraid!

Many paths lead to Wagner, and I suppose none of them is entirely smooth. But must everything be easy and smooth immediately? 'Wagner to go' is not on the menu: you have to want his music enough to invest time, patience and concentration in it. Three more arguments in its favour. Those who take a little trouble will be richly rewarded. They will discover strange, bizarre worlds, strong women, wicked beings, sad heroes. At the same time they will learn both to know and to forget themselves.

Ideally they first get a taste for Wagner at home or at school. A single good (or bad) music teacher often decides whether your whole life will be lived with or without classical music, with or without Wagner. That doesn't mean that you can't catch up later. The TV transmission of an opera, a public viewing of Bayreuth, 'Opera for All' in Munich or Berlin, perhaps a colleague at work who subscribes to an opera house and can't use a ticket that comes up at short notice – all kinds of opportunities may arise. You just have to take them. There are stories of such lucky chances: for instance, a supermarket check-out girl who is given a ticket to the opera, doesn't know what has hit her when she hears the Prelude to *Lohengrin*, and becomes an enthusiastic fan of opera and Wagner. I always like to hear such anecdotes.

If you are going to approach Wagner systematically, you will probably want to go to books. For those able to tackle German sources, there are guides to his operas written with great empathy by Attila Csampei and Dietmar Holland (who can be found online at www.opernfuehrer.org). Those with more knowledge of the subject can go to the five-volume guide *Opernführer für Fortgeschrittene* (*Opera Guides for Advanced Students*), by Ulrich Schreiber.*

But don't be afraid to go straight to the sources. Those who can't read music will probably not want to start learning from Wagner. However, there is always the libretto. Wagner wrote his own libretti, and if it is true that they represent an early stage of his music, a 'language of sound' in the truest sense, then they tell you more than just what is happening on stage. And you will be glad to be reasonably familiar with the libretto before a performance, because once it begins there is so much that is potentially demanding to take in. The audience is expected to listen and watch, bring everything together and understand it: the text, the statement it makes, the director's interpretation, the conductor's interpretation, in fact the whole opera at an epic length of four, five or six hours. That is a lot to cope with.

I am often asked why Wagner's operas had to be so long. To be honest, I can't entirely explain, apart from saying that personally I wouldn't want to miss a single note. Two hours for the first act of *Twilight of the Gods*! Two for the first act of *Parsifal*! Seven hours for the original version of *Rienzi*: it is a great deal to expect of an audience. But Richard Wagner wanted his music dramas to create a world, and you don't usually do that by administering tiny homeopathic doses. He aims to take possession of his audience and leave his mark on their lives. He does that by means of the intensity of his operas, but their sheer length also has something to do with it. And if we think of the ancient Greeks or the classic German dramatists, Wagnerian drama does not seem so excessively long. The *Oresteia* of Aeschylus, performed in full, lasts a good 10 hours, and Goethe's *Faust* (both parts) as directed by Peter Stein at Expo 2000 in Hanover took all of 22 hours. By comparison, the length of *Twilight of the Gods* is positively modest.

---

* Translator's note: in the English-speaking countries, good reference libraries will have copies of the 29-volume *New Grove Dictionary of Music and Musicians*, published in 2001, also available online for a subscription. An earlier work, the four-volume *New Grove Dictionary of Opera* (1992), covers operatic subjects very fully. One of the consulting editors, Barry Millington, writes on Wagner's operas. Magazines such as *Opera* and *Opera Now* publish up-to-date reviews. Opera houses such as, in the United Kingdom, the Royal Opera House and English National Opera have their own websites, and so do radio channels for classical music.

The message

Wagner's dramas are always about power and love and power *or* love. Wotan's domain falls apart because his daughter Brünnhilde breaks the law that he, as father of the gods, has made, and he has to punish her; King Marke's plan for a lasting peace between Cornwall and Ireland is thwarted by a magic potion; and although Elsa of Brabant is rehabilitated when her brother Gottfried, the rightful Duke of Brabant, thought to be dead, reappears, she pays for it with the loss of Lohengrin. Wagner's heroes tend to come from outside or from above, and that is part of the programme: it is not entirely easy to explain all these swan knights, captains doomed to sail the seas for ever and pure fools. Who they are, what they want and where they finally go are often questions shrouded in mystery and the miraculous. The important factor, so it seems to me, is that they act as catalysts. They set change in motion, expose conflicts, release society from outdated rules and rituals, break taboos. They are all manifestations of the *alter ego* of their creator Richard Wagner, they embody his artistic soul – a character like Stolzing tending more towards its bourgeois aspect, a character like Parsifal more towards its religious side. Only the artist, says Richard Wagner, can save the world from itself. He does it, in his own metaphysic, by creating another world through and by his art, a kind of second life – or at least the perfect illusion that there could be such a thing.

Of course the claim that Wagner makes is monstrous. The Bayreuth master does not make crochet doilies and perform little comedies for us; instead, he speaks of the creation of the world. From the first he plays the part of creator. But ultimately, and this is how I have always understood his monomania, that makes his art human. It is the work of a single human being. The Wagnerian artist follows no divine mission of mercy, and certainly no political programme, only his own inspiration. With this creed, Richard Wagner balances on the line between the Romantic and the modern periods in music, between fairy tale and psychoanalysis. He is one of the last who credibly seek the supernatural – and one of the first to touch our subconscious and unconscious minds deeply.

Wagner goes to the limits. His music dramas are full of murder and violence, incest, revenge, betrayal, obscenity, sexual subservience, none of them admirable things. Yet we go home after them feeling stronger. By projecting our fears on Wotan and his companions, we learn how life is played out, and in Wagner it always goes on. What happens at the end of *Twilight of the Gods*? First the world goes up in flames – and then it begins all over again. A funeral pyre burns outside the hall of the Gibichungs, Brünnhilde has thrown a torch on it in honour of the dead Siegfried, but suddenly the flames die down, and Wagner writes: 'The Rhine has risen high above its banks, and its waters flow above the fire to the threshold of the hall.' The conflagration of the world is extinguished as if the powers of nature were fighting with one another. And who knows, perhaps Brünnhilde and her horse Grane leap through the fire only to cool down in the water beyond it? Alberich anyway, the dwarf also described as a 'black elf', survives, so do the daughters of the Rhine – and suddenly the situation is back where it began 14 or 15 hours before, 'on the riverbed of the Rhine' at the beginning of *The Rhinegold*.

The message is not banal. It does not offer any truism about endurance, any cliché saying that life goes on despite its horrors, so we must not worry. Instead it contains a great challenge. With other operatic composers, catharsis may operate as it does in Greek tragedy: first grief, then horror, and when Tosca finally leaps from the battlements of the Castell Sant'Angelo, or Aida and Radames are buried alive, those emotions lead to purification and we feel cleansed. As a spectator, I go through the suffering of the characters on stage with them – and end by feeling a better and more reasonable human being because I have been through all these excesses of passion and emotion, and will have better control over them in future. The tragic ending of many operas is also – indeed, above all – a warning not to let matters come to such a pass: Don Giovanni going to hell, Rigoletto stabbing his daughter Gilda, Mimi in Puccini's *La Bohème*, for whom there is no hope from the first.

The same effect is found in Wagner. *Tristan and Isolde* shows us so terrible and urgent an image of disaster that we say afterwards: not me! I will never let it go as far as that! But Wagner does yet more: the final chord dies away, the curtain falls, and not only is the music drama not over, it is only just beginning. The spectator takes it home. That, too, is part of the total work of art. Live with it, says Wagner, suffer with it, I will give you time enough – but the stage will not absolve you of working out what you make of the experience. Wagner sets fuses to ignite in the future, thus contravening all operatic conventions. For the fuse to catch fire it needs sparks, the remains of embers, a sign that not everything is cold and destroyed. That is why Alberich survives in *Twilight of the Gods* (and perhaps his son Hagen as well), why the Pope's staff puts out leaves at the end of *Tannhäuser*, why Eva and Walther von Stolzing find that they are right for each other in *The Mastersingers*. Wagner was a Utopian. For all his aberrations and confusions, for all his nihilism and decadence, he never gave up hope. I can draw a good deal from the satisfying ends of his operas; they do not gloss over things, they say: good survives – and so does evil.

None of Wagner's music dramas, as I have said above, ends in a minor key. All of them, from *Rienzi* to *Parsifal*, end in the major. But we do not have to understand that in a simplistic way. Major keys are not simply to be equated with cheerfulness and minor keys with sorrow. A major key has sharper edges and clearer lines than a minor key; it is more unequivocal. If Wagner makes all his worlds end in the major, it speaks for the clarity of his vision. We have to face this or that final situation, there is nothing to quibble about and nothing to be covered up. Not even in *Tristan*, which ends with a B major chord (five crosses on the stave, F sharp, C sharp, G sharp, D sharp, A sharp), a key that Hector Berlioz was to describe as 'sublime, sonorous, radiant'. A bright and almost glistening light floods the stage. 'The bystanders are moved and transported', says the libretto, and after all the harmonic wanderings and convulsive changes of time in the *Liebestod*, the score itself comes to rest, *morendo, rallentando*, dying away, slowing down. Three characters are left on stage dead. What about Isolde? 'As if transfigured, she sinks gently, held in Brangäne's arms, on the body of Tristan.' Does she die, too? Is it total catastrophe, or is there a glimmer of light left at the end after all?

The characters

Wagner's characters sometimes remind me of the late-eighteenth-century sculptor Franz Xaver Messerschmidt's 'character heads'. All the types are represented: stupid people, brooding people, the wise, the damaged, the tolerant, the intolerant, those greedy for power, those tired of power, beings of the underworld, beings of the world above, the brilliant and the simple, gods, men and dwarfs – the entire range. The audience can easily see themselves in relation to this company. They are reflected in it, recognize themselves and assemble their own personalities from the most diverse of its facets. But so far as the voices of Wagner's characters are concerned, they strike me as less stereotyped and conventional than those of Italian (or Russian or French) opera, which tend to come down to triangular situations with naïve sopranos notoriously caught between radiant tenors and sinister baritones. Wagner's conflicts are more widely conceived, more global and mythic, which of course is because of the subjects of the operas. And where they do not arise from the subject, as in *The Mastersingers*, Wagner plays with operatic convention in a very intelligent and enjoyable way.

A brief summary of the Wagnerian bestiary follows below, in chronological order:

RIENZI is not only the last of the tribunes (of the Roman people), as the subtitle of the opera tells us, but also a tenor and Wagner's first solitary hero. He dies in the flames of the Capitol (we need not dismiss parallels with *Twilight of the Gods*), and with him died any ambitions of Wagner's to write grand opera.

THE FLYING DUTCHMAN has no name, and is the embodiment of the restless, unredeemed soul. His story also reflects Wagner's experiences in flight from Riga to London over the storm-tossed ocean. The register of his voice is baritone, and what he seeks is the steadfast love and constancy of a woman. Only she can release him from his eternal wandering over the high seas. He thinks he has found this woman in SENTA (soprano), and indeed she falls in love with his picture before he ever sets foot on land. But the young huntsman ERIK (tenor) also shows a strong interest in Senta, and now we find ourselves in the familiar love-triangle – see above. That is not so serious because the opera still follows the conventional form, and counts to some extent as one of Wagner's number operas: aria follows aria, ensemble follows ensemble. In contrast, Wagner's later music dramas are through-composed as a single 'never-ending melody'.

TANNHÄUSER is Wagner's second eponymous hero to be a tenor, and he vacillates – like Wagner himself? Like every man? – between the Apollonian and the Dionysian principle, between Eros and Agape, sensual lust and pure love. He is offered the latter by the devout ELISA-BETH, he enjoys the former with VENUS in the Venusberg (located as the real-life Hörselberg in the Thuringian forest). Elisabeth sings soprano, Venus is in the mezzo register, but the two women are not musically differentiated very much, so that Wagner can easily lose sight of them in the third act. Elisabeth's 'Hall aria' is famous: *Dich, teure Halle, grüss' ich wieder* ('I greet you, my dear hall, again'), and after singing it she prays, telling the beads of her rosary, and dies. WOLFRAM is Wolfram von Eschenbach, the poet of the Middle High German *Parzifal* epic, and in *Tannhäuser* he sings what is perhaps the most beautiful aria that Wagner ever composed, his 'Song to the Evening Star'. Wolfram is the most lightweight baritone part in Wagner's operas, and the evening star, of course, is Venus.

LOHENGRIN, too, a tenor and the Knight of the Swan (he crosses the River Schelde in a boat drawn by a white swan, a scene that gave rise to countless caricatures), has no name for two acts. But then he is forced to reveal his identity, because ELSA cannot keep the promise she made never to ask his name. She is driven to ask it by ORTRUD. Unlike the two women in *Tannhäuser*, Elsa and Ortrud are a very disparate pair: Elsa is the naïve and not particularly complex heroine who believes in 'love without regrets', but the evil intriguer Ortrud and her husband TELRAMUND, who is subservient to her, have the most exciting and progressive music in the whole opera. That is often the case in Wagner: the higher voices are given to the characters who, to put it mildly, are not very complex, while the cleverer, wittier and more fallible characters sing in the lower register. Ortrud is a dramatic soprano or mezzo-soprano, Telramund is a baritone. KING HENRY, a bass, who stirs up trouble between the various parties, belongs in that category, like his royal colleague the bass King Marke in *Tristan*.

TRISTAN and ISOLDE are the Wagnerian lovers par excellence: the Heldentenor and the dramatic soprano, the Irish king's daughter and the vassal from hostile Cornwall, the murderer of Morold (formerly betrothed to Isolde) and the woman who is a healer, the wanderer by night and the avenger. In real life there is little to make them seem made for each other, but in their erotic desire, aroused by the love potion, they literally know only one another: *Tristan ich, nicht mehr Isolde* ('Tristan am I, no more Isolde'), sings Isolde, and *ich Isolde, nicht mehr Tristan* ('Isolde I, no more Tristan') Wagner writes for Tristan: the effect is of a cabinet of mirrors. Only at the end do the lovers' ways part: he dies of a genuine wound, partly inflicted by himself in a struggle, while she dies, well, of love in the *Liebestod*. Wagner's female characters are an interesting subject. Isolde is a tremendous role (like Ortrud, Brünnhilde and Kundry), there is no doubt of that, and musically she is in no way inferior to Tristan. But from the point of view of their profiles and psychology, Wagner's women often seem to me shallower, less fully rounded and deeply realized, than his men, and further away. It is a very interesting distinction. Wagner's viewpoint is inevitably a male one: he may see woman as the 'woman of the future' on whom he projects all his Utopian hopes, but ultimately she still remains an unknown, mysterious being, a kind of saint – to be on the safe side.

I have always wondered why KURWENAL, Tristan's confidant, has to die too at the end of the opera. Because he has nothing left to live for after Tristan's death? Because Tristan dies not of his wound but of the non-fulfilment of his love? Then he would have been beyond Kurwenal's reach long ago. *Tot denn alles! / Alles tot?* ('Dead then, all! Are they all dead?') mourns KING MARKE, who has been betrayed, and that also means that the world is divided – divided into those ready to give everything for their passion, and those who remain true to their social avocations, their kingdoms and wars. Wagner himself, making use of his liaison with the businessman's wife Mathilde Wesendonck in *Tristan*, did not come down entirely on either side. But as an artist, he did not have to.

To my mind, HANS SACHS in *The Mastersingers* is one of the greatest of all operatic roles, a craftsman and a poet in one person, Wagner's perfect *alter ego*. He is a bass-baritone, and his vocal register in itself marks 'the Germans' favourite cobbler' (as *Der Spiegel* magazine once remarked with some malice) as a complex character. He can be ironic and self-ironic, he thinks cleverly and strategically, and also has very lively emotions. Of course Sachs plays with the idea of whether, as a widower, he might not pay court himself to the master goldsmith's daughter EVA, or his renunciation of her would be neither effective on stage nor interesting. That renunciation is no stupid resignation to the inevitable. *Lieb' Evchen! Machst mir blauen Dunst?* ('Dear Eva! Don't pretend to me') runs his answer to Eva's famous: *Ei was, zu alt! Hier gilt's der Kunst: / wer sie versteht, der werb' um mich* ('You're not too old! Art alone counts. Let him who knows that seek my love'). And the score underlines this little daydream with directions like *dolcissimo*, very sweetly, and *ausdrucksvoll*, with expression. So it is not an entirely absurd notion. However, Hans Sachs withdraws – and yet remains a happy man. That is what makes him great. By comparison WALTHER VON STOLZING, who sings for Eva's hand and wins it with a beautiful but rather naïve Prize Song, appears like a typical tenor.

The Ring of the Nibelung rests on a complicated network of relationships that seems to reach its peak in situations involving two people: we have WOTAN, the father of the gods, and his wife FRICKA, whose arguments fall rather short of the divine, as might be natural for an old married couple; he sings baritone and she sings mezzo-soprano or alto. Then there are two sets of siblings, SIEGMUND and SIEGLINDE, tenor and soprano; and GUNTHER and GUTRUNE, bass and soprano; one pair divine and (unwittingly?) incestuous, the other brutally avid for power and in that extremely human. Then there are fathers and children: Wotan with his favourite daughter BRÜNNHILDE, who is in rebellion against him and Fricka, and also ALBERICH the dwarf with his son HAGEN (singing high bass and low bass respectively). Alberich, as mentioned above, survives *Twilight of the Gods*, but what becomes of Hagen? The DAUGHTERS OF THE RHINE, we are told in the final and almost ironic stage direction, 'wind their arms round his neck, and thus, swimming back, draw him down with them into the depths'. Perhaps he will emerge some day? And last but not least there are the lovers Brünnhilde and SIEGFRIED (the incestuously conceived son of Sieglinde and Siegmund), a high dramatic soprano and a Heldentenor, the Valkyrie and the saviour of the world. The emphasis on their love makes them extremely vulnerable. He is treacherously murdered, she goes willingly to her death. *Nur wer der Minne / Macht entsagt, / nur wer der Liebe / Lust verjagt, / nur der erzielt sich den Zauber / zum Reif zu zwingen das Gold* ('He who denies / the power of love, / he who will have / none of love's joys, / that man alone may forge / a ring from the gold') sing the daughters of the Rhine at the beginning of *The Rhinegold*. The loss of love is the price that Brünnhilde and Siegfried pay.

There remains Wagner's last work, *Parsifal*, composed for Bayreuth and described as 'a festival drama to consecrate a stage'. Oddly enough, the female characters find themselves confined here to the roles of whore (the FLOWER MAIDENS) and/or witch (KUNDRY). The male characters and the company of the Grail are sad and sickly: the old Grail king TITUREL cannot die because the festering wound of his son AMFORTAS will not heal, the faithful knight GURNEMANZ is also at his wits' end, and even KLINGSOR the magician, who castrated himself in order to join the chaste company of the knights, suffers severely from his fate. Unusually, they all have deep voices, and sing bass or baritone. Salvation, therefore, can come only from a tenor – and so it promptly does: his name is PARSIFAL and he is the 'pure fool'. He drives his mother to her death, shoots peaceful swans out of the sky, all in complete innocence. It takes Parsifal two attempts and a few years to understand what human (male?) company means: empathy, fellow feeling, the right questions to lead him to know sympathy. Then he is crowned the new Grail king.

With which of his characters did Richard Wagner identify most? With each of his heroes in their time. He is Tristan with his distant beloved Mathilde Wesendonck; he is Wotan bringing Bayreuth into being and, like the father of the gods, disappearing from his own creation as a 'wanderer'; and most of all, like any restless genius, he would surely like to be Hans Sachs and stop being driven by his own artistic imagination, instead finding peace, a place to rest, and contentment.

Conversely, however, literature and above all the cinema find it extremely difficult to deal with Richard Wagner the man. In films about King Ludwig II made by famous directors – Helmut Käutner,

Luchino Visconti, Hans Jürgen Syberberg – the composer hardly ever shakes off a cliché-ridden image of himself. Somehow these film versions always end like the American film *Magic Fire* (1955, directed by Wilhelm Dieterle), shot at Herrenchiemsee, King Ludwig's royal palace on an island in the Bavarian lake of Chiemsee, and in Bayreuth itself. At least the composer Erich Wolfgang Korngold takes the part of Hans Richter in that film, conducting abstruse arrangements of Wagner's music in the Festival Theatre pit, while Carlos Thompson plays Franz Liszt in a strange wig, and in the end Wagner dies with a longing look at Venice. It out-soaps soap opera.

III

Wagner's Music Dramas

INFANT PRODIGIES EASILY FIND ACCEPTANCE. Don't Mendelssohn's String Symphonies foreshadow the elegance of the *Midsummer Night's Dream* music? Don't Mozart's violin sonatas KV 6 and 7 (written by a child of eight) already allow us to guess at his Dissonance Quartet, KV 456? Yes, they do. However, the musical world makes things difficult for all other beginners. Most composers' first attempts seem to blur the view of their real, later masterpieces rather than cast light on the history of their development. They appear uncertain, awkward, rough-hewn – and no one takes much notice of them.

Richard Wagner's is an extreme case. If you are lucky, your standard guidebook to his operas will begin with *Rienzi*, his third opera to be completed, given its première in 1842. Its predecessors *The Fairies* of 1834 and *The Ban on Love* of 1826 may at best be mentioned in the introduction – let alone his earlier work. A glance at Wagner's artistic biography shows how hard he had to toil on his way to music drama. In the catalogue of his works, the *Wagner-Werk-Verzeichnis* (*WWV*), Opus 1 is the 'great tragedy' *Leubald* (1826–8), and we have only the text of this Shakespearian pot-pourri. It was followed in 1830 by the fragment of an unnamed 'pastoral opera' based on Goethe's *Die Laune des Verliebten* (*The Mood of the Man in Love*), none of which has been preserved, and two years later *Die Hochzeit* (*The Wedding*), described as a 'horror opera'. Wagner destroyed the manuscript when his sister Rosalie confessed that she didn't like either the subject or his treatment of it. The plot described the tragic reconciliation of two patrician families: first the bride throws a secret admirer off a balcony on her wedding day, then she goes mad and sinks to the ground 'as if lifeless', something of a habit with many of Wagner's women characters. All that survives of *The Wedding* is a vocal septet.

However, first attempts ending in failure are typical of Wagner, and not only in his early work. The line from *The Flying Dutchman* to *Parsifal* is not a straight one, masterpiece following masterpiece without interruption. Wagner was a seeker, an explorer, and his work expressly includes shots that missed their mark and aberrations. They had names: *Männerlist grösser als Frauenlist, oder Die glückliche Bärenfamilie* (*Male Cunning Greater Than Female Cunning, or: The Happy Bear Family*), 1838; *Friedrich I*, 1846–9; *Jesus von Nazareth*, 1849; *Luthers Hochzeit* (*Luther's Wedding*), 1868; and an attempt simply entitled *Eine Kapitulation* (*A Capitulation*), 1870.

But why is so little attention paid to Wagner's early work? Why, in his of all cases, does archaeological curiosity remain well within bounds? Are those early pieces not distinguished for any of the dramatic features – characters, subjects, connecting themes – that we encounter again and again later?

It is worth looking at the following possible reasons:

1. Richard Wagner was a child of the cult of genius. But a genius meant a genius born, with no roots and no genesis. Wagner, however, began as a good, imaginative and rather philosophical young man, an able craftsman and practical man of the theatre. If we try listening to *The Fairies* and *The Ban on Love* without any preconceptions (which of course is impossible), we have to admit that the young Saxon musician might never have amounted to much. Only with *Rienzi* do his potential and his will to succeed in the field of drama come to light more clearly. Wagner's early work is redolent of the workshop – and that endears him to me. He himself may even have guessed what was fermenting in his mind; hence his courage in writing unfinished works and quickly discarding them. But that did not make things easy for posterity.

2. We have become used to judging a creative œuvre from its end, so to speak, as if it were all of a piece, making from the first for an imaginary culmination at its peak. We hear Beethoven's First Symphony with the Ninth in mind; we listen to Schubert's early songs under the spell of *Die Winterreise*. I consider that problematic, and here, for once, I am on the side of historically influenced performance practice. Wagner, of all composers, reached such a unique level with his trio of works *The Flying Dutchman*, *Tannhäuser* and *Lohengrin* as to cast all other contemporary opera, including his own early work, into the shade. To that extent, it is not only unfair to assess a grand

opera like *Rienzi* by the sophisticated operatic standards of *Twilight of the Gods*, it simply cannot be done. Anyone who nonetheless tries will never be able to appreciate those early works. What is better is, and always will be, the enemy of what is best.

3. Wagner also had yet to win his spurs in the field of drama. As we see it today, the plot of *The Flying Dutchman* is clearly better and more tightly constructed than the plot of *The Fairies*. However, that is not just to do with Wagner; it is also due to the globalization of the operatic repertory. Until the 1930s and 1940s, works like Karl Goldmark's *Die Königin von Saba* (*The Queen of Sheba*), François-Adrien Boieldieu's *La Dame blanche* (*The White Lady*), Marschner's *Hans Heiling* and Lortzing's *Undine* were still being performed from Rudolstadt to Tallinn. This repertory, embracing light or comic opera of the genre known in German as *Spieloper* (denoting an opera usually with spoken dialogue between musical numbers), as well as certain works of German Romantic opera, has fallen out of fashion today. There may be reasons of style and public taste for that – not every period, after all, is suitable for every repertory, although I would never rule out possible revivals. For the reception of Wagner's early works, however, the development had far-reaching consequences. In the absence of works like those listed above, we miss out on an entire plane of experience, emotion and comprehension. We feel impatient when we hear *The Fairies* or *The Ban on Love*, and fail to understand them. Or we understand too little. Or we get the wrong idea of them.

4. And then there are sound practical reasons for not putting on Wagner's early works. All the sung parts are extremely demanding. Directors would have to find singers prepared to learn and sing those parts, often knowing that in the end there would be only one or at the most two performances. Why, the singers may think, should we go to the trouble of studying the parts of Eglantine de Puiset or Count Lysiart in Weber's *Euryanthe*, which we shall probably never be asked to perform again, when we could be singing Ortrud and Telramund in *Lohengrin*? (The musical similarities between those two operas, incidentally, are striking.) The same is true of economic considerations: only half the house will be full for Wagner's *Ban on*

Love even if its cast consists entirely of top-ranking singers. And even then there is no guarantee that the opera will gain an established place in the repertory.

The transitions in the young Wagner's work are interesting. In 1840–41, with *The Flying Dutchman*, he suddenly knew what opera needs – a good plot, catchy arias, effective choral scenes, a gripping production. He had not yet grasped that in *Rienzi*, where he relied on sheer size and gigantic effects. He had tried to follow the fashion of the time and the formal requirements of French grand opera: he succeeded. Promptly he did everything differently in *The Flying Dutchman*. *Rienzi* lasts nearly seven hours, *The Dutchman* two and a half. *Rienzi* meanders from one large tableau to the next, *The Dutchman* rises to high points. And then there is the instrumentation: *Rienzi*, *The Ban on Love* and the *Faust* Overture are all extremely loud; the early Wagner liked noise. To our ears, even *The Dutchman* may still sound loud, particularly in its original version – but compared to Wagner's earlier works it is kept down on an entirely different dynamic level. However, I must not anticipate, but begin at the beginning.

I

Die Feen (The Fairies):
A First Look Inside Wagner's Botanizing Drum

Origin

Paradoxically, Wagner's first completed opera had its première posthumously – over 50 years after he wrote it, on 29 June 1888, at the Munich Cuvilliés Theatre (in the version prepared by the young Richard Strauss, and with Franz Fischer, the Bayreuth conductor, on the podium). At this time Wagner had been dead for five years. It had been written in 1833, just after Wagner had moved from Leipzig to Würzburg as choirmaster. In 1834/5 he was still trying by every means he could think of to get a première of this first work in Leipzig. When nothing came of it, he seems to have forgotten the opera. At Christmas 1865 he gave the score to King Ludwig II, along with the original manuscripts of *The Ban on Love*, *Rienzi*, *The Rhinegold* and *The Valkyrie*; in 1939 these treasures came into the possession of Adolf Hitler, and since 1945, as mentioned above, they are all regarded as lost. Today *The Fairies* is very seldom staged, and when it is, mainly in concert performances.

Cast and orchestration

The leading roles are those of the fairy Ada (soprano) and Arindal, King of Tramont (tenor). There is nothing strikingly unusual about the orchestra, which features a piccolo and double woodwind instruments (two flutes, two oboes, two clarinets and two bassoons), with four horns, two trumpets, three trombones, drum and harp. They are joined by a relatively large number of instruments played on stage: two more flutes, two more clarinets, a trumpet and three trombones.

Plot

Wagner wrote his own libretto, which goes back to Carlo Gozzi's drama *La donna serpente* (*The Snake Woman*) and reads rather like a blend of favourite mythical, classical and Romantic operatic plots in general. The human King Arindal, who has fallen hopelessly in love with the fairy Ada while out hunting, has to go through a number of trials to show himself worthy of her. They include a ban on asking her name for eight years, and vowing never to curse her. Arindal fails on both counts and goes mad. Ada too has to do penance, and is turned to stone for 100 years. However, with the help of magic weapons and a magic lyre Arindal wins her back, gives up his children, his crown and the earthly world itself, and amidst rejoicing on the part of the immortals moves into the fairy realm.

Music

The young composer's botanizing drum contains borrowings from Gluck's *Orpheus* and Mozart's *Magic Flute*, from the fairy music and magic horns in Weber's *Oberon*, and from the popular horror factor in the same composer's *Der Freischütz* (*The Free-shooter*).* The effect is of inspiration in some parts and simply of clever theft in others. However, there is no denying the awkward and long-winded nature of the score.

Recordings

There are some rather second-rate recordings of the work, but the only one to be seriously recommended is the first, made with the Bavarian Radio Symphony Orchestra under Wolfgang Sawallisch in 1984 on the Orfeo label. Linda Esther Gray sings Ada, and John Alexander Arindal.

---

* Translator's footnote: one of the two usual English versions of the title of Weber's opera; the other is *The Marksman*. To win his bride, the young forester Max is tempted to shoot with magic bullets that never miss their mark, but the Devil is involved.

2

A Sin of Wagner's Youth and a Hymn to Carnival:
Das Liebesverbot oder Die Novize von Palermo
(The Ban on Love, or The Novice of Palermo)

Origin

1834 was a significant year for Wagner. He became music director of the (touring) Bethmann theatrical group, making his debut as its conductor with Mozart's *Don Giovanni*, he met his future wife, the actress Minna Planer – and he travelled to Bohemia, where he had the idea for his next opera. This was to be an excursion into *opera buffa* territory, based on Shakespeare's comedy *Measure for Measure*, and also inspired by Wilhelm Heinse's satirical novel set in Italy, *Ardinghello* (1787) and by Heinrich Laube's libertine love story *Das junge Europa* (*Young Europe*) of 1833. Wagner admired Laube, who later became director of the National Theatre in Vienna and was the figurehead of the free-thinking literary movement known as Young Germany, which had its roots in the French July Revolution, and flourished in the years leading up to the March Revolution of 1848 in the German states. In line with the ideas of Young Germany, Wagner's libretto for his new opera was bold and indeed risqué, but all the same, surprisingly, it escaped censorship. Wagner finished the score of *The Ban on Love* early in 1836, and it had its première on 29 March (in the middle of Holy Week!) at the Magdeburg City Theatre, the winter quarters of the Bethmann company, in disastrous circumstances. The company was facing financial ruin at the time; Wagner, conducting the opera himself, had only 10 days for rehearsals, and the singers had not learned their parts properly. On stage, said Wagner later, a 'musical shadow-play' took place, 'with the orchestra doing its best to accompany the inexplicable effusions of the libretto, often with excessive noise'. Only a handful of opera-goers attended the second performance, whereupon the production was dropped from the company's programme.

Cast and orchestration

The orchestration was conventional up to a point, with a piccolo, two flutes, two oboes, two clarinets and two bassoons. But Wagner embellished the brass, adding to the four horns other instruments in the shape of four trumpets, three trombones and a bass tuba. The percussion, represented by a large drum, was also colourful and indeed suitable for the carnival theme. The *banda militare sul Theatro*, as Wagner described the musicians on the stage at the end of Act 2, with reference to Bellini and Italian opera, consisted at this time of whatever the theatre concerned could provide, probably on the basis of three (or preferably six) clarinets, two trumpets, four horns and a small drum. The main roles are Friedrich, Governor of Sicily (baritone), the handsome young nobleman Claudio (tenor) and his sister the novice Isabella (soprano). In operatic literature Friedrich is regarded as the first typical example of Wagner's heroic and character parts for baritone voice. 'Inflamed solely by ambition,' we are told in the first act, he scorned 'the quiet happiness of love'. Who would not be reminded of Alberich cursing love in the opening scene of *Rhinegold*?

Plot

The scene of this 'great comic opera' in two acts is Palermo in the sixteenth century. The German governor Friedrich issues a decree banning love, intended to curtail the sexual licence usual at carnival time. First to fall foul of the new law is Claudio, condemned to death for getting his lover Julia pregnant. The novice Isabella, Claudio's sister, begs for mercy for her brother, and succeeds, but only on condition that she gives herself to the governor. In the end the people free Claudio from prison, the bigoted Friedrich is deposed, and power reverts to the king. The ban on love ends in a revolution of love, and the young Wagner bursts into a paean to the kind of hedonism that he could no longer indulge so wholeheartedly in Tannhäuser: *Verbrennt zu Asche die Gesetze! / Herbei, herbei, ihr Masken all, / gejubelt sei aus voller Brust, / wir halten dreifach Karneval / und niemals ende seine Lust!* ('Now burn to ashes all decrees! / Come here, come here, you maskers all! / Let us

At the piano

With Herbert von Karajan at rehearsals in 1982 for the studio recording of *Der fliegende Holländer* [The Flying Dutchman], also with, from left to right, Peter Hofmann, Peter Alward, Michel Glotz, José van Dam

Liebestod in a rowing boat: *Tristan und Isolde*, Act 3, in the staging by Ruth Berghaus at the Hamburg State Opera in 1988 (left, Gabriele Schnaut as Isolde, right, Hanna Schwarz as Brangäne)

Richard Wagner in 1871, photographed by Franz Hanfstaengl

Siegfried's fight with the dragon: illustration for the
production of Wagner's *Ring des Nibelungen* [The Ring
of the Nibelung] at La Scala, Milan, in 1899

Richard Wagner
conducting, silhouette
by Willi Bithorn of the
year 1870

The 'Rogues' Gallery' in the Bayreuth Festival Theatre

Wagner's 'barn': the Bayreuth Festival Theatre

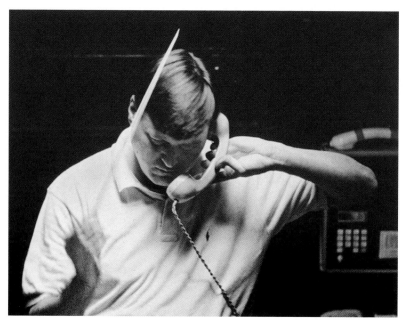

On the telephone during rehearsals in the orchestra pit at Bayreuth

In Bayreuth (2002)

With Wolfgang Wagner on the stage of the Bayreuth Festival Theatre
in 2002, after a performance of *Die Meistersinger von Nürnberg* [The
Mastersingers of Nuremberg] under his direction

Felix Mendelssohn-
Bartholdy, water-
colour of the year
1829, by James Warren
Childe

Adolf Hitler in conversation with Winifred Wagner and Joseph Goebbels at
the Bayreuth Festival Theatre, 23 July 1937

Tristan und Isolde: beginning of Brangäne's watch song in the second act

Götz Friedrich's famous 'time tunnel': photograph on stage from
Götterdämmerung [Twilight of the Gods] in 1985 at the German Opera in
Berlin (with René Kollo as Siegfried)

With Martha Mödl (2000)

Lohengrin with the swan, fresco by August von Heckel (1881) in
Neuschwanstein Castle

Richard Wagner in Paris, c. 1841, drawing by Ernst Benedikt Kietz

Première of *Tannhäuser* in Dresden, October 1845, with Wilhelmine
Schröder-Devrient as Venus and Joseph Tichatschek as Tannhäuser, drawing
by Paul Tischbein (c. 1852)

Rats at Bayreuth: production of *Lohengrin* by Hans Neuenfels at the Bayreuth
Festival, 2010, with Annette Dasch as Eva

Mathilde Wesendonck, portrait of 1860 by Johann Conrad Dorner

Cosima Wagner in a drawing by Franz von Lenbach of the year 1870

Première of the *Ring* at Bayreuth in August 1876: draft of stage set for the second act of *Die Walküre* [The Valkyrie] by Josef Hoffmann

The centenary *Ring*: Patrice Chéreau's production of the *Ring* for the Bayreuth Festival, 1976, Act 3 of *Siegfried* (left, Manfred Jung as Siegfried; right, Gwyneth Jones as Brünnhilde, 1979)

The first page of *Parsifal*, dated 23 August 1879 in Wagner's hand (top right)

The New Bayreuth aesthetic: Wieland Wagner's production of *Parsifal* for the 1951 Bayreuth Festival, Act 3 (from back to front: Ludwig Weber as Gurnemanz, Ramón Vinay as Parsifal, Martha Mödl as Kundry)

rejoice with a full heart! / Thrice let us hail the Carnival / and may its joys never depart!')

Music

First and foremost, according to the musicologist Martin Geck, *The Ban on Love* is a real mishmash, a typical early work in search of itself. There are reminiscences of Beethoven, Weber, Bellini, and above all of French *opéra comique*; and if the castanets click merrily at the beginning of the grandiose Overture it is also to mark the composer's protest against all the ossified revivals of older music then taking place in Germany. Musically and harmonically, however, the score has something of its own to offer. For the first time, Wagner was working with what he called 'memory motifs'; individual characters and situations were, so to speak, labelled and guided through the score in this way. Although the young Wagner was trying to make a work formally complete in itself, this early opera found no favour in his own eyes and ears later. *Ich irrte einst, und möcht' es nun verbüssen / Wie mach' ich mich der Jugendsünde frei? / Ihr Werk leg' ich demütig Dir zu Füssen, / Dass Deine Gnade ihm Erlöser sei* ('When young I erred, and now I hope to meet, / With pardon for this work, my youthful sin, / By laying it before your royal feet, / Hoping it may your royal favour win') – with these words, half remorseful, half boastful, Wagner presented the score to 'his' king 30 years later.

Recordings

Anyone wanting to make the acquaintance of *The Ban on Love* has a choice between two recordings. The first, of 1962, features the Great Viennese Radio Orchestra under Robert Heger (Documents). The second is later, made in 1983, and as with *The Fairies* it is conducted by Wolfgang Sawallisch, this time with the Bavarian State Orchestra. Hermann Prey sings Friedrich, Robert Schunk is Claudio, and Sabine Hass sings Isabella (Orfeo). This early Wagnerian work obviously benefited from the Wagner year of 1983, commemorating the centenary of the composer's death.

3

Defeating Grand Opera with its Own Weapons:
Rienzi, der letzte der Tribunen
(*Rienzi, the Last of the Tribunes*)

With *Rienzi* we are on more familiar ground. However, one cannot count on any wide general knowledge of this 'great tragic opera' in five acts. All that most people know is the Overture – and that generally from radio and television (in Germany it has been used as a theme tune), or as part of a film score. The non-musical associations that hang like a millstone round the neck of modern perceptions of Wagner arise here for the first time. Together with *Lohengrin*, *Rienzi* is thought of as Adolf Hitler's favourite opera, and to this day the work, a young man's vividly conceived opera, has never fully recovered from being saddled with that label. According to Albert Speer's *Spandau Diaries*, when he attended a performance of *Rienzi* in Linz Hitler was inspired to think 'that I too would succeed in making the German Reich great and unified'. Add the rallies of the National Socialist Party, which opened with a performance of the Overture, and the work is irretrievably stigmatized. That fact is reflected, not least, in the history of its recent productions: as directed by David Pountney in Vienna in 1998, Katharina Wagner in Bremen in 2008, and Philipp Stölzl in Berlin in 2010, no modern staging (I mean dating from after 1945) escapes references to fascism. Is that fair?

Cuts are also often made to the score of *Rienzi*. Is *that* fair? Wagner's third completed opera may be to some extent a half-baked work, difficult to digest, a typical 'youthful sin' of its composer and, as the master himself later recognized, much too noisy. It would be a considerable task to do it real justice – if only because here Wagner is so much more clearly himself than in *The Fairies* and *The Ban on Love*.

Origin

From Magdeburg to Königsberg, from Königsberg to Riga, from Riga full tilt to London and Paris and from Paris, finally, to Dresden: Wagner's life now gathered speed, showing the chaotic features of his later years. Never any money, always in flight, always thinking himself under-estimated, and off again with 17 suitcases on the next train, to the next hotel, to his next experience of homelessness: a frightful experience! The work accompanying him on all his travels between 1837 and 1842 was *Rienzi, the Last of the Tribunes,* from the novel of the same name by the English writer Edward Bulwer-Lytton, which Wagner had read in its recent German translation. He wrote the draft libretto for his opera in Königsberg, composed two of the five acts before moving to Paris, and the other three while living there in 1840. At first Wagner obviously intended *Rienzi* for Berlin, where the Italian Gaspare Spontini was general music director of the Berlin Court Opera (which accounts for Wagner's many echoes of Spontini's successful *Fernand Cortez* of 1809 in his score). But then he changed his mind, aiming for Paris: hadn't Spontini acquired his international reputation there? And didn't Giacomo Meyerbeer hold undisputed rule over the grand operas of that city? Even before finishing the composition of the opera, Wagner was having its libretto translated into French (and also the libretto of *The Ban on Love,* just in case).

However, the French metropolis brought him no luck. Wagner did not succeed in getting either *The Ban on Love* or *Rienzi* produced at the opera house, and the 'sweeping dimensions' of the latter in particular confounded his dreams. His idea of defeating grand opera with its own weapons, indeed surpassing it, was hubris and he failed in Paris. In this situation, rescue came from his native land: in the summer of 1841 the Semper Opera House in Dresden expressed itself willing to produce *Rienzi.* Wagner was delighted, and even managed to win over Minna to return there, unhappy as she was at the prospect of yet another move. 'Everything promises great success,' he wrote to Robert Schumann, 'and may God grant it. I have been yearning to emerge from obscurity for ten years now.'

Rienzi had its première in Dresden on 20 October 1842, and it was Wagner's first conclusive success. He had a prominent singer for the title part in Joseph Tichatschek, and the equally famous Wilhelmine Schröder-Devrient took the trouser role of Adriano. 'There was the excitement of revolution all over the city,' Wagner wrote breathlessly. 'I received four tumultuous ovations. I am assured that Meyerbeer's success with the production of his *Les Huguenots* here is nothing by comparison with that of my *Rienzi*.' Was the main consideration to outdo Meyerbeer?

As early as the second performance, considerable cuts were made on stage, and a little later the whole work was divided to be performed over two evenings: *The Greatness of Rienzi* and (with a prelude of its own) *The Fall of Rienzi*. In future, too, the huge work was fated to suffer from such problems, resulting in its arbitrary treatment. It is true that *Rienzi* triumphed in the musical world (in Stockholm, Rotterdam, Paris, Ghent, Venice, Budapest, Madrid, New York, London and St Petersburg), but it was to be 50 years before the next complete production, under Richard Strauss in Weimar in 1899. Cosima's attempt to give the work more of the nature of a music drama after Wagner's death, playing down its bel canto character, seems to have made it less rather than more likely to be well received. The fact that the original score has been lost since 1945 has long been an obstacle to a critical revision of these and other adaptations (even the early printed editions already contained considerable cuts). When the BBC proposed to produce all three of Wagner's youthful operas in 1976, over a thousand bars from the sketches for the composition of *Rienzi* had to have new instrumentation.

Cast and orchestration

The enormous leading roles (enormous in their length and their technical demands alike) are those of the Papal notary Cola Rienzi (tenor), his sister Irene (soprano), Stefano Colonna, head of the Colonna family (bass), and his son Adriano (mezzo-soprano). With four horns, four trumpets and three trombones, the orchestra in the pit is a large one, and also includes percussion (large drum and small drum, field drum, cymbals, triangle, a gong called a tamtam), as well as a serpent (a historical woodwind instrument in the shape of a snake), and an

ophicleide, the fashionable precursor of the tuba, known to us from
the *Symphonie fantastique* of Hector Berlioz. The music performed on
stage calls for a trumpet, an organ, bells, and an extra twelve trumpets,
six trombones, four ophicleides, ten small drums and four field drums
for the warlike third act.

Plot

The opera depicts five successive days in Rome in the fourteenth century. The papal notary Rienzi succeeds in giving the Roman people
a constitution and disempowering the two ruling noble families, the
Orsinis and the Colonnas. They avenge themselves with an assassination attempt on the tribune of the people, but are pardoned. Paolo
Orsini and Stefano Colonna fall in battle, and Rienzi is acclaimed as
the victor. More trouble threatens him from Adriano di Colonna, who
is paying court to his sister Irene, and who now wants to avenge his
father's death. With the help of the Church, Adriano intrigues against
Rienzi, and the people rebel. In the end the Capitol burns down, Rienzi
and Irene walk into the flames with heads held high, and the despairing
Adriano follows them.

This brief summary makes Wagner's *Rienzi* sound as if it were
concocted like a recipe: take one historical subject, contrast the fate
of individuals with mass movements, provide long ballet interludes,
mingle political and private themes – and you should have the perfect
grand opera. It was only with the dimensions, as mentioned above,
that Wagner overreached himself. The Lucretia mime in the second
act and the closing tableaux, which often take up half an act, strain the
audience's patience too far.

Music

Rienzi, said Hans von Bülow once, ironically, was 'Meyerbeer's best
opera'. A hundred years and more later, the American musicologist
Charles Rosen countered that remark by calling it 'Meyerbeer's worst
opera'. They are probably both right. And so are all those who cite
Spontini, Auber and Bellini, writing the popular Italian opera of the

time, as criteria of excellence. Carl Friedrich Glasenapp, Wagner's
first biographer, records the following declaration of intent on the
composer's part: 'My artistic ambition was not to imitate grand opera
[...] but to outdo it with whole-hearted extravagance exceeding all its
manifestations so far.' That ambition may ultimately have been greater
than his musical and dramatic skills. Tableaux, ballets, processions,
mimes, full-blooded arias, ensembles brimming over – the score knows
no moderation. As if the young Wagner were setting Beelzebub to
drive the Devil out.

But as I see it, the way in which he intensifies his personal style in
this work, for all its length and indeed its *longueurs*, is fascinating. He
continues the work that he began in *The Ban on Love*, with its motifs
conjuring up memories, setting out from the single fanfare note that
opens the action in the Overture, and returns to permeate the whole
work as a warning (one might almost think that Beethoven had taken it
as the model for his trumpet call in *Fidelio*).The sound profile with the
very strong wind instruments, the differentiation of the orchestration,
the rhythmical variety – all these things are typical of the budding
Romantic composer. But above all, the content shows Wagner finding
his themes: the impossibility of reconciling power and love, the solitary
hero, the downfall of the world depicted in the opera. Cola Rienzi is, if
I may put it in that way, an early stepbrother of the Flying Dutchman,
Lohengrin and even Siegfried.

The only real jewel in the score is the Overture: an overwhelmingly
attractive, vital and indeed virile *perpetuum mobile* tracing the entire
musical range of the opera, in 10 minutes that are positively bursting
with the will to find expression in song. The main theme, Rienzi's emotional hero motif with rising sixths, the dotted rhythm of a descending
cadenza, a returning upward movement and a hovering seventh chord,
is first performed *piano* by the strings, a little later by the entire orchestra
fortissimo. It is a melodic stroke of genius. And the young Wagner works
cleverly with it, changing the instrumentation, dynamics rising by stages,
constant *crescendi* and *decrescendi* – it all suggests that the whole world
revolves around this motif like the stars round the sun in a planetarium.

Recordings

The Overture has been recorded again and again, the entire opera, however, only a few times. I will start with a 1964 recording from La Scala, Milan, conducted by Hermann Scherchen, the old master of New Music, and the whole work, interestingly, displays not so much analytically dry qualities as a delightful expression of *italianità*. Giuseppe di Stefano, the long-term artistic associate of Maria Callas and a true powerhouse of the bel canto style, sings Rienzi, Raina Kabaivanska is Irene. The recording is on the Connaisseur label. It was followed, 10 years later, by my favourite: Heinrich Hollreiser's 1975 version with the Dresden Staatskapelle and the choruses of Leipzig Radio and the Semper Opera House in Dresden. It is brilliantly conducted, with Hollreiser casting light into the concentrated music of many dark places. René Kollo sings the title role with silvery radiance, Siv Wenneberg is Irene, Theo Adam a villainous Paolo Orsini, Janis Martin a passionate Adriano tormented by self-reproach (EMI). It would score 10 out of 10 on my own scale. But Wolfgang Sawallisch, obviously an inevitable choice for Wagner's early work, also gives a good account of the opera (if much louder than Hollreiser's) in a Munich recording again from the Wagner centenary year of 1983. Kollo sings Rienzi here as well, with the young Cheryl Studer as Irene, the rather pallid Jan-Hendrik Rootering as Colonna, and the part of Adriano, as sometimes happens, is taken by a male singer, the baritone John Janssen (Orfeo).

I have conducted the Overture to *Rienzi* several times myself in the concert hall, and recorded it with the Vienna Philharmonic (Deutsche Grammophon). I conducted the whole opera for the first time in Bayreuth in 2013, although not at the Festival Theatre – that would not have suited Wagner's intentions, and would have been counter-productive in view of the covered pit. It was given at the Upper Franconian Hall in Bayreuth, directed by Matthias von Stegmann, with the American tenor Robert Dean Smith, of whom I think highly, in the title role, and the Leipzig Gewandhaus Orchestra. The whole project was a co-production with Leipzig Opera, and on Wagner's bicentenary was to emphasize the axis between the city of his birth and the places with which his work is most associated. *The Fairies* and *The Ban on*

Love were also on the jubilee programme. As the basis of my *Rienzi* I took a thoughtfully cut version that gave the whole opera a tolerable length, and still did justice to its effect as a colourful, youthful work running riot: in short, an interpretation that did not shrink from taking inspiration from Italy and France, and also kept an eye on German *Spieloper* and Wagner's own inner workshop.

4

Plain, Meagre, Gloomy?
Der fliegende Holländer, oder der Fluch des Willens
(The Flying Dutchman, or the Curse of the Will)

How best to approach Richard Wagner? Perhaps by listening to two or three excerpts from *The Ban on Love* and *Rienzi*, the *Faust* Overture – and then enjoying *The Flying Dutchman*. This is where truly great music drama suddenly comes into its own. In part a numbers opera, in part through-composed, the *Dutchman* is quite short at two and a half hours of playing time, but allows the audience to become accustomed to its style: a stormy, intense, dark piece. A burning wind blows through the opera. The instruments are already playing in a highly exposed register in the Overture, almost hysterically, the music whistling, rattling and sweeping all before it, and the characters all seem to be on the verge of a nervous breakdown: the Dutchman in his eternal damnation, Senta in her illusions, Daland in his avarice, while the whole situation is beyond the understanding of Erik the tenor. Ghosts sing from the hull of the ship, women fall in love with oil paintings, Nature is beside herself, and it all ends in a great apotheosis.

In *The Flying Dutchman*, Wagner is already looking back to the German *Spieloper* genre, for that is where it comes from. Its roots are there, in the work of Heinrich Marschner, Carl Maria von Weber and Albert Lortzing. It cannot be said too often that without knowing about Lortzing's *Zar und Zimmermann* (*Tsar and Carpenter*), we cannot really understand *The Mastersingers* properly. The more open form, the fast dialogue, the loose orchestral writing, the hazy, airy effect that Wagner never entirely loses, even in the *Ring* – all of that comes from the *Spieloper* and its rather more substantial sister, German Romantic opera. In the *Dutchman*, Wagner moved some way from that tradition, setting off for new shores, although he did not yet know where those shores would lie. That was the state of the composer's inner workshop at the time, and it is what makes an encounter with this 'romantic opera', as Wagner himself calls it, such an exciting experience.

Origin

Wagner got the libretto of the *Dutchman* down on paper in May 1841, in only 10 days, and the draft score followed in only six weeks between July and November that year. In contrast to *Rienzi*, Wagner is not trying to improve on Meyerbeer here; in contrast to that opera, this time he presents himself as a genuinely German artist. The idea did not come to him out of nowhere. In the summer of 1841 Weber's *The Free-shooter* had its first performance in Paris, and Wagner enthusiastically promoted this favourite work of his. Let the French only put their hearts into 'breathing the fresh, fragrant air of our forests', he urged, writing in Maurice Schlesinger's *Gazette musicale* (and foreshadowing the uselessness of the attempt). The intention behind his words speaks volumes: once *The Free-shooter* had gone down well in France, he thought, the French would welcome his own 'romantic opera' – another reason was that one of the ideas for his plot came from a story entitled *The Memoirs of Herr von Schnabelewopski*, by that popular German exile Heinrich Heine, who had chosen to live in Paris.

Wagner's own experience also contributed to the plot: in 1839, on their dramatic flight from Königsberg to London on board the *Thetis*, Richard and Minna Wagner ran into a storm at sea. It raged for seven days, and all on the ship feared for their lives (including Wagner's beloved Newfoundland dog Robber). However, the composer spent the rest of the crossing, which lasted for about three weeks, in observing the crew and getting them to spin him seamen's yarns – thus gathering material for the *Dutchman*.

However, *The Free-shooter* was a flop in Paris, and no one there wanted *The Flying Dutchman*. That did not deter the German composer, if anything the opposite: the fact that this was not a commissioned work, so that Wagner did not have to keep an eye on actual circumstances of performance, seems to have spurred on his composition of the score.

He did, in financial need, sell his prose draft of the libretto to the Paris Opéra (Pierre Louis Dietsch's *Le Vaisseau fantôme*, based on it, was the next flop of the season), but he had been pinning his hopes on Berlin. Wagner composed three numbers before the rest, as advertising material, so to speak: Senta's ballad, the sailors' chorus *Mit Gewitter und Sturm* ('With tempest and storm'), as well as the chorus for the Dutchman's crew, *Johohe! Johohe! Hoe! Hoe! Hoe!* All three were well received, and so Wagner, now living in Dresden, sent the complete score to the Berlin Court Opera.

When, contrary to his expectations, the Berlin opera house made difficulties, Dresden came to the rescue again. The *Dutchman* had its première there on 2 January 1843, with the composer conducting – and the public did not like it. Was this 'plain, meagre and gloomy' work, as Wagner himself later described it, from the pen of the man who had given them sheer magnificence two months earlier in the form of *Rienzi?* The critics were not enthusiastic either, and after only four performances the opera was taken out of the repertory. This initial failure did not affect its subsequent history of success (in Riga, Kassel, Berlin, Zürich, Prague, Vienna, Munich and Rotterdam). Wagner soon set about retouching the score, generally where the instrumentation was concerned, but not until 1860 were there two major revisions. Although he regarded his fourth completed opera as the earliest of his works to be suitable for Bayreuth, it was a long time before the Festival Theatre staged it: only in 1901, almost 20 years after the Master's death, did it produce the *Dutchman*. The production was directed by Siegfried Wagner, with Felix Mottl conducting, and for the first time the three-act opera was given as a work in a single act without an interval.

Cast and orchestration

The title character (bass) has no name, nor does the small part of the Steersman (tenor), while the rest of the cast have only first names. Senta (soprano) is the daughter of the ship's captain Daland (bass), her suitor is Erik (tenor), and her nurse is Mary (alto). The chorus represents sailors, girls and the members of the Dutchman's crew. Wagner specifies two valve horns and two natural horns in the orchestra, two trumpets, three trombones, an ophicleide, a kettledrum, a harp and strings. The music on stage for the first act calls for six horns, a tamtam and a wind machine. I am constantly amazed by the fact that this is far and away the smallest orchestra required in the 10 operas that make up the Wagnerian canon, but makes far and away the most noise. Wagner was certainly giving his audience what they wanted, no doubt as a throwback to his early years.

Plot

The action takes place on the Norwegian coast in the middle of the seventeenth century, and of all Wagner's plots is certainly the most gripping and exciting.

Act 1: Daland's ship is in distress at sea, and steers for a bay in which the Dutchman immediately casts anchor as well. This dark figure is doomed to sail the seas and come on land only once every seven years (*Die Frist ist um*, he sings, 'the time is up'), where only the love of a faithful woman can break the curse on him. Daland, stupidly, is dazzled by the Dutchman's wealth and treasures, and promises to give him his daughter Senta's hand in marriage.

Act 2: The local girls spend the time in spinning as they wait for their lovers to return from sea. Only Senta's mind is elsewhere. She is spellbound by a painting of the Flying Dutchman, and indulges in ardent fantasies of redeeming him: *Traft ihr das Schiff im Meere an* ('If you should meet the ship at sea'). Meanwhile Erik, who is in love with her, is tormented by bad dreams. All of a sudden the Dutchman in person is standing before Senta – what a theatrical coup! The man who is under a curse recognizes the young woman as his saviour, she vows to be faithful to him unto death, and Daland agrees to their betrothal.

Act 3: The sailors celebrate their safe return: *Steuermann, lass die Wacht!* ('Steersman, leave your post'), but only a dark, echoing sound comes from inside the Dutchman's ship, and a storm rises. Erik takes Senta to task, reminding her that she once swore to be true to him. The Dutchman overhears them, and makes haste back to his ship, not without first telling Senta the story of the curse on him: *Erfahre das Geschick* ('So hear my fate'). However, Senta will not leave him, and throws herself off a cliff into the sea as a sign of her wholehearted devotion. Here there are alternative endings: in the first version the Dutchman's vessel sinks beneath the waves for ever – he and his men thus find release in death. In the second version, the Dutchman and Senta reappear 'far away' above the waves, and disappear, as specified by the libretto, 'in a transfigured state'.

What is all this about? Perhaps the *Dutchman* does not have such a powerful mythical and philosophical message as its companion pieces and the later works of Wagner. I for one would not read too much mystery into the action. As I see it, the work has a clear, simple message: if you want something too much in life, you will never get it; if you want something too much you will only harm yourself. The Dutchman comes on shore after seven years of wandering and stakes everything on a single card – what does he have to lose? However, he also expects everything of a girl who is not really free to be his. The backstory is that he is supposed to have blasphemed against God when he did not succeed in rounding Cape Horn. It is obviously for that reason that he is doomed to sail the seas of the world for all eternity. His restless, driven nature must have struck a familiar chord in Wagner, whose professional appointments had so far ended in failure in Magdeburg and Riga – and trouble was already brewing for him again in Dresden. Why? Because he wanted too much; because his boundless ambition drove him on. I am not sure, but if he really did identify with the character of the Dutchman as much as many people claim, then he ought to have learnt something from the story; he should have said to himself: I don't want to end like that, I must and will go more carefully. But then would there have been a *Dutchman*, a *Tristan*, a *Ring*? Probably not. *Die Kunst ist lang! / Und kurz ist unser Leben*, we are told in Goethe's *Faust*: 'life is short and art is long'. In practice, Wagner was not so wise in life as in his art.

Music

The past and the future of Wagner's œuvre meet in the *Dutchman* as in no other work; their origins and their Utopian ideas. He holds the loose threads of the early works in one hand, in the other the strand of the music dramas to come. As an ill-assorted couple, Senta and the Dutchman still show features of Ada and Arindal from *The Fairies*, and at the same time Elsa and Lohengrin cast their shadows ahead of them – so even do Tristan and Isolde in their unconditional love. Themes characteristic of Wagner are also intensified: the impossibility, as in a fairy tale, of uniting two worlds (as we also know from *The Fairies*, from *Lohengrin* and from *Tristan*); the woman who sacrifices herself (Ada, Elisabeth); the man as lonely hero and exotic saviour (Arindal, Lohengrin); death and love as equal ways to redemption; the heroine as a 'woman of the future' (Isolde, Brünnhilde). In 1860, when Wagner turned back to the *Dutchman*, he had just finished composing *Tristan*. It is hardly surprising, therefore, that his reworking of the earlier score aimed for the effect of transfiguration (see the second conclusion of the opera). The fact that he was able to achieve it without doing violence to the genre of Romantic opera also shows the full potential of the *Dutchman*.

Wagner himself was naturally aware of that. 'I struck out along a new path,' he wrote later, as if describing someone else choosing the path 'of revolution against the public art of the present'. In the process, his subversive thinking turns against everything French on principle, but also against the conventions of the *Singspiel* in German operatic tradition. Wagner is fighting an aesthetic war on two fronts in the *Dutchman*. Characteristically, he overdoes it. The score has, in all, eight great numbers, each in its own turn containing such elements as introductions, recitatives, arias, ballads, choruses, duets, and so on. Wagner himself claims the opposite. He had, he says, to abandon the 'modern way of chopping up the music into arias, duets, finales, etc.' in order to tell the legend of the Dutchman 'continuously' – favouring a more or less through-composed whole.

Perhaps this was a case of the wish being father to the thought. However, there is no mistaking his attempts to break out of the corset of the numbers opera in the *Dutchman*. For instance, the duet between the Dutchman and Senta in the second act – *Wie aus der Ferne längst vergangner Zeiten* ('As from the depths of long-forgotten times') – expands into a form combining recitative and aria on a grand scale. And the two orchestral interludes (which allow the opera to be performed without an interval) point the same way. But at the same time, as if Wagner wanted to keep the wound open, reminiscences of the musical past persist. For instance Erik's third-act cavatina, *Willst jenes Tags du nicht mehr dich entsinnen?* ('Will you no longer think back to that day?'), inappropriately holds up the development of the dramatic action, making it feel as if someone had accidentally opened the wrong window, an Italian one in the Rossini style, a bel canto window, which of course makes a fantastic contrast to the following finale. Numbers like the spinning chorus, or Daland's *Mögst du, mein Kind, den fremden Mann willkommen heissen* ('My child, welcome this stranger to our house') in turn draw almost provocatively on the tradition of the comfortably bourgeois *Spieloper*. However, it is to outrageous effect that Wagner interrupts the extraordinary tension after the first meeting between Senta and the Dutchman with this light aria from Daland. And it is particularly interesting when the styles overlap and permeate each other, most convincingly in the opening spectacle of the third act, when the ghostly chorus of the Dutchman's crew overwhelms the conventional sailors' chorus, so to speak, and breaks it apart.

In 1860, when Wagner was preparing a concert performance of the *Dutchman* in Paris, he not only moved the finale in the direction of transfiguration but also extended the Overture, giving it a positive conclusion. This version is the one usually performed today, particularly as it also contains some improvements and refinements to the instrumentation. However, I would not like to play off the two versions against each other. The original version is certainly extremely interesting, because it allows us deep insight into Wagner's musical workshop. It is rougher, harsher, with more brass in it. Seen in that light, the second version is not necessarily better, it is simply different, with smoother contours and above all more practical relevance. We must not forget that in 1860 Wagner had already conducted the *Dutchman* himself several times, in various places, so he could fall back on his own auditory experience. He knew where the balance was not quite right and the singers were overtaxed, and reacted accordingly.

Recordings

Oddly enough, the Overture of the *Dutchman* is almost never given a concert performance, unlike the Overtures to, for instance, *Rienzi* and *Tannhäuser*, although it is so effective. The Dutchman's demonic theme, Senta's theme of redemption expressed by horns, the cor anglais and other woodwind instruments, and the sound of the turbulent sea: a more vivid atmosphere could hardly be created. And there are only a few recordings of the Overture alone. However, recordings of the whole opera amount to an embarrassment of riches. My own favourite is probably the one under Hans Knappertsbusch: a recording from the 1955 Bayreuth Festival, with Hermann Uhde as a noble Dutchman, Astrid Varnay giving a dynamic performance as Senta, and Wolfgang Windgassen as Erik (Orfeo). The old conductor draws from the 'mystic abyss' of the covered pit a sensational account of the work, notable for its romantic intensity of depth and psychological internal tension, with the austere yet soft-edged sound of the brass, the sinewy strings defying saltwater at every turn, and tempi fit for a cathedral. There are several recordings from Bayreuth on the market, for instance one of 1942 under Richard Kraus, with Maria Müller as Senta and Franz Völker as Erik (Preiser), and of course the 1961 recording under the baton of the young Wolfgang Sawallisch (Philips). This recording is not only to be recommended for Anja Silja's Senta and the indestructible Josef Greindl in the role of Daland, but is also interesting because of the version it uses, a mixture of the 1841 and 1860 alternatives, with a harsh conclusion to the Overture and no orchestral interludes. A recording of 19 September 1936 from the Teatro Colón in Buenos Aires has also, rightly, won praise: Fritz Busch conducts in the pit of that famous opera house, setting about the task heatedly and in expressionistic colour, while Alexander Kipnis sings Daland (Pearl). In contrast, a more measured account is given by Clemens Krauss in March 1944, with the orchestra of the Bavarian State Opera, Hans Hotter as the Dutchman, and that fine singer Viorica Ursuleac as Senta – a recording made in Munich's small Wagnerian opera house, the Prinzregent Theatre (Preiser).

In 1961 Franz Konwitschny was able to call on fine performers from both West and East Germany for a studio recording: Gottlob Frick

as Daland, Rudolf Schock as Erik, Fritz Wunderlich as the Steers-
man, accompanied by the Berlin Staatskapelle (Berlin Classics). Only
Dietrich Fischer-Dieskau lacks the dramatic stature for the Dutchman.
Recordings also worth mentioning are Antal Dorati's London studio
production of 1960 (with the great George London in the title role,
Decca), and Otto Klemperer's interpretation of 1968 with the New
Philharmonia Orchestra, again with Anja Silja and the magnificent
Martti Talvela as Daland. And anyone wishing to hear the original
1841 version may turn to Bruno Weil and the Cappella Coloniensis
(DHM, 2005).

In Bayreuth, incidentally, the original version does not work: the
Festival Theatre is calibrated for a much softer, more discreet sound.
That explains why, towards the end of his life, Wagner thought of
making a thorough revision of the *Dutchman*. There is no doubt that
he wanted to stage it in Bayreuth – but in a different form. I think we
can be grateful to history that such a revision was never made. The
challenge of making the *Dutchman* sound good in Bayreuth anyway
is all the greater, and means muting the sound to the point where it is
not too explosive, too piercing, too loud. The only chance of succeeding
in that endeavour is with the 1860 version.

5

Tannhäuser und der Sängerkrieg auf der Wartburg
(Tannhäuser and the Singers' Contest on the Wartburg):
The Art of Moderation and Wagner's Failure to Achieve It

I have always felt that, of Wagner's early works, *Tannhäuser* is musically the easiest and most logical in terms of emotion. In content, however, its structure is distinctly creaky. It stands between the world of fairy tale and legend typical of German Romantic opera, and the future Wagnerian drama of ideas, and that may account for certain inconsistencies. In point of fact the eponymous hero is redeemed at the end, Elisabeth has sacrificed herself for him, the Pope's staff puts out buds in token of the salvation of his soul – but all the same Tannhäuser has to die. Why? And why does Wagner write such an apotheosis of a conclusion, with surging choral music fit for an oratorio? Is it a finale for the sake of a finale, music for music's sake – hadn't he long ago left all that behind him? It is said that during the *Parsifal* period, Wagner exclaimed that after creating the invisible orchestra (the Bayreuth orchestral pit, where the audience does not see the musicians), he next wanted to achieve the 'invisible drama'. I always think of that when directors grit their teeth on tackling the conclusion of *Tannhäuser*. Perhaps that finale simply cannot be staged, perhaps we should leave it cloaked in its invisibility. Then again, Richard Wagner was 32 years old when he wrote *Tannhäuser* – we can hardly expect a masterpiece as perfect as if it were written by Goethe in his late period.

Origin

In February 1843, Wagner was appointed court Kapellmeister to the King of Saxony – a position that he owed primarily to the success of *Rienzi*. He shared it with Carl Reissiger. The double appointment was a good choice: while Reissiger devoted himself chiefly to everyday organization, Wagner was keeping a sharp eye on the innovations introduced by Mendelssohn in neighbouring Leipzig as conductor of the Gewandhaus Orchestra. He swiftly set about the 'artistic reorganization of musical life here'. Soon Bach and Palestrina were being played in his concerts, as well as Gluck, Mozart, Beethoven and his own contemporaries, and Wagner is regarded, along with Mendelssohn and Berlioz, as one of the first star conductors of musical history.

Tannhäuser and the Singers' Contest on the Wartburg, Wagner's second 'romantic opera', falls into his early successful and eventful period at Dresden. The initial plans for it were laid in Paris, and Wagner described his feelings when he first saw the Wartburg on his return journey to Dresden: 'I immediately envisaged a distant mountain ridge to one side of it as the Hörselberg, and thus, as I went down into the valley, I constructed the setting of the third act of my *Tannhäuser*.'

The question of sources is rather confused. Broadly speaking, Wagner combines two sets of themes: the tale of the minstrel Tannhäuser in the Venusberg, and the legend of the historical singers' contest on the Wartburg in the time of Hermann I of Thuringia. Wagner studied everything to do with this contest of the Middle High German period, from Romantic versions of both sets of themes (by Tieck, von Arnim and Brentano, the brothers Grimm, E.T.A. Hoffmann and de la Motte Fouqué) to those of his contemporaries like Heine and a certain C.T.L. Lucas – an enormous workload in view of all his concerts and conducting duties. I have always found the double-edged nature of the subject, including the actual content of the new opera and the contrast between the Venusberg and the Wartburg, an exciting symptom of Wagner's unresolved attitude to the spirit of *Sturm und Drang*, the 'storm and stress' movement, and the receptivity of his creative mind.

The comparatively slow progress the young composer made with his new idea also shows what heavy burdens he had to bear in his position at Dresden. The libretto was in fact ready in April 1843, but it was not until two years later that Wagner finished the score of the Venusberg act, and only now was the opera rechristened *Tannhäuser and the Singers' Contest on the Wartburg*. The Court Opera began rehearsals in September 1845, and they proved unexpectedly complicated. Joseph

Tichatschek, formerly a brilliant Rienzi, had difficulty with the title role, and of all things the important stage sets for the second act, the minstrels' hall on the Wartburg, were not ready in time. Wagner himself conducted the première on 19 October 1845, the audience applauded the first two acts but could make little of the tedium of the third, and the production closed after eight performances. Wagner took that as a call to make various revisions, some of them major; the first was staged in a revival in Dresden in 1847, the second in Paris in 1861. Meanwhile, however, the work had known success after success: under Franz Liszt in Weimar in 1849, under Louis Spohr in Kassel in 1853, and in Munich in 1855: the 'model production' following Wagner's own long-distance instructions. Berlin gave the opera in 1856, Vienna in 1857, and New York in 1859 – the first American production of any of Wagner's operas.

Cast and orchestration

The title role of Tannhäuser is regarded as one of the most difficult of all Wagner's tenor parts. He is supported by Hermann (bass), the Landgrave of Thuringia, and the two women: Elisabeth, the Landgrave's chaste niece (soprano), and Venus, the fiery-eyed temptress (mezzo-soprano). The singers are led by Wolfram von Eschenbach, a lyric baritone. The chorus and ballet dancers represent the Landgrave's courtiers, as well as sirens, naiads, nymphs and bacchantes in the lustful atmosphere of the Venusberg, and a company of pilgrims returning from Rome (in the Paris version there are also three graces, youths, amoretti, satyrs and fauns). The orchestra is large and highly romantic. There is a strong body of woodwind in the pit: three flutes, two oboes, two clarinets and a bass clarinet, two bassoons; plenty of brass instruments (two valve horns and two French horns, three trumpets, three trombones, a bass tuba); strong percussion (kettledrum, large drum, cymbals, triangle, tambourine) as well as a harp and strings; on stage a cor anglais, four oboes, six clarinets, four bassoons, twelve (!) French horns, twelve (!) trumpets, four trombones, a drum, cymbals and a tambourine, and also castanets and a harp in the Paris version. A weighty musical apparatus for what is a remarkably quiet score.

Plot

The action is set at the beginning of the thirteenth century on the Wartburg in Thuringia and its surroundings.

Act 1: In the interior of the Hörselberg, Tannhäuser is lying in the arms of Venus: *Dir töne Lob! Die Wunder sei'n gepriesen* ('May praise be yours! Such miracles be praised!') but all the same he longs to be back in the world of humanity. When the goddess of love refuses to let him go, he calls on the Virgin Mary, whereupon the Hörselberg sinks into the ground and Tannhäuser finds himself back outside the Wartburg. A chivalric hunting party happens to be passing, led by the Landgrave. When Wolfram von Eschenbach recognizes his old friend Tannhäuser, and tells him of Elisabeth's love for him, the hero follows his former companions to the castle: *Zu ihr! Zu ihr! O, führet mich zu ihr!* ('To her! To her! O, lead me back to her!').

Act 2: Elisabeth, the Landgrave's niece, anticipates her reunion with Tannhäuser: *Dich, teure Halle, grüss ich wieder* ('I greet you, my dear hall, again'). They confess their love to each other. In honour of the day Hermann decrees a feast at which the assembled minstrels will compete with one another in praising the nature of love. There is a violent altercation between the men, and at the end of it Tannhäuser, beside himself, praises the joys of Eros: *Dir, Göttin der Liebe, soll mein Lied ertönen!* ('To you, love's goddess, may my song ring out!'). Elisabeth throws herself in front of the man she loves to protect him, and he is sent by the angry society of the Wartburg on pilgrimage to Rome as penance for his sins.

Act 3: Tannhäuser is not among the pilgrims returning from Rome, and the despairing Elisabeth dies. Wolfram sings her one last greeting (in the number known as the Song to the Evening Star). Then Tannhäuser staggers in after all and describes his sufferings on pilgrimage ('the Rome story'). The Pope has refused to absolve him of his sins, and in his pain the singer calls once more on Venus. Her appearance is disturbed by the approaching funeral procession with Elisabeth's corpse. Tannhäuser dies on her coffin, but pilgrims bring in the staff of St Peter, which has put out fresh green buds as a sign of his pardon and redemption.

Phew. All of it rather confused and violent.

What is it really about? About the artist – and once again about Wagner himself. It is about the balance between emotion and reason, the conflict and harmony of sexual instincts and the mind. And thus, in fact, the mystery of Wagner himself. How can anyone be so shamelessly calculating and at the same time such a spontaneous musician? Too much feeling, too much sensual heat – that is Venus; too much reason – that is the theme of the pilgrimage to Canossa, or in this case to Rome. In the end both cannot be equally valid. Tannhäuser fails, and perhaps Wagner *could* not have left us a successful version of his fifth opera because in principle there is no solution to the conflict it presents. There can never be a stable synthesis between the Wartburg and the Venusberg, Dionysus and Apollo, Eros and Agape, opera and drama, instinct and morality, only movement back and forth between them: in a state of vital tension and turmoil, first one of them causes more suffering, then the other.

I think that Wagner first felt this for himself in *Tannhäuser*: on the one hand he wanted to give a more philosophical view of the world, and on the other he could not yet manage that without the support of operatic convention. He masters the balancing act best in the Overture, but it too follows a relatively traditional pattern. The pilgrims move in the stable rhythm typical of them, the Venusberg entices hearers with wild *rubati* and *accelerandi* – and in the end the audience has tasted one without abandoning the other. However, Wagner does not manage to maintain that equilibrium throughout the length of the entire opera, or at least not dramatically and in terms of its content. To be sure, the music tells us right to the end: 'Listen to this, I can do it, and guess what, I could do anything!' But the plot comes seriously to grief.

Tannhäuser also, to some extent, contains a warning to conductors of Wagner: you must learn to tread a middle way, even when you are standing on the podium. You must neither abandon yourself entirely to intoxication, nor imagine that analysis can reveal Wagner's whole art.

Music

Tannhäuser is always popular with audiences. It has enchanting melodies, a magnificent Overture, it is easy to understand its musical construction, and the third act is a dream anyway. Nonetheless, in this score we are looking at a typically transitional work. Unlike the *Dutchman*, it is not divided into separate numbers, but is regarded as a through-composed opera – which is not to say that it does not contain passages resembling numbers. Examples are Elisabeth's 'Hall' aria and her prayer, Wolfram's wonderful Song to the Evening Star, and Tannhäuser's account of his journey to Rome. However, there is a crucial innovation: these 'numbers' are not bravura pieces in the traditional sense. Instead, they merge into the course of the action and carry it forward. Wagner treats the choruses in the same way (the entry of the guests in the second act, the Pilgrims' Chorus in the third), and does the same with the music performed on stage. One might say that in *Tannhäuser* he sets about liquefying what remains of operatic conventions.

It is not so easy to follow this process – the more so because the various versions do not lead to any one distinct and final form of the work. Even in the year of his death, Wagner famously told Cosima that he still 'owed the world' a *Tannhäuser*. However, I will try to trace a path through the confusion of different versions. In 1847, for the revival of the opera in Dresden, Wagner added to the 1845 score a real – and not just imaginary – appearance of Venus in the third act, as well as a real – and not just reported – funeral procession for the dead Elisabeth. What was originally meant to be taking place solely in Tannhäuser's mind (and the audience's imagination) finds its way back into what is actually shown on the stage. However, Wagner was not yet satisfied. In Paris in 1861, he expanded the Venusberg scene in the first act by adding a large-scale Bacchanale with a ballet and a mime, and cut Walther von der Vogelweide's song in the second act. But after the extraordinary number of 164 rehearsals, the production at the Paris Opéra proved to be one of the major scandals of Wagnerian history: he had satisfied the demand for a major ballet interlude with the Bacchanale, the kind of thing that Parisian audiences were used to, but unfortunately he put it in the wrong place – at the beginning of the first act and not, as usual, in the middle of the second. How were the members of the notorious Jockey Club of fashionable young men to observe their usual ritual of enjoying a leisurely dinner, and only then, as if to aid digestion, strolling over to the opera house to feast their eyes on opulent female forms in the Venusberg ballet? After three chaotic performances Wagner indignantly withdrew his score. In spite of the scandal (or perhaps because of it?), Wagner's popularity spread through France as swiftly as a viral infection.

We are left with a curious hybrid. The Dresden version may seem disconcerting because the Venus episode is so short, the Paris version because of its stylistic inconsistencies. Of course the Paris version shows how close it is to *Tristan*, almost as if it were enamoured of that opera, which Wagner had completed in 1859: we have the luxuriant chromatic palette of musical colour and the impressionism of the Bacchanale, and the fidelity to the diatonic scale of the ossified and self-righteous society of the Wartburg can hardly compete with that. The audience has difficulty in keeping up as well: first a conventional Overture in the style of the Dresden version, then the Venusberg with all its Tristanesque magnificence and morbidity – and after that are they to be content with the Dresden version? It is almost too much to ask.

For the sake of equilibrium I would always argue in favour of the Dresden version. When I conducted *Tannhäuser* at Bayreuth in 2001, it was the longest Dresden version of all time. We expanded the shepherd's song in the first act (intriguingly, the musical notation for that longer version was in the Bibliothèque Nationale in Paris), and found 20 or 25 more bars for the chorus to sing in the finale of the second act. Naturally Tannhäuser sang all three verses of his aria in the first act, and as prescribed he sang *Erbarm dich mein* ('have mercy on me') seven times in the large ensemble scene of the second act. (Cuts are often made in both cases today out of consideration for the singer's stamina.) The audience is expecting these passages, and as dramatic outbursts going all the way up to high A they are a severe test for any tenor.

That was exactly where Joseph Tichatschek failed in the première of *Tannhäuser*. On the one hand he incurred Wagner's displeasure because he obviously had 'no idea of his task as a dramatic actor', and on the other he could not, or would not, 'hurl out' the tenor's pleas for mercy with the requisite passion. Finally Wagner had to cut the passage, and with it 'the central point of the entire drama'. A little later, however, in a letter of 1851 to Franz Liszt, he says that the key passage lay in Tannhäuser's lines just *before* that outburst, lines in which he describes Elisabeth's appearance as God's envoy sent to save him while he raised sinful eyes to her, wishing to touch her with vicious intent. So Wagner cannot have been as cross as all that about the shift of emphasis.

That does not alter the fact that fundamentally two voices are needed for the part of Tannhäuser: a lyric tenor for the beginning and a weightier voice for the second and third acts of the opera. There are similar inconsistencies later in the parts of Isolde and Brünnhilde. Wagner did not give a great deal of thought to composing for his singers. He was concerned with the effect of the music drama. As a conductor, however, I am bound to wonder what use is a Tannhäuser whose voice is feeling the strain even before he gets to the story of his pilgrimage to Rome? And what use is my entire interpretation if it does not reflect the technical, mental and emotional sensitivities of the others involved and the condition of their voices? A good conductor *lets* his singers perform as easily and with as little strain as possible. He ought to support his singers, breathe with them, have a sense of the fact that today Tannhäuser's voice has more stamina than usual, and if that means he has to depart from a certain tempo, then so be it.

Recordings

Tannhäuser has a turbulent performance history. Siegfried Wagner's Bayreuth production of 1930, for instance, attracted attention chiefly for the Bacchanale, which was very much in the style of German expressionist dance; for the presence of several horses and 32 hounds on stage; and also, of course, for the conducting of Arturo Toscanini. A live recording of August 1930 (Naxos) has been preserved, although with Karl Elmendorff on the podium. As that season's *Ring* conductor, he was obviously stepping in here for Toscanini, whose fanatically meticulous approach to the score can perhaps be sensed in the orchestra, but Elmendorff was not quite the same thing. To get some idea of how sensational Toscanini's unpretentious, sober image of Wagner must have seemed on the Green Hill in the early 1930s, one can go to YouTube to see him conducting the Overture with his NBC Symphony Orchestra in 1948: his gestures are wide-ranging, his treatment of the Venusberg music almost puritanical, and he is uncompromising and radical when conducting the *piano* passages that are called for.

The history of *Tannhäuser* at Bayreuth continues with recordings of 1954 (Josef Greindl as the Landgrave, Ramón Vinay as Tannhäuser, and the young Dietrich Fischer-Dieskau as Wolfram, on the Archipel label), and 1955 with Wolfgang Windgassen as Tannhäuser (Orfeo). On the podium are the 'Latin' Wagnerian conductors preferred by Wieland Wagner, Joseph Keilberth and André Cluytens, musicians who liked a slender sound and very taut tempi. They were joined a little later by Wolfgang Sawallisch, conducting Wieland's new production of 1961. The American mezzo-soprano Grace Bumbry was a sensation here as a 'black Venus', singing in the 1961 recording beside Victoria de Los Angeles as Elisabeth (Myto), and in the 1962 recording beside Anja Silja (Philips). Exactly 10 years later Götz Friedrich, with a *Tannhäuser* almost reminiscent of Samuel Beckett's *Endgame*, gave the Festival Theatre one of its greatest scandals since 1945. The conductor was the experienced Erich Leinsdorf (whose two recordings from the Met, of 1939 and 1941, have been preserved). Gwyneth Jones sang Elisabeth *and* Venus, something that few sopranos can or should trust themselves to do. There is a recording of this 1978 production under Colin Davis on DVD (Deutsche Grammophon).

Other recordings worth mentioning are those of George Szell in 1954, live at the New York Met, because he was trying to compete with Toscanini (with the fabulous cast of Astrid Varnay, Ramón Vinay and George London; Myto); Franz Konwitschny in 1960 with the Berlin Staatskapelle – for the sake of Fritz Wunderlich as Walther von der Vogelweide, and again Dietrich Fischer-Dieskau who (in the studio) gives surely the most beautiful, sensitive and modern account of Wolfram in music history (EMI); and for my choice also Herbert von Karajan in early 1963, live from the Vienna State Opera, because it shows what an excellent theatrical conductor the supposed jet-setting star was (Deutsche Grammophon). Those who like the Paris version must go either to Georg Solti and the Vienna Philharmonic (1970, with

René Kollo in the title role and Christa Ludwig as Venus; Decca) or Giuseppe Sinopoli and the Philharmonia Orchestra – a studio production of 1989, although it suffers from Plácido Domingo singing in a very non-idiomatic accent.

It must be said in general that conducting the *Dutchman* in Bayreuth is difficult because its volume does not suit the mixed-sound aesthetic of the Festival Theatre. *Tannhäuser* is not a loud score, far from it; there is hardly another Wagner opera where the instruction *piano* is found so frequently. All the same, the covered orchestra pit again does it no special favours. There are passages in the second act for violins where the murderously difficult cascades of semiquavers can hardly be heard distinctly outside the pit, because the cover blurs them. The audience gets the impression that the chorus here is singing whole notes (*Freudig begrüssen wir die edle Halle*/ 'We joyfully greet this noble hall'), that the violins are playing whole notes, the same melody nicely in unison – and the conductor himself hears the chorus, especially when it is right at the back of the stage, that notorious fraction too late. The only solution is for the chorus master to tell him: just go on conducting, playing your part, keep it clear and distinct, but don't expect to work magic.

But one thing does reconcile the conductor of *Tannhäuser* to Bayreuth: the Pilgrims' Chorus. In any other opera house in the world you have to work very hard on the orchestra here, making it play softer, softer, softer! The score says *piano*, so please, bassoonists and horn players, play appropriately but with no accents. 'Coming slowly from far away', Wagner wrote in his stage directions, and that applies to more than the sound. It doesn't work with an open pit, where the sound is much too direct. In Bayreuth, however, the orchestra sounds indirect of its own accord, as if the pilgrims really were coming all the way from Rome over the Alps. It is important for the orchestra to stick to the line rather than the rhythm of the music here, it must not forget to breathe, must move steadily on rather than marking every step. *Beglückt darf ich nun dich, O Heimat, ich schauen* ('Happily now may I see my homeland again'). It is awe set to music, a sacred moment anticipated with a shudder of fear. The absolved pilgrims, Wolfram as mediator and observer, and the disappointed Elisabeth: nowhere but on the Green Hill does all this sound so beautiful.

6

A Floodlight on the World Beyond, Love without Regret:
Lohengrin

Lohengrin is a rat-catcher of an opera. Wagner does extraordinary things to the psyche of his audience simply by means of the instrumentation. It is the purest eroticism expressed as sound. The mixture of registers, the various sound values, absolutely take your breath away. Suddenly you don't know exactly which of the strings are playing. Or when Wagner combines horn and cello, in itself an old trick, he likes to support them in the lower register with the trombones and in the higher register with the trumpets – and you start to wonder if you are listening to wind instruments or strings. Such amalgamations send a shiver of delight running down the spine. *Lohengrin* is the emancipation of sound from workmanship. The music strikes something in me that sends my senses spinning, and I think it must be the same for the audience.

Wagner composed *Lohengrin* realizing that it was a case of once and never again! At least, there are far more connections running from the *Dutchman* and *Tannhäuser* to the *Ring* than from *Lohengrin*, which points, rather, to *Parsifal* (if only through the family relationship of the two eponymous heroes), but even so not in a very marked and concrete way. After *Lohengrin*, Wagner wiped the slate clean and began again from the beginning with *The Rhinegold*. In *Lohengrin*, he seems to be saying: I am now writing the most beautiful and melodious opera that you can imagine, you can all wallow in milk and honey, I am giving the world a real theatrical sensation and writing parts for the singers that they will be grateful to perform and go down well with them (which is not my usual way), I am making the chorus a protagonist, and you, the audience, shall have everything you require – but then there must be an end to it. Then you will dance to my tune, and I will show you what the 'work of art of the future' is really like.

Lohengrin is like a catalyst in the middle of Wagner's œuvre. The master is not yet even dreaming of the Bayreuth Festival Theatre – but this early score already anticipates it. This, too, is Wagner's genius and his internal workshop.

Origin

When *Lohengrin*, Wagner's third and last 'romantic opera', had its première on 28 August 1850 under Franz Liszt, the intelligentsia of Europe came flocking to Weimar: Giacomo Meyerbeer, Bettine von Arnim, the writer Karl Gutzkow, critics from London and Paris and many more. Expectations were high, and reactions guarded. The one man who could not be at the première was the composer himself. As court Kapellmeister to the King of Saxony, he had taken part in the May rebellions in Dresden in 1849 (put down with bloodshed after four days); he had leaflets printed, transported hand grenades; in short, he was freelancing for the revolution. Wagner's last official performance was to conduct a concert on 1 April 1849 including Beethoven's Ninth Symphony. 'All men shall be brothers'? It is easy to imagine the emotion and hectic theatricality of that performance. To this day scholars argue over what Wagner really saw in the revolution of 1848/9: a genuine political issue, the chance to realize ideas of radical democracy? Or the elevation of a collective passion concentrated in art, as he was to formulate and encourage it a little later in his theoretical writing? I cannot make up my mind.

After 16 May 1849, Wagner was a wanted man in Germany. With the aid of Liszt and a false passport, he went to Switzerland, and then travelled straight on to Paris. There, circumstances had changed, and not to his advantage. 'As matters now stand, Meyerbeer has everything in his hands – that is to say in his moneybags; and the slough of intrigues to be waded through is too great, so that other and cleverer fellows like me have long ago given up the attempt.' Meyerbeer's opera *Le Prophète* made him more than a million francs in Paris, and with his ballet *Les Patineurs* and the spectacular introduction of electric light into the theatre, Wagner's chances in that city were finished, and his lifelong hatred of the other composer sealed. 'When robbers and murderers set fire to a house, it may well seem to us a vicious and disgusting act,' he writes in a letter to Theodor Uhlig in October 1850, 'but how will it appear when the great city of Paris is burnt to ashes [...] and we ourselves turn enthusiastically to the impossible task of mucking out this Augean stable to get some fresh air?'

Back to Switzerland, then, back to Zürich. Minna, complaining, followed him in the autumn of 1849. His next few years were marked by marital crises and existential fears. Wagner felt that it was humiliating to be going from door to door abroad, at a distance from his operas, unable to concentrate on their artistic interests. All the same, he needed money. And all the same, in the first few years after the première of *Lohengrin*, it was being performed in over 20 opera houses. The composer himself heard his work for the first time in Vienna in 1861, in the same year, incidentally, as the 15-year-old Crown Prince of Bavaria heard it in Munich. In 1864 the latter came to the throne of the Wittelsbachs as Ludwig II and, having admired the composer enthusiastically for a long time, he invited Richard Wagner to his court.

Wagner's first interest in the Lohengrin legend goes back to the time of his first visit to Paris in 1839. The sources of the opera are regarded as Wolfram von Eschenbach's epic poem *Parzifal*, which Wagner studied in Karl Simrock's translation while taking a cure in Marienbad in 1845, as well as texts by Joseph Görres and Jacob Grimm. The genesis of the work is rather disjointed: the libretto was finished at the end of 1845, the first sketches for its composition were written by the summer of 1847 (the last of them being the Prelude). So that he could concentrate better, Wagner went to the countryside in Graupa near Pirna, to stay in a manor house that is now a Richard Wagner Museum. He completed the score in a euphoric frenzy of creativity from January to the end of April 1842, and nothing then seemed to stand in the way of its première in Dresden.

Cast and orchestration

The singing parts divide neatly into 'good' and 'bad' characters: the Knight of the Swan, Lohengrin (tenor) and the innocently naïve Elsa of Brabant (soprano) are an effective contrast to Friedrich of Telramund (baritone) and his wife Ortrud (mezzo-soprano). The weakness of the German King Heinrich, known to us as Henry the Fowler (bass), is evident in the fact that he always stands between the two fronts. There are large double choruses representing Saxons, Brabantians and their wives. An orchestra that is typically romantic in its size and constitution plays in the pit: three flutes, two oboes, a cor anglais, two clarinets, a bass clarinet, three bassoons, four horns, three trumpets, three trombones, a bass tuba, a kettledrum, percussion, harp and strings. On stage, Wagner emphasizes the grandeur of the ruler's court with a large body of wind instruments: four trumpets, three flutes, three oboes, three clarinets, two bassoons, four horns, eight to twelve additional trumpets, as well as the kettledrum, cymbals, organ, harp, bells and snare drum. They do not impair the fairy-tale quality of the opera, if anything the opposite.

Plot

The incidents of the legend take place in the early tenth century, on the banks of the River Scheldt near Antwerp and in Antwerp Castle.

Act 1: King Henry is dispensing justice. Count Telramund accuses Elsa of the treacherous murder of her brother Gottfried in order to take the throne of Brabant for herself. Elsa appears distracted, and tells the horrified onlookers about her dream of a knight who will come to her defence (*Einsam in trüben Tagen* / 'Alone in dismal days'). The king suggests appealing to the judgement of God, and Telramund declares himself ready to fight any champion of Elsa's in single combat. Sure enough, a knight – Lohengrin – appears at the last minute, drawn over the water by a swan. He is ready to fight for Elsa and marry her on condition that she never asks his name and origin. Lohengrin defeats Telramund, but spares his life.

Act 2: Ortrud goads Telramund on to further hostility to Elsa, and sows the seeds of doubt in Elsa's innocent heart. Outside the cathedral the two intriguers bar the way of the wedding party and demand information about Lohengrin's identity. Elsa reaffirms her faith in the knight she loves, and the procession goes into the cathedral.

Act 3: In the bridal chamber, Elsa is overwhelmed by her doubts, and finally asks Lohengrin the forbidden question of his name and origin. Telramund, who has been eavesdropping, rushes in, and Lohengrin kills him. At last he reveals his secret in the Grail Narrative (*In fernem Land, unnahbar euren Schritten* / 'In a far land, beyond your human steps'). He is the son of Parzifal the Grail king, sent out to save the innocent, but in so doing he must remain unrecognized. Triumphantly, Ortrud drops all pretence and confesses that it was she who turned little Gottfried into a swan. That breaks the spell, and Elsa dies in the arms of her brother, the rightful ruler of Brabant. Lohengrin's boat, however, now drawn by a dove, disappears with him to where he came from: into nothing.

What is at the heart of this story? Lohengrin as Wagner's closest alter ego, a variant of the artist in his relation to the world? 'Genius is always at odds with traditional ideas of life, art and morality,' says Hans Mayer. In that reading, Lohengrin is not only a saviour, the bringer of well-being and happiness, but also someone who comes from nowhere and causes great disturbance and change in the society where he finds himself. Wagner has a great deal of sympathy with nonconformists and outsiders, as we know from Ada and Arindal in *The Fairies* and from Senta and the Dutchman. Someone turns up – a fantasist, a purist, a man possessed, an artist if you will – and everything goes wrong. The conflicts that had been neatly swept under the carpet break out again.

However, we should be careful not to confuse *Lohengrin* with *Twilight of the Gods*. The Grail envoy is not young Siegfried, whose mission is to save the world (and art with it), and *Lohengrin* is still a romantic, indeed highly romantic opera, not a music drama. Knights in shining silver armour being drawn over the water by swans or doves, maidens who must buy love at the price of a forbidden question – the story is redolent of fairy tale. We have to respect that unconditionally and see it in the right light. As a child, incidentally, I thought swans were kind and delightful creatures, which was all Richard Wagner's fault. Only later did life teach me better.

Personally I find it hard to forgive Elsa for asking her question and destroying everything. Why does she do it? Everything is going so well in the third act with its wedding march and wedding night, sparkling wine flows, the fire crackles on the hearth, the sheets are freshly starched. *Das süsse Lied verhallt; wir sind allein, / zum ersten Mal allein, seit wir uns sahn* ('The sweet song dies away, we are alone, / alone for the first time since when we met'), sings Lohengrin 'very calmly' – the line is marked *piano*. Certainly, Ortrud has been spitting venom, and now it is taking effect. But if Elsa were brighter and more experienced she would not let it irritate her and lead her astray. A sophisticated wife would bury the doubts gnawing at her and wait to see what life would bring. She could always ask the question later, even in three or four years' time, when the Saxons and Brabantians had won their war against the Huns and matters had settled down. But unfortunately, as Wagner knew, the Elsas of this world are not like that. And then again, such a bourgeois and pragmatic set of circumstances would not make for a gripping opera.

What is the message of *Lohengrin*, then? In the end, at least, for Gottfried and the others left behind, it runs: we must be able to forget. We must accept the notches and scars left on our lives, pain, guilt, malice and loss. Otherwise we cannot live on. We must be aware of our past history, but we must not neglect to look forward. *Weh!* ('Woe!') cries the chorus at the end, as Lohengrin disappears 'with head bent, sadly leaning on his shield'. Which is to say that there is no future for the hero as a hero. Hence that cry of woe, *fortissimo* and in the key of darkest F sharp minor. The world that Lohengrin is leaving, however, certainly has a future; its name is Gottfried, the new ruler of Brabant. The key changes to A major and the curtain slowly falls.

Music

The score of *Lohengrin* is very straightforward *and* very sophisticated, it is naïve in the sense of being instinctive *and* sentimental in the sense of being thoughtfully reflective, melodious *and* advanced. Wagner may have had difficulty with *Tannhäuser* all his life; he succeeded with *Lohengrin* from the first. In *Tannhäuser* he is saying goodbye to the *Spieloper*; in *Lohengrin* he erects a memorial to German romantic opera and at the same time surpasses it. A hero who may not speak his name, the Grail as a higher authority situated somewhere ineffable, inaccessible, indeed divine – already, these features have so much of the artistic mythology of *Parsifal* in them that we cannot be surprised to hear of the audience's bewilderment at the 1850 première in Weimar.

In form, *Lohengrin* is Wagner's first truly through-composed work. Here he concentrates more strongly than in *Tannhäuser* on the art of the transitional: the motifs and harmonies of the three acts are so densely interwoven, the orchestral composition is organized so much like a symphony, that apparent 'numbers', like Elsa's somnambulistic entrance in the first act, or the wedding march, the love duet and the Grail Narrative in the third act arise from the material as if of themselves. Wagner also allocates certain musical features to the characters: the key of A major belongs to Lohengrin and the world of the Grail in their 'silvery blue beauty', as Thomas Mann put it, while the dark, wild, parallel key of F sharp minor is associated with Lohengrin's antagonists, Ortrud and Telramund, and all that the king says is written in the striking but ultimately empty key of C major. Similarly, in the orchestration the king has the brass on his side, Ortrud and Telramund are supported by woodwind and the lower strings, and Lohengrin is surrounded by the glistening radiance of violins playing in several parts. At the same time the motifs of Lohengrin and Elsa reflect each other, and even Ortrud's sphere is concealed there. We are living in a single world, says Wagner – good will never exist without evil, we can never have heaven without hell.

Lohengrin is also the first opera for which Wagner did not write an Overture, but a Prelude. I would not want to make too much of this change of term, but it clearly expresses his turning away from Italian and French operatic conventions. Wagner wanted to establish a tradition of his own, and now found himself well on the way to it. In addition the Prelude to *Lohengrin* – unlike the Overtures to the *Dutchman* and *Tannhäuser* – has no definite ending to catch the attention. 'Continue without a break', writes Wagner under the transcendent string music of its conclusion, and it goes straight on to King Henry and his men in the first scene of the first act.

The floodlight from the world beyond with which the Prelude begins has been enormously admired. Franz Liszt spoke of 'a kind of magic spell', Tchaikovsky saw it as anticipating Verdi and 'the final yearnings of the dying Traviata', and Thomas Mann called the entire opera 'the summit of Romanticism'. Anyone who studies the score will notice the incredible power of imagination with which Wagner set to work on it, the extent of his poetic feeling, craftsmanship and chutzpah! Some of the violins play with flageolet notes (light stopping), others do not, gradually the rest of the strings join in, also playing in different parts, then the oboes and flutes – taken all together, the effect is of a silvery glittering and flickering, as if one were dazzled by the sight of sunlight on waves. With a good conductor, incidentally, you do not notice when the woodwind comes in, as with the bassoons and horns in the Pilgrims' Chorus of *Tannhäuser*. Wagner did not want to climb steps but to mingle colours. He does it in *Lohengrin* with the massive orchestral pedal effect achieved by the sound of all the instruments, from very high to very low and back up again; you sense it from your hair to the tips of your toes and back by way of your internal organs, and it is extraordinary.

Equally magnificent is the close of the scene in the bridal chamber. *Weh! Nun ist all unser Glück dahin!* ('Alas, this is the end of all our joy!') sings Lohengrin, 'deeply distressed', after Elsa has asked the forbidden question and Telramund has fallen dead. The attentive listener will be reminded of an earlier passage, the second part of Lohengrin's warning to Elsa never to ask *woher ich kam der Fahrt, / noch wie mein Nam' und Art* ('from whence to here I came, / nor ask my rank and name'). We have the same motif, the same harmonies, but twice as slowly and creating an entirely different atmosphere, with more depth, more like a requiem, with muted cello music. And then the bell sounds, like a death knell from some galactic distance. Incidentally, whenever Wagner has brought suspense to an absolute boiling point, all of a sudden nothing happens. We hear only the solitary bell, or after the death of Telramund a drum roll. Only then is there tremendous tumult, Elsa cries, *Rette dich! Dein Schwert! Dein Schwert!* ('Save yourself! Your sword! Your sword!'), and then only silence, silence. Four bars of nothing but the kettledrum. Listening, we think our hearts will stop, and then what does Wagner do to counteract the burden of this crippling depression? We get the cavalry march, rousing fanfares, *Heil, König Heinrich! / König Heinrich, Heil!* ('Hail, King Henry! / King Henry, hail!'), with 10 or 12 trumpets on stage. What a crazy, terrific contrast, like something out of a film! What a trick to play!

It is known in Bayreuth that with *Lohengrin* Wagner was aiming for sound effects that he could not achieve until much later, on the Green Hill. Seen in that light, the opera is a Utopian project – which I am afraid does not mean that it works particularly well in the Festival Theatre. The limitations of the Bayreuth pit are unfortunately obvious, particularly in the Prelude to the third act. 'Very fiery, but never in too much haste', was Wagner's stage direction, and it should be taken to heart. The heavy brass, the virtuosity of the entire orchestra – it must race along, it must sometimes be explosive with all those triplets and dotted notes, but you must not overdo it. An experienced conductor will always say: I conduct the Prelude 3 per cent more slowly at Bayreuth than in an open pit so that the music will still be distinct. The 'mystic abyss' mingles sound where perhaps it should not be mingled. It also swallows up the overtones, and a score groomed to such perfection as the score of *Lohengrin* will always sound less brilliant here than in Munich or Vienna.

For the conductor, an important question thus becomes very clear for the first time in relation to *Lohengrin*: how much structure does Wagner's music need? How much will it bear? How do I solve the contradiction between atmosphere and clarity, mixed sound and distinct sounds? Only craftsmanship, feeling and experience will provide the answer.

Recordings

In the early days of the Bayreuth Festival Theatre, *Lohengrin* was produced on the Green Hill only at very infrequent intervals. Felix Mottl was its first conductor there, in 1894, followed by Siegfried Wagner in 1908/09. After that there was another break, this time of 27 years. However, in 1936 the next production of *Lohengrin* was Bayreuth's official contribution to the Olympic Games being held in Germany, and to the millennium celebrations of the German Empire. Wilhelm Furtwängler conducted, Heinz Tietjen was the director, Franz Völker sang Lohengrin and Maria Müller Elsa. The recording of 19 July 1936 that has come down to us in excerpts reveals a great moment in musical history. The tender ease of the singing is satisfying and clear, and the orchestra sounds magical in the true sense of the word. Soon afterwards a 'best of' selection from the opera was given a studio recording by Telefunken with the same cast, this time conducted by Tietjen, and it too is worth hearing (Malibran Music). The tradition that the parts should be sung, not spoken, shouted or bawled, in fact that Wagnerian singing has its roots in Italian bel canto, was continued first and foremost in Bayreuth after the war in this opera. The protagonists of that production were Sándor Kónya and Leonie Rysanek (in the recording of 1958 under André Cluytens; Myto), and four years later Jess Thomas, Ramón Vinay, Astrid Varnay and, not quite so sweetly sung, Anja Silja, with Wolfgang Sawallisch conducting (Decca).

Remarkable for its singing is the often ignored 1953 studio recording under Wilhelm Schüchter with the NDR Symphony Orchestra, unfortunately mono, but with Gottlob Frick as the king, Rudolf Schock as Lohengrin (in 1936 he had sung in the chorus in a series introducing new singers to Bayreuth), Margarete Klose as a malicious Ortrud and Josef Metternich as a Telramund with a lyrical voice (Walhall Eternity). There are certainly some very decent later recordings. If you want to play safe in your choice of a *Lohengrin*, however, you should still pick Rudolf Kempe's studio production of 1964 with the Vienna Philharmonic (EMI). It is exemplary for the reliable Jess Thomas in the title role, for Elisabeth Grümmer's virginally ardent Elsa, and a couple of villains who can hardly be outdone for guts and lyrical and dramatic sharpness in Christa Ludwig and Dietrich Fischer-Dieskau. And with Gottlob Frick as King Henry we know we are in good hands.

I cannot give the whole history of productions of the opera here. Since the 1960s, however, it has been a favourite of what is known as 'director's theatre'. Productions such as those of Götz Friedrich (1979) and Werner Herzog (1980) on the Green Hill have been great sensations, and at the Hamburg State Opera in 1998 Peter Konwitschny simply transplanted the feverishly adolescent aspect of the opera to a school classroom. The current Bayreuth *Lohengrin*, a new production of 2010, is the work of Hans Neuenfels, a director known for surrealism and symbolism, with his designer Reinhard von der Thannen. The chorus wear rat costumes, Elsa and Ortrud appear as white and black swans in opposition to each other, at the end Rosemary's baby (freely adapted from Roman Polanski) comes into the world instead of Gottfried – and in this laboratory of the emotions Lohengrin himself becomes a surface on which everything and nothing is projected. The production, conducted by the young and very gifted Latvian Andris Nelsons, today enjoys cult status.

7

Tristan und Isolde:
The Chord of Life

The harmonies of *Tristan* arouse feelings in me that I can hardly describe: sensuality, excitement, watchfulness, the wish for enjoyment. When I first heard the Tristan chord I knew: this is the chord of life. It contains everything: tension, longing, desire, melancholy, pain – and also relaxation, peace and deep pleasure. I shall probably have all the music theorists up in arms against me, since that chord is regarded as the very image of the hopelessly strife-torn individual, definitively restless and dissatisfied. To this day I can't share that opinion. And isn't it more interesting, I ask myself, to show someone in a state of internal strife who makes peace with himself and the world – without denying his former condition? This dialectic (although that is not a term I like) is what, as I see it, Wagner presented in composing *Tristan*.

For decades *Tristan and Isolde* was far and away my favourite opera. I swore that nothing would ever oust it from that position. But at some point *The Mastersingers* drew ahead of *Tristan*. I would never have thought that possible. Can there be any greater imaginable contrast than between *Tristan* and *The Mastersingers*? The nightmare work that should be locked in the poisons cupboard and Wagner's only comic opera? But that is Richard Wagner all over: he is always starting out in a different direction, he forces us to look at something new. It is perfectly possible that, after *Parsifal*, he might have written nothing but symphonies.

All the same, *Tristan* remains the peak of operatic art, the opera of operas, the incunabulum, *the* key work. *Tristan* is the sum of everything *and* the exception to it. With *Tristan*, Wagner begins where he left off with the Prelude to *Lohengrin*: with music that seduces us, leads us astray and makes us deny our limitations. Jump, Wagner whispers in my ear, trust yourself, it's only one last little step. And already I see myself standing on top of the Radio Tower in Berlin, staring longingly at the depths below. It is the way that Wagner plays with fire, plays games with life itself, that makes him the greatest creator and visionary of his time – and also the greatest destroyer. For what can endure when it is set beside *Tristan*? What has endured since? The hubris of this, his seventh opera, can hardly be expressed better by anyone than the Master himself, in a letter to Mathilde Wesendonck. 'Child, this Tristan will be amazing! That last act!!! [...] I fear the opera will be banned – unless a poor performance makes the whole thing a parody of itself – only run-of-the-mill performances can save me! Really good ones would be bound to send people mad – I cannot think otherwise. I had to go to these lengths!!'

Origin

Here the chronology becomes rather complicated. Since 1849, as mentioned above, Wagner had been in exile in Switzerland, where he first wrote several of his central prose works, *Art and Revolution*, *The Work of Art of the Future*, and in the autumn of 1850 *Opera and Drama*. How was his life to go on, in exile abroad as he was, cut off from the theatrical world at home, without financial means, unhappily married and out of a job, 'adrift from everything'? Writing, coming to terms with himself on paper, was an outlet: all of a sudden Wagner's mind was clear again. He began work on a new project, a 'heroic opera' entitled *Siegfrieds Tod* (*Siegfried's Death*), which was soon to grow into *The Ring of the Nibelung*, a 'stage festival drama' in four parts. A vast conception, entailing the expense of a vast amount of strength. Wagner began setting the libretto at the end of 1853, while alternating between painful attacks of facial erysipelas and following drastic water cures to treat it. Nothing seemed to do him any good: 'No wine, no beer, no coffee – only water and cold milk. No soup, everything has to be cool or lukewarm. Early to bed, three to four glasses of cold water, then I wash and have a cold enema.' Wagner was reading Schopenhauer, mingling in German revolutionary circles, and in 1854 he conducted a few concerts in London for which he was poorly paid. Meanwhile his friendship with his patron, the Rhineland merchant Otto Wesendonck and his wife Mathilde, was becoming ever closer. In 1857 the Wagners rented a house from the Wesendoncks in the garden of their newly built villa close to Zürich, with a view of the lake.

Was Mathilde Wesendonck more than Richard Wagner's platonic lover? The correspondence between them does not tell us, and only fragments of it are preserved. But perhaps the question does not really matter. The relationship was certainly passionate, they had a highly erotic sense of being kindred spirits, discussed it with each other, sometimes wrote one another letters several times a day. She gave him a gold pen, and he used it to write coded phrases like 'I. l. d. gr.!!' (*Ich liebe dich grenzenlos!!* / 'I love you boundlessly!!') on the score of *The Valkyrie*. In addition Mathilde wrote poetry, and he set some of her poems to music; the result was the *Wesendonck Lieder* of 1857/8, which are musically close to *Tristan*. Minna had been jealous for a long time anyway, and soon so was Otto Wesendonck. But this was far from being the same as Wagner's later affair with Cosima von Bülow, who became his second wife in 1870 after the births of their three children; Wagner did not envisage a future with Mathilde – or she did not envisage one with him. His material situation was and remained hopeless, and in addition he had a guilty conscience over Minna, who was suffering from heart trouble. So many dreadful emotional complications! In December 1854 Wagner was already writing to Liszt: 'As I have never in my life known real happiness in love, I intend to set up another monument to that loveliest of all dreams, one to be satiated with love from the beginning to the end; I have an idea in my mind of Tristan and Isolde, the simplest but most full-blooded musical concept, and then I will take the black flag flying at the end of the opera, cover myself with it – and die.'

So was it to be art rather than life, music instead of love? Caution is advisable in approaching such posturing, especially as there was another and tangible reason for Wagner to write *Tristan*. After failing to find a publisher for the *Ring*, he needed money, and fast. In August 1857, when he was in the middle of the composition of the second act of *Siegfried*, he put the *Ring* aside and turned to his *Tristan* project. The libretto was ready that autumn; he took his sources and inspiration from Gottfried von Strassburg's medieval epic *Tristan und Isolt*, Novalis's *Hymnen an die Nacht* (*Hymns to the Night*), August von Platen's poem 'Tristan', and Karl Ritter's drama of the same name. On 1 October Wagner began composing the music. He was not allowed much peace for it: in January he fled briefly to Paris – obviously the Mathilde situation was too precarious – and in April disaster struck: one of his letters to Mathilde fell into Minna's hands. In August, after much indecision, they moved out of the house in the Wesendoncks' garden, and that was the end of their marriage. Wagner went to Venice, Minna to Dresden. All the same, the composer managed to finish the first two acts of *Tristan* in the spring of 1859. After that he briefly returned to Switzerland, where he completed the score in Lucerne on 6 August. Meanwhile, Otto Wesendonck had bought the rights to the *Ring*, thus giving Wagner, a genius living on credit, some financial breathing space.

However, it was almost six years before the successful Munich première of *Tristan and Isolde*, on 10 June 1865. Strasbourg, Karlsruhe and Paris all declined to stage it. The demands made by the work seemed insuperable. A last attempt in Vienna was abandoned after 77 rehearsals; it cannot be said that the world did not try hard to stage the 'work of art of the future'. 'I need a good, truly helpful miracle now,' groaned Wagner, 'or it's all up with me!'

The miracle came to the Bavarian throne in the shape of King Ludwig II, on 10 March 1864. Ludwig was 18, and had been waiting eagerly for the time when he could officially forge links with Richard Wagner. Since seeing *Lohengrin*, he had thought of little other than Wagner's writings, libretti and stage sets. As one of his first official actions he sent a messenger to visit the composer in Stuttgart, and the somewhat bewildered Wagner found himself the possessor of a diamond ring and a coloured photograph of King Ludwig. Next day, 4 May 1864, Wagner was in Ludwig's royal residence in Munich – and it was a case, as Hans Neuenfels puts it, of mania at first sight. But that mania was to be very fruitful for the history of European music. Wagner was immediately rescued from all unpleasantness and hardship. 'Our meeting yesterday was a great love scene that seemed as if it would never end,' he enthusiastically told his friend Mathilde

Maier in Mainz. 'He has the deepest understanding of my nature and my requirements. He offers me all I need in order to live, to create, to get my works performed. I am to be his friend, that is all he asks – no court position, no functions.'

An amnesty granted by the King of Saxony in 1862 made it possible for Wagner to move first to Starnberg, then to Munich, and Ludwig 'commanded' his court opera to stage the première of *Tristan*. The finest talents were engaged: the court Kapellmeister Hans von Bülow was the conductor, the Dresden stars Malvina and Ludwig Schnorr von Carolsfeld sang the title parts, and the first horn in the orchestra was played by the father of Richard Strauss, who had just been born. Audience reactions were mixed, but that did not trouble Wagner. Other factors in his life were also beginning to change. On 10 April 1865, the day of the first rehearsal of *Tristan*, a daughter was born in Munich to Cosima von Bülow. The little girl was to be called Isolde, and was Richard Wagner's first child. Von Bülow, the cuckolded husband, was furious, but kept his mouth shut.

Cast and orchestration

Tristan is one of the most demanding tenor roles in all Wagner's operas (legend has it that Ludwig Schnorr von Carolsfeld, who was not yet 30, died of over-exertion soon after the première). The same can be said of the part of Isolde, which calls for a highly dramatic soprano voice with terrifying high Cs in the second act. A crazy couple hovering on the verge of what is musically possible. The rest of the ensemble is of manageable size, comprising Tristan's servant and confidant Kurwenal (baritone) and Isolde's maid and companion Brangäne (mezzo-soprano), with King Marke (bass) and his vassal Melot (tenor). A shepherd, a steersman and a young sailor deliver the few messages and perform the few services linking the internal action of the opera with the outside world. The chorus represents sailors, knights and squires in the first act.

The orchestra in the pit is similar to the orchestra for *Lohengrin*: three flutes, two oboes, a cor anglais, two clarinets, a bass clarinet, three bassoons, four horns, three trumpets, three trombones, a bass tuba, kettledrum, triangle, cymbals, harp and strings. The music on stage, however, almost entirely dispenses with the blaring sound of brass: only the homeopathic effect of three trumpets, three trombones, six horns and a cor anglais are called for.

From the point of view of cast and orchestration, we are told that Wagner said *Tristan* was a good opera for a city opera house: almost no chorus, not much on-stage music – there would be nothing for theatrical managers to worry about. Both then and now that is, of course, an audacious claim.

Plot

The action takes place first at sea between Ireland and Cornwall, then in the garden of King Marke's castle, and finally at Tristan's citadel of Kareol in Brittany. No date is suggested.

Before the opera: during the war between Ireland and Cornwall, Tristan has killed the Irish King Morold, whom Isolde was to marry, and sent her his head. Severely wounded, he is cast up on the coast of Ireland, where he is received and nursed back to health by none other than Isolde herself. Although she recognizes the stranger who calls himself Tantris as Morold's killer, she cannot bring herself to murder him.

Act 1: Tristan is escorting Isolde to Cornwall to marry King Marke. She feels humiliated, and tells Brangäne her story (*Weh! Ach, wehe! Dies zu dulden!* / 'Woe, ah woe, to suffer this!'). Her companion reminds her of the casket of magic potions that Isolde's mother gave them, and Isolde determines to be revenged on Tristan by giving him the death potion. She will take it too in order to avoid a forced marriage to Marke. Tristan approaches, they drink reluctantly – and fall into one another's arms. (*Tristan! – Isolde! Treuloser Holder!* / 'Tristan! – Isolde! Faithless dear one!'): Brangäne has switched the death potion for the love potion. Intentionally or by accident? The ship reaches Cornwall.

Act 2: In the garden outside King Marke's castle, the lovers meet for a tryst (*O sink hernieder, / Nacht der Liebe* / 'Sink down on us / O night of love'), while Brangäne's urgent warnings as she keeps watch are ignored. At the height of their ecstasy, Tristan and Isolde are taken *in flagrante*, so to speak, by the arrival of King Marke. The king is shattered by this double breach of faith (*Tatest du's wirklich?* / 'Would you do that?') and Tristan falls on his former friend Melot's sword.

Act 3: Kurwenal has taken his severely wounded master to Kareol, where they are both waiting for Isolde. Fantasizing, Tristan has hallucinations (*Isolde kommt!* / *Isolde naht!* / 'Isolde is coming! / She is close now!'). But as soon as his beloved arrives at last, he dies. Marke, having heard the true background of the betrayal from Brangäne, also comes too late. Kurwenal and Melot fight, and kill each other, and Isolde dies her *Liebestod* or erotic death (*Mild und leise* / *wie er lächelt* / 'Mildly, gently / see him smiling').

What is all this really about? Intensity, nothing else. An intensity of emotion that cannot be lived out in reality. It is about an exclusively personal perception that *must* end in death, about the magic of that desire for death, it is about anarchy and the deepest depression. To me, *Tristan* is an object lesson in how things ought *not* to be. Wagner shows us all the facets of this nightmare – and then closes with a pensive, placatory touch, relaxing and positively uncomplicated if not actually banal, in the key of B major. Isolde's erotic death builds a bridge to this development: a 'hymn to the night' of human consciousness, a long – too long – *diminuendo* at the end of which we are aware that day will return, and soon *must* return. And life goes on. I do not think Isolde really dies at the end of her *Liebestod*. Wagner writes, in his last stage direction, that 'in Brangäne's arms, Isolde sinks gently onto the body of Tristan, as if transfigured'. This is almost literally reminiscent of Elsa and looks ahead to Kundry in *Parsifal*. 'Slowly, looking up at Parsifal, Kundry sinks to the ground before him, lifeless' – the word is *entseelt*. It is a typical fate for Wagner's women characters. However, one should not ignore a potentially subversive element. Could it not be that Isolde avoids death because of the fact that she has music in her, indeed *is* music? And that the whole opera does not end in disaster and total dissolution, but in music and art?

I do ask myself why it is so essential for Tristan to die. 'He tears the bandage off his wounds,' we are told in the third act, and, 'no longer in control of himself,' rushes to meet Isolde. That would be suicide. Because only death can unite what life divides for reasons of origin, fate, social convention and morality? Because perhaps Isolde does not love Tristan as ardently as he loves Isolde? Because she preserves her composure while he loses his and tears himself to pieces? Compared to the Utopian frenzy of the music, that thinking does seem to me a little too petty, too romantic, too much in the spirit of *Lohengrin*. It is true that light could be cast even on *Tristan* by the preceding operas of Wagner's storm-and-stress period. But what Hugo von Hofmannsthal called the 'dreadfully autobiographical' aspect of this music composed in 1958/9 is more strongly evident in *Tristan* than its predecessors. Hoffmansthal's comment suggests a simple calculation, with Mathilde Wesendonck as Isolde, Otto Wesendonck as King Marke, and of course Wagner himself as Tristan (Minna, typically, comes nowhere). By sentencing Tristan to suicide and Isolde to her erotic death in the 'surging torrent', the 'musical sound', the 'flowing universe', Wagner is saying: I may die as a man and a lover – I shall survive as an artist and a composer. In a way, *Tristan* is programme music with unfulfilment as its theme.

The genre is given simply as a *Handlung* – an action, plot or narrative – in three acts. There are two provocative ideas behind this description. One is that almost nothing in the way of an outward operatic plot occurs in *Tristan*. The voyage, the night of love, waiting and death – nothing else happens. No swans swim across a river, no pilgrims' chorus comes from Rome, no sea captain's daughter leaps into the sea from a high cliff. All that happens in *Tristan* is that the characters talk, reflect, wax enthusiastic, complain and talk again – mainly at odds with each other rather than to each other. That leads to the second provocative idea. Even the lovers do not actually do anything, they do not make physical love, so there is no real 'action', it is all words. As a result, the tension lasts for four hours, unresolved. Also as a result, the Prelude to the first act is nothing but an imagined version of the ardent opposite of unfulfilment, and the discovery of the lovers by King Marke in the second act is like a case of *coitus interruptus*. Thomas Mann calls Tristan the classic *opus metaphysicum* of art. Everything happens, but only in fantasy.

Music

F, B, D sharp, G sharp: at first sight an unremarkable four-note chord. Yet in the second bar of the opera it opens the gates to hell and heaven alike. This chord, known as the Tristan chord, is the password, the cipher for all modern music. It is a chord that does not conform to any key, a chord on the verge of dissonance. A chord standing alone, hovering in the air and not trying to go anywhere. The Tristan chord does not seek to be resolved in the closest consonance, as the classic theory of harmony requires; the Tristan chord is sufficient unto itself, just as Tristan and Isolde are sufficient unto themselves and know only their love. No promise of marriage, no pledge of faithfulness, no past, no fear, not even the fear of death. If we want to fit Wagner's biography so sweepingly to his work of art, we could say that what was not given to him with Mathilde Wesendonck in real life is crystallized in the Tristan chord, obeying the claim of their feelings to absolute validity.

To this day, musicologists have come to no clear conclusion in the analysis and exegesis of this chord. What is it supposed to be? A modified three-four chord, the reverse form of a double dominant seventh chord with a diminished fifth, a subdominant triad with *sixte ajoutée*, or a diminished dominant ninth chord? I think that all this rummaging around in the theoretical toolbox shows mainly our own inadequacy. The same could be said of the music of *Tristan* as a whole: it can hardly be defined by traditional parameters. In harmonic terms, there is no major or minor tonality here, and formally not the slightest trace of the old numbers opera. Dramatically, too, the old conflict between the artist and the social reality in which he lives seems to have been faded out for once. Instead, we have chromaticism and free counterpoint, and the singing voices fit into the symphonic and opiate tissue of the music as a whole like instruments. With *Tristan*, Wagner crossed a border that would come to light only half a century later. *Tristan* is the music of Freud's psychoanalysis, the literature of Thomas Mann, the factor that ignited the musical thinking of Gustav Mahler, Arnold Schönberg, Alban Berg, Claude Debussy and their contemporaries. 'The most important part of the action here is what goes on in the human mind,' Wagner notes of his attitude in almost plain and simple terms. In Cosima's diary of 1870, we find the principle of composition to match it: 'In the carriage, R. speaks of putting several motifs together in the music; the ear perceives only one, but the addition of the others as accompaniment enormously sharpens and enhances the impression of that one perceived melody.' Music as an expression of the unconscious mind, a reflection of our memories, dreams and premonitions.

In *Tristan and Isolde*, Wagner wrote his first real total work of art. As a practitioner, he was obviously profiting by theory, or at least he successfully strips off any corset of operatic convention in this work. For the first time, the content radically dictates the form. The Prelude is called simply an introduction, and runs on naturally into the first scene (no one dares to applaud after the last *pizzicato* from the cellos and double basses), and it is impossible to single out individual passages, let alone 'arias', ensembles, and so on from the sound as a whole. The score is a single tissue of sound, a torrent of 'sweet and spine-chilling infinity', as Nietzsche put it.

Already, in the Prelude to *Lohengrin*, we feel it would be better if it came not at the beginning but at the end of the first act – the musicians are often still nervous at the beginning of a performance, and it is not easy for the conductor to get instruments divided into so many sections playing cleanly and precisely *pianissimo* here. However, a failed introduction to *Tristan* can ruin the whole evening. If it sounds casual, tedium threatens, and that tedium cannot easily be corrected in the first act; if it sounds overheated, the conductor may exhaust all his powers in the first 10 minutes. *Tristan* goes rapidly from zero to 300, hence its explosive nature. Such explosive material demands great subtlety of feeling, as much delicacy as you might need to crack a safe. Either you set off the alarm, or you find the right combination of numbers.

From the first I felt that *Tristan* was a touchstone. I remember sitting at the piano as an adolescent, playing Brangäne's night watch song, her '*Habet acht!*' ('ah, take care!') in the second act – just the harmonic links. I was trying to work out how Wagner achieves such hypnotic sound – and to be honest, to this day I am not quite sure. Here again, much but not all can be neatly analysed. In his autobiography, Wagner writes that it took him almost two weeks to compose the five minutes of the watch song. They must have been two dismal, terrible weeks, until at last he had found what he wanted. Sometimes Richard Wagner strikes me as a version of Dr Jekyll and Mr Hyde: one side of his personality sees visions and staggers from one insanely somnambulistic state to the next (Mr Hyde), the other constructs and refines, mixes and discards ideas, simmers and tastes them (Dr Jekyll). It is part of his genius that each side knows about the other.

And one further factor has always particularly fascinated me; it occurs when Tristan, in his great recapitulation in the third act, complains of the sunlight, of his inability to die of the love potion that only drags out his suffering and torment. *Für dieser Hitze / heisses Verschmachten / ach! keines Schattens / kühlend Umnachten!* ('In the sun's heat dying, / ah, that I might / feel the cool / of surrounding night'), runs the libretto, and the woodwind plays needle-sharp triplets, *pipipi pipipi pipipi pipipi* – only at this one place, as if the bright light were perforating the retina of the hero's eyes. The strings accompany the woodwind in wild chromatic movement, half in a *tremolo* effect, half twitching, *molto crescendo* – in terms of composition this is Wagner taking pure pleasure in his own virtuosity. How far can I go, he seems to ask himself here, how can I drive the world out of its mind? Just like that, is the answer, through this crazed *notturno*. It is the Paganini effect, demonic, art for art's sake, simply because he could do it.

Much as this sunlight passage always grips me, I have to keep a cool head conducting Tristan's lament. Its waves break higher and higher for over three-quarters of an hour, and must be organically constructed like the ebb and flow of a tide, without letting the music stop, or come out all in a rush, or allowing the tenor to run out of breath in the middle of it. It is the maximum challenge to my sensitivity, my concentration, my knowledge of the opera as a whole, and my powers. Not for nothing is the third act of *Tristan* considered incomparable in the extremity it depicts (a depiction continued, however, in the second act of *Parsifal*).

The intensity in which *Tristan* deals also corresponds to the intensity that Wagner demands of the interpreters of the opera. That is the crazy aspect of the work: seductive, dangerous, diabolical and sacred. One ought not to sing, play or conduct it too often, and it should always be approached with great care: with awe, respect, devotion, love and a touch of fear. On the one hand, we musicians are not about to do ourselves violence, like Tristan himself, to find satisfaction and release in our own death; if we did that, there would be no music. On the other hand, musicians who take it seriously risk infection by certain borderline symptoms.

The successful interpreter of *Tristan* needs – paradoxical but true – mental armour, something to buoy him up while the waves break over him. The successful interpreter of *Tristan* is the pharmacist who carries the key to the poisons cupboard on him at all times – and the successful interpreter of *Tristan* knows how to defuse bombs.

Recordings

I previously conducted *Tristan* in 2002 at the Vienna State Opera. After that I voluntarily took a break from the work. I suddenly felt afraid that my favourite opera might leave me in a psychological and emotional state that would make me a stranger to myself. A sense of emptiness and exhaustion spread through me as if I would have no more to say – indeed, would never have anything more to say. I had to get myself out of that situation when I conducted *Tristan* at the 2015 Bayreuth Festival. The 13 years of abstention did me good; at least, I began to feel a wish to conduct it again. And I was open to the idea of doing everything differently this time.

There is a recording of that Viennese production (Deutsche Grammophon), with the American tenor Thomas Moser singing Tristan. Casting such a lyrical tenor makes discipline necessary: the conductor must take care not to make the great culminating passages (the conclusion of the first act, the conclusion of the night of love) sound too compact, too rich, or the tenor's voice may give out, and we shall not hear very much from him in the third act. I hope I succeeded in Vienna. The casting under Herbert von Karajan in the Bayreuth production of 1952 was very different, and for me it is still one of the greatest of recordings (Orfeo). Ramón Vinay sings Tristan with a velvety, dark timbre, and from the first has something of the Knight of the Sorrowful Countenance about him, and Martha Mödl, at the height of her powers, is Isolde – what a huge voice, what a woman! Ira Malaniuk sings Brangäne, radiating such unconditional authority in the watch song that you wonder why the lovers do not immediately do as she says. Karajan was 44 years old at the time of this recording, and handled his singers as if he had never conducted anything but *Tristan*. It is pure atmosphere, light, shade, colours never known before. But it always feels as if Karajan were the director, in charge of the whole production. In the orchestral introduction to the third act he relishes the tender Bayreuth sound, letting the cellos lead without being overpowering and noisy, so that you might take them for violins – there is a sensitivity and clarity about it hard to find elsewhere.

The discography of *Tristan* is full of milestones. Thomas Beecham's recording of 1937 in London is one of them, because he makes the orchestra a protagonist, just as Wagner wanted (EMI). His Isolde is Kirsten Flagstad, the ideal dramatic soprano and *the* Isolde of the 1930s, 1940s and early 1950s. Her name also appears in the cast at the Met under Erich Leinsdorf, in 1948 under Erich Kleiber at the Teatro Cólon – and in Wilhelm Furtwängler's legendary London studio production of 1952 with the Philharmonia Orchestra (Ludwig Suthaus sings Tristan; also EMI). Flagstad was 57 years old at this time, and it would be wrong to say one can't tell that. Her Isolde has seen and known everything, and acts retrospectively rather than out of immediate experience. I feel the same about Furtwängler here. For all the incomparable depth of his musical sensitivity, all his magnetic feeling for sound, all his psychological mastery, there is a sense of sunset and the golden mean about this late recording. Two years later Furtwängler was dead; I sometimes think that he did not come to terms with events in Germany between 1933 and 1945 nearly as easily as he was said to have done.

In the next generation I like Wolfgang Sawallisch's recording best, made in 1957 with the ideal New Bayreuth couple of Birgit Nilsson and Wolfgang Windgassen – young but not simply passionate. And of course there is Carlos Kleiber and his legendary recording from the Church of St Luke in Dresden, made in 1980 to 1982, which ended with several disagreements (Deutsche Grammophon). An argument with René Kollo, singing Tristan, was the deciding factor. Because of the singer's indisposition, Tristan's laments had to be added later in the studio (with Kollo singing solo, which was current practice), and it took some time for them to be mixed in any way that suited Kleiber and integrated with the rest of the material. In spite of the conductor's furious dissatisfaction, the result is brilliant. To my mind Kleiber comes close to Karajan: Apollonian and drawing sparklingly transparent playing from the orchestra, with extremely lyrical casting (Margaret Price, who could never have sung Isolde on the stage, does so here with youthful rejoicing that shows the part in a positively defiant light), and very risky in many of the tempi. Carlos Kleiber was a musical erotomaniac. His *Tristan* kindles images in the mind that make any staged performance seem almost obsolete. In any case, the sets of *Tristan* productions on stage, from Adolphe Appia by way of Alfred Roller and Wieland Wagner to Erich Wonder, prefer an empty and symbolically abstract space.

8

A Plea for Tolerance:
Die Meistersinger von Nürnberg
(*The Mastersingers of Nuremberg*)

I see *The Mastersingers* as the pivot and central point of Wagner's entire œuvre. On the one hand it is a reaction to *Tristan*; on the other, he had found himself in a blind alley with *Siegfried*, and together those two works showed him the way out of it. The fascinating thing about *The Mastersingers* is that you can find everything in it. Hero and anti-hero, comedy and tragedy, upper-class and lower-class lovers, burlesque and reflection, the old and the new, in short a whole world.

The magic words summing it up for me are 'atmosphere' and 'poetry'. How can I, as a conductor, make the music glitter in its exaggerations and parodies, and at the same time lend it authority? Conversely, how can I make its emotionalism sound not false but genuine, emphasizing the deeply felt popular note in the music? Wagner is fundamentally asking his interpreters to square the circle, which is what makes *The Mastersingers* such a difficult work to perform. Perhaps it can succeed only by osmosis, if we open ourselves up entirely to all its moods, colours and aromas, inhaling them so deeply that they naturally emerge from us again at the right moment.

Origin

The weeks and months up to and after the première of *Tristan* in June 1865 Richard Wagner a happy man: he seemed to have found the right publisher in Bernhard Schott (the Mainz music publisher bought the rights to the *Ring* from Otto Wesendonck, and held out the prospect of an advance on *The Mastersingers*), Ludwig II granted his every wish, and in the form of Cosima von Bülow a woman had come into his life who united all the qualities of a lover, a companion and a partner who appreciated his art. Cosima was 24 years younger than Wagner (and 15 centimetres taller), sophisticated, multilingual and very well educated: Franz Liszt's daughter by Countess Marie d'Agoult. She had been married to the conductor Hans von Bülow since 1857 (ironically, their honeymoon journey took them past the Wagners when they were renting the house in the Wesendoncks' garden). Richard Wagner had last seen his wife Minna in Dresden in November 1862, and Minna died over three years later, in January 1866, abandoned and alone. Wagner was unable to come to her funeral, since by now he had fallen out with the Bavarian court, and had to ask for asylum in Switzerland again. His expensive lifestyle, which put a great financial strain on the Bavarian state coffers, his disrespectful political comments about the 'useless, emasculated aristocracy that had sunk to such depths', and not least his notorious affair with Frau von Bülow all asked too much of the patience of the public.

In March 1866, Wagner moved to the Villa Tribschen on Lake Lucerne, near the city of Lucerne itself. Ludwig paid the rent, and Cosima – still married to von Bülow – kept house there for Wagner. In February 1867 their second child, Eva, was born, to be followed in June 1869 by their son Siegfried. Not until the autumn of 1870 did Cosima ask Hans von Bülow for a divorce. On 25 August 1870, Cosima and Richard finally married in Lucerne. King Ludwig was far from happy about the marriage, feeling, with latent homoerotic inclinations, that he had been betrayed and deceived. But that did not detract from his lifelong admiration for the work of Wagner.

The next admirer came knocking on Wagner's door at Tribschen in 1869; he was Friedrich Nietzsche, the 24-year-old Professor of Philology at Basel University and future philosopher. They had met in Leipzig the previous year at one of Wagner's popular 'readings' from *The Master-singers*, in which the composer slipped into all the roles and imitated their various voices. For the young Nietzsche, Wagner was 'a fabulously lively and fiery man', and anyway, as he once wrote, he could never have endured his youth without Wagner's music. Nietzsche stayed at Tribschen 22 times; there were discussions of politics and aesthetics,

Nietzsche played with the children or ran errands for Cosima. All the same, Wagner kept a certain distance from his disciple, perhaps feeling that the borderline between mania and madness is not always easily discerned. After the founding of the Bayreuth Festival in 1872, the friendship cooled, and indeed turned to outright hostility on the philosopher's part.

A first prose draft of *The Mastersingers* dated back to Wagner's visit to Marienbad to take the waters when he was composing *Tannhäuser* and *Lohengrin*. The sources are regarded as Johann Christoph Wagenseil's *Buch von der Meister-Singer holdseligen Kunst* (*Book of the Fair Art of the Master-Singers*) of 1697, Johann Ludwig Deinhardstein's play *Hans Sachs* and Lortzing's opera of the same name, Gervinus's *Geschichte der deutschen Nationalliteratur* (*History of German National Literature*), Jacob Grimm's *Über den altdeutschen Meistergesang* (*On Old German Master-Song*), and E.T.A. Hoffmann's story *Meister Martin, der Küfner, und seine Gesellen* (*Master Martin, the Cooper, and his Journeymen*). When did Wagner read all those works? 'Just as a tragedy was followed by a merry satyr play in ancient Athens, the idea of a comic piece suddenly came into my mind, one that could in fact follow my Singers' Contest on the Wartburg,' he wrote in a 'Message to My Friends' in 1851. But it was another 10 years before he produced the second prose draft. In 1861, after the débacle of *Tannhäuser* in Paris, Wagner seems to have remembered his comic opera again. The libretto was finished in January 1862, and he finally completed the score in October 1967. Ultimately *The Mastersingers* is not only the satyr play to go with *Tristan*, but also desensitizes it. We might almost say that after the most intoxicating chromatic narcosis in music history, Wagner provides the right smelling salts to counteract it.

The Mastersingers of Nuremberg had its première in Munich on 21 June 1868. Wagner sat in state beside Ludwig II in the royal box of the National Theatre, and was enthusiastically acclaimed.

Cast and orchestration

The ensemble of singers is enormous, assembling no less than 12 master craftsmen alone, from a soap-boiler by way of a pewterer to a grocer and a stocking-weaver, chief among them the cobbler Hans Sachs (baritone) and the goldsmith Veit Pogner, Eva's father (bass). In accordance with operatic convention Eva (soprano), also known as Evchen, and Walther von Stolzing (tenor), a knight from Franconia, are the high-born lovers, Eva's nurse Magdalene (mezzo-soprano) and the jaunty David (tenor), Sachs's apprentice, are their plebeian counterparts. The chorus forms large tableaux of more apprentices and journeymen, local girls and citizens from all the craft guilds. All these crowds have to be kept moving on stage.

The *Mastersingers* orchestra is not large, but it can sound very earthbound and, above all, loud. That is the problem. Wagner writes for two flutes and a piccolo, two oboes, two clarinets and two bassoons, four horns, three trumpets, three trombones, a bass tuba, kettledrum, large drum, cymbals, triangle, glockenspiel, harp, as well as a steel or Beckmesser harp, and a large body of strings. On stage there are various trumpets and horns, an organ, drums, and for the finale of the second act an 'ox's horn' for the night watchman.

Plot

The setting is Nuremberg in the middle of the sixteenth century.

Act 1: In the Church of St Katherine, divine service is just coming to an end. Walther von Stolzing, who wants to become a citizen of Nuremberg, was a guest of the goldsmith Veit Pogner the day before and fell in love with his daughter Eva. She tells him that she must marry the winner of the singing contest announced for the next day, or live single for the rest of her life. A meeting of the Mastersingers is held in the church, Stolzing introduces himself as a new suitor for Eva's hand (*Am stillen Herd* / 'Beside the hearth'), and is now to sing to the Masters. Sixtus Beckmesser, the town clerk, who fancies his own chances in the contest, has the task of acting as 'marker' – the referee who notes down all a singer's mistakes according to the rules of Mastersong. At the end the verdict is clear: the aristocratic Stolzing has sung badly and lost.

Act 2: In the street between the houses of Pogner and Hans Sachs. David tells Magdalene how Stolzing fared with his test song, while Eva tries to find out more from Sachs. He seems to let her beguile him (*Was*

duftet doch der Flieder / 'How sweet the lilac smells'). When Stolzing
appears, the lovers decide to defy the Masters' verdict and run away.
Eva puts on Magdalene's clothes – but Sachs, going about his handi-
work undeterred, prevents their flight. Meanwhile Beckmesser comes
along to serenade Eva (*Den Tag seh' ich erscheinen* / 'I see the day now
dawning'). The cobbler's hammering and Beckmesser's tuneless singing
finally wake the neighbours, David thinks he has caught Magdalene
out in an assignation with Beckmesser, and the scene degenerates into
a mass brawl. But it is all over when the night watchman goes on his
rounds at midnight.

Act 3: In the cobbler's house on the morning of Midsummer Day.
Sachs reflects on the events of the night (*Wahn, Wahn! / Überall Wahn!*
/ 'Folly, folly! All of it folly!'), David reminds him of the day's duties.
Stolzing describes a dream he has had, and with Sachs's help turns it
into a song (*Morgenlich leuchtend* / 'Bright in the morning'). Believing
that he has found a poem by Sachs, Beckmesser steals the lines quickly
jotted down on paper. Sachs describes Stolzing's song as a 'blissful
morning-dream interpretation', the lovers and the master join in a
quintet (*Selig, wie die Sonne* / 'Blessed, like the sun'). The scene moves
to the festive meadow, with all the apprentices and masters of the guilds
making merry. Beckmesser opens the singing contest with the song he
has stolen. As he has failed to memorize it properly, he makes himself
the butt of mockery. Singing the right version, however, Stolzing wins
the contest and Eva's hand. When Sachs explains the Masters' responsibility for art to him, the knight, originally hesitant, allows himself to
be accepted into their guild (*ehrt Eure deutschen Meister* / 'honour your
German masters').

As I see it, *The Mastersingers* is a plea for tolerance. The end of the
opera is extremely interesting, and is often, unfortunately, misunderstood. 'All present join in the people's singing', Wagner notes, and I do
not feel that is by any means a prescription of unanimity, a 'chalybeate
bath in C major', as Hans Richter, conductor at the première, put it,
but is rather a collective confession of faith. Stolzing has sung a song
that breaks the constraints of the former rules, yet one and all are
happy to hail him as the victor. They know that you achieve something
only together, not fighting against each other. Seen in that way, *The*

Mastersingers can almost be regarded as an opera of integration. Stolzing is the outsider, an immigrant from a different (aristocratic) background who sings in what is ostensibly the wrong way, but is accepted into the bourgeois society of Nuremberg – and immediately changes it. The Masters must free themselves from their ossified, narrow-minded ideas if they want to continue their achievements. And as politics always have their private side, Wagner also presents the conflict in a private light: Hans Sachs himself must accept the inevitable and acknowledge that Eva loves the foreign knight and not him, the widower. Even worse, he must ensure – *Hier gilt's der Kunst* ('This is the art of it') – that the knight wins the singing contest, to that end disregarding his personal interests and feelings. The reminiscence of *Tristan* in the third act is very significant – here Sachs is speaking to Eva, but above all he is showing what a close thing his decision not to court her himself was: *Mein Kind: / von Tristan und Isolde / kenn' ich ein traurig Stück: / Hans Sachs war klug, und wollte / nichts von Herrn Markes Glück* ('My child, of Tristan and Isolde / a sad tale I could tell. / Hans Sachs was wise, and did not want / the fate that Marke befell'). It was time, he concludes, that he faced facts instead of heading for misfortune.

There remains the fascinating question of what becomes of Beckmesser. The town clerk makes a fool of himself by stealing the song, 'peals of laughter' greet him on the festive meadow, and finally he rushes away in a rage and 'loses himself among the people'. As I see it, Beckmesser is still around in Nuremberg; he is not summarily disposed of like Kaspar, the villain of the piece in *The Free-shooter* ('Throw the monster into the Wolf's Glen'), nor is he killed like Mime in *Siegfried*. *The Mastersingers* is not an aggressive or dark work in general, in fact Wagner would have needed very different instrumentation to give that impression, and he would really have wanted to present the opera in a different light. The brawl in the finale of the second act certainly results in bumps and bruises, but the tone of it is definitely comic and ironic. Where else would one find the anger of the people vented in strict counterpoint, in the form of a fugue? And there is plenty of discontent in 'the Masters' bourgeois society', as Wagner himself calls it; there are troubled moments and grey shades, glances into the abyss. But at the end the mood is overwhelmingly cheerful, merry, in an atmosphere of festive delight, and if we cannot see and hear that properly today, we ought to chalk it up to our own discredit and not blame the opera.

Music

The Mastersingers is the ultimate German festive opera. Art is, yet again, thinking about itself – in a typically Wagnerian or typically German way? – and doing so in a very contradictory manner, or at least so it seems at first glance. The ensemble of characters suggest Italian *opera buffa* and German *Spieloper*, the three large-scale finales are reminiscent of Meyerbeer's grand opera, and if we are to believe Wagner the whole thing should sound like 'Bach in practice [...] old and yet so new'. In order to achieve that effect, he dispenses here, for the first and only time, with all gods, extra-terrestrial heroes and mythical backgrounds. The cast of *The Mastersingers* consists of flesh-and-blood human beings, well-behaved bourgeois citizens. And the mixture works. It is made up of fictional realities and closely observed traditions, real and invented, and the score is notably intelligent. The list of opera houses that have opened, or been reopened, with productions of *The Mastersingers* is a long one: the Munich Prinzregent Theatre in 1901, the Nuremberg Opera in 1905, the Freiburg Opera in 1949, New Bayreuth in 1951, the Berlin State Opera in 1955, Leipzig in 1960, the Munich National Theatre in 1963, the Essen Aalto Theatre in 1998, and it may be hoped there will be many more in the future.

Wagner's understanding of art is expressed with particular clarity in Hans Sachs's 'lilac' monologue in the second act: *Ich fühl's – und kann's nicht verstehn; – / kann's nicht behalten – doch auch nicht vergessen; / und fass' ich es ganz – kann ich's nicht messen* ('I feel and cannot understand it / cannot hold it fast, nor can I forget it / and if I do understand I cannot measure it'). Art, Wagner is saying, is immeasurable, and that can be so only if it is aware of its effect *and* comes from the heart. In my opinion the secret of Wagner's work as a whole mystery draws on this tension, this gauging of powers. *The Mastersingers* is the opera in which he makes it his subject. Hans Sachs is, as Carl Dahlhaus puts it, his 'self-portrait as a classic figure'. And an imposing figure he is: artist and craftsman, cobbler and poet combined – the parallels are clear.

But what about the musical context of early modernity? The Prelude, with its three-part counterpoint, could pass as a Baroque overture; the scene of the brawl is technically a double *fugato* in which polyphony features prominently – in short, it is archaic or archaizing. Listen, Wagner is saying, I know my way around, I know the tradition in which I stand, and I will show you what I can do. *The Mastersingers* always reminds me of Richard Strauss's *Rosenkavalier*, because in both works there is great sophistication behind apparent simplicity, and the 'naïve' aspect can only be the work of a 'sentimental' spirit (that is to say, a deliberately thoughtful one). Just as Strauss transfers the waltz to the Maria Theresia period, *The Mastersingers* bears the stamp of the nineteenth century. Lilac, for instance, would not have been growing in Nuremberg in the sixteenth century, but elder (for which the same German word can also be used) was possible. And how exactly was a nobleman, Walther von Stolzing, supposed to be teaching the Masters the secret of true art? That hardly fits the patriotic spirit of the years before 1871 or Wagner's own fundamental revolutionary convictions. Yet somehow it seems all right. Life, after all, is not without its contradictions.

'The art of being art must conceal the fact that it is art and appear natural,' says Carl Dahlhaus, hitting the nail on the head. Not for a single bar do we consciously notice the workmanship and montage of *The Mastersingers*, it all flows apparently naturally together, including no less than 45 leitmotifs. It sounds odd, but this score could have been logically dictated. So to this day I am convinced that a conductor does not need a 'concept' for the work. You just have to lay yourself open confidently to its humour, its wit, and the tricks that it plays.

Let us take the Prelude to Act 3, with its gloomy cello cantilena disappearing as if into the void of a dungeon. What kind of music is this? The opposite of all the splendour of the festive meadow that is yet to come? The dungeon of the soul? A collective headache after the previous night's brawl? 'Bourgeois philosophy' is what Thomas Mann calls it, for the beginning of the third act is the world of Hans Sachs, far more so that his cobbler's workshop and the scent of lilac (or elder); it reflects his own business in accounting for himself, ruminating, writing poetry, singing, all to gain clarity about life. Ernst Bloch sees a basic melancholy in it. And how does Wagner find his way out of this departure from the mood? First, in comes Stolzing with his 'morning dream' song, then the quintet follows – and then the grandiose transition to Beckmesser's mime, the scene in which the town clerk tries to get the hang of the verses he has stolen. Groaning and limping, he announces himself as if Wagner had composed music for every one of his bruises separately; scraps of the brawl motif are at odds with his failed serenade from the second act, Sachs's cobbling song comes in briefly, the shadow of Stolzing haunts the room: life is a merciless pastiche, is parody and travesty and truth all at once. And the music is as progressive and clear-sighted as never before. But that is often the case with Wagner: the villainous and difficult characters, the Ortruds, Beckmessers and Klingsors, have the most daring music of all.

Such layers of reality are also present on the festival meadow. Standards are carried around, the craftsmen chant in rhyme, we hear snatches of waltzes and ländlers, we hear drums and trumpets. There is a glittering tableau at an angle of 360 degrees in C major, and at its culminating points you can look in vain for interruptions or doubts. Wagner built in no disadvantages here, and in fact that opened up the way to a problematic reception of the opera, which very soon came to be regarded as the showpiece opera of the Third Reich. Especially notorious were the performances of it given at Bayreuth in 1933 in the presence of Hitler and Goebbels, and at Nuremberg in 1935 as a festive celebration at the Reich Party rally. Wagner's bourgeois drama as a nationalist portent, the writing on the wall?

I have been asked several times how I could conduct *The Mastersingers* in Nuremberg or Bayreuth, and my answer was always: very easily. For one thing, public reaction to the opera did not stop in the 1930s, and for another, it is not an artist's job to let his view of a work be dictated and distorted by its previous performance history. We ought to know who made use of a work of art, and when, there is no doubt of that, but we must also stand by our own experience and our own reaction to it. In my case, obviously, it is not the same as the reaction of a conductor in 1933 or 1935.

And, speaking of Bayreuth, yet again the Festival Theatre is not the best place in which to perform *The Mastersingers*. The staggered arrangement of instruments in the pit is suitable for the elaborate *parlando* style of the score only with reservations. There are passages that will never be entirely satisfactory on the Green Hill, for instance the brawl scene, which will not be as clear as it should because all the little notes so easily lose their distinct sound under the cover of the pit. At the same time, however, Bayreuth is the place where you can most easily succeed in conveying the lightness and poetry of the score. The *Midsummer Night's Dream* atmosphere of the second act, the cobbler's workshop in the third do not sound so luminous and elfin, so redolent of lilac, anywhere but in the Festival Theatre, and that reconciles one to it.

Recordings

At four and a half hours' playing time, *The Mastersingers* is far from being a short comic opera. The conductor has to be well in control, and there are several dangers lying in wait. First, if you are young you may think you should conduct it from memory, but then you can easily find yourself floundering. Any number of things can go wrong with Beckmesser's serenade in the second act, with all its interruptions and sideswipes, and above all with his mime in the third act. It is better to concentrate on finding the right tempo for the mime. Second, if you conduct the Prelude as if it were part of a concert or an encore, you will have used up too much energy already. Third, if you confuse the sensitive Mendelssohnian intensity of the Prelude with boisterous sound and volume, you will immediately have difficulty getting the orchestra to play quietly right through the first act. We see how necessary that is at the beginning, in the first scene after the hymn. The swift exchanges of words between Stolzing and Eva, Eva and Magdalene must be fluid, and for that very reason are seldom precise. *Verweilt! – Ein Wort! Ein einzig Wort!* ('Oh, stay! One word. A word for me!'), *Mein Brusttuch! Schau! Wohl liegt's im Ort?* ('My kerchief! Look! Where can it be?'). This is pure *Singspiel* such as Lortzing might have written. In addition, Wagner keeps writing *forte* on the score, which is impossible. Orchestras of the time probably just did not play so loudly, or that is my rather simple explanation. Today you have to negotiate between the stage and the pit in such passages.

And you must not lose sight of the mountain range as a whole. The first act is infernally difficult, purely from the technical and manual point of view (and is also the one that takes most rehearsal); the second is the dramatic plumb line, the centre, a delicate masterpiece, and the third is so long – almost two and a half hours – that it can finish the performers off physically. The only solution is to resort to calm conducting here. For that reason the recordings by the great conductors of the past appeal to me most: Hermann Abendroth and Wilhelm Furtwängler in the wartime summer of 1943 in Bayreuth, Rudolf Kempe in Dresden in 1951, Hans Knappertsbusch in Munich in 1955, Fritz Reiner the same year in Vienna, and Karajan's alert studio recording of 1970, again with the Dresden ensemble. Later recordings either, like Eugen Jochum's with the orchestra of the German Opera House in Berlin, suffer from unnecessarily showy casting (Plácido Domingo as Stolzing), or like Wolfgang Sawallisch's in 1993 with the Bavarian State Orchestra fall into too complacent a style of music-making. The difficulty is that a conductor of *The Mastersingers* must have both a sense of humour and a quick wit *and* no fear of melancholy and emotion, must observe counterpoint passages strictly *and* be supple in adjusting the tempi to each other.

The 1937 recording under Arturo Toscanini at the Salzburg Festival is also legendary. It is springy, airy, no question of that, and Toscanini catches Wagner's conversational tone magnificently, while his singers articulate naturally and precisely (Hans Hermann Nissen as Sachs, Maria Reining as Eva). For me, however, a little of the atmosphere in between the notes is missing, although that can be blamed on the extremely poor technical quality of the recording. Until the 1960s it was usual to cast the roles of *The Mastersingers* with rather heavyweight voices. Nissen as Sachs was followed by Paul Schöffler (under Abendroth, Knappertsbusch and Reiner), Jaro Prohaska (under Furtwängler), Otto Edelmann (under Karajan in Bayreuth in 1951) and Ferdinand Frantz (twice, under Kempe). In 1970 Herbert von Karajan tried casting singers who would do justice to the transparency of the work, which almost resembles chamber music in that respect, and in keeping with that aim they had lyrical voices (Theo Adam as Sachs, René Kollo as Stolzing, Peter Schreier as probably the best David in recording history). This aesthetic has rightly become the accepted norm, and you will find it in more recent recordings under Georg Solti and Daniel Barenboim. However, that hardly makes the general requirements of casting any less arduous. It is difficult these days to find a Sachs who has the right vocal stature, is in command of the rhetoric of the part and remains relaxed. The same can be said of Stolzing and Beckmesser (whom Cosima Wagner replaced in 1888 with an actor).

The Mastersingers holds up the mirror to us musicians as well. What succeeds here will succeed in all the works of Wagner, both for those who are early in their careers and those at a later stage, for youthfully inexperienced musicians as well as the more mature.

9

Money, Power or Love?
Painting the World in Sunset Colours:
Der Ring des Nibelungen (*The Ring of the Nibelung*)

From 2006 to 2010 I spent about 300 hours in the Bayreuth orchestral pit with the *Ring* alone, Wagner's 'stage festival play for three days and a preliminary evening', and that is counting only dress rehearsals and performances. I looked forward to the task again every year, and I do not think I have entirely finished with it yet. The *Ring* has such musical variety that your curiosity and desire to make new discoveries are never exhausted. Because of the different worlds through which you move for 15 hours in all, and the four very different atmospheres of the operas in the tetralogy, the conductor of the *Ring* feels like a battery being constantly recharged. It is true that the music is set for a huge orchestra, including a contrabassoon, a bass tuba and eight horns, but Wagner handles the whole apparatus with great subtlety and delicacy. In the orchestral *parlando* of *The Rheingold*, there is still a good deal of Mozart and Mendelssohn; in *The Valkyrie* we may think most readily of Beethoven; in *Siegfried* of Carl Maria von Weber; and the music of *Twilight of the Gods* is moving firmly in the direction of Brahms and Bruckner – although Wagner would murder me for that comparison. Seen in this light, the *Ring* cuts a path through what is known as the 'German sound', illustrating its extremes and its facets from the light and playful to the weighty, serious and significant. The German sound, so Wagner teaches us, is never just one thing and never just the other. It is a principle that the apologists of the notion that 'anything goes' might well take to heart.

The *Dutchman, Tannhäuser, Lohengrin, The Mastersingers*: then, with the *Ring*, Wagner begins at the beginning once again. In the technique of its musical setting, in the orchestral treatment, in its dimensions and its harmonics, everything is different. When he was composing the *Ring*, Wagner did not have an orchestra ready to hand so that he could check whether what he had thought of would work. The whole thing was being played only in his head. When he did hear it in 1876, he made a good many alterations, and would surely have liked to make a few more at a later date. However, I consider it pointless to speculate on that. We have to take the work as it is, and that is difficult enough.

Origin

When and where do we first meet the creator of the *Ring*? Is it in Dresden, before the May Revolution of 1849, where Wagner was studying the *Edda* and the *Nibelungenlied*, Nordic sagas and Hegel's *Philosophie der Geschichte* (*Philosophy of History*), and dreaming of a society that would no longer be divided into 'the powerful and the weak, those with rights and those without, the rich and the poor'? Is it in his first exile in Switzerland, where he formulated his views of art and encountered Utopian love in the person of Mathilde Wesendonck? Or in Munich, where his political opinions ran counter to his life as court artist to Ludwig II? In his second Swiss exile, where he lived with his new wife Cosima, read Schopenhauer and met Nietzsche? Or not until he was living in his new Villa Wahnfried in Bayreuth, in 1872, where, as its name suggests, he found a peaceful resolution to his illusions and institutionalized his thinking?

The answer has to be everywhere. The Wagner of the *Ring* is the complete Wagner. His cycle reflects everything: *Spieloper* and fairy-tale opera, music drama and the 'invisible orchestra', myths of the gods and heroic sagas, revolution and prestige.

The creation of the tetralogy took almost three decades. Wagner was 34 and an anarchist when the idea of a 'heroic opera' entitled *Siegfried's Death* began to haunt him – and he was 63 and a 'musician of state', as Karl Marx put it, unkindly, when the *Ring* had its première. Think of the energy he needed not to abandon such a huge work. To go on spinning the thread of it, even after leaving it untouched for almost 12 years while he was writing *Tristan* and *The Mastersingers*! What a strong will the man had, what Herculean strength of character! And we should not deceive ourselves; Wagner felt the enormous weight of his project. In 1872, Cosima quotes him as saying, 'This Nibelung composition ought to have been finished long ago; either it's madness or I should have been born as wild as Beethoven.' I don't think he was being coy; I believe that like any artist he suffered under the weight of the responsibility he imposed on himself. At least, I can well imagine it. 'My inclination would have been to live for my own education and enjoy my happiness,' Wagner went on, adding with what sounds like a heartfelt sigh, 'It was different in the past.' In the past he wanted to change the world, now he would like to satisfy himself – is that what he meant?

His first sketches for the composition of *Siegfried's Death* (which was to become *Twilight of the Gods*) was followed in May 1851 by the prose draft of *Der junge Siegfried* (*Young Siegfried*, later to be *Siegfried*), and Wagner realized that he would need the entire myth to tell his hero's story. He began planning a trilogy with a prelude, four operas that were to be a total work of art. Interestingly, he wrote the libretti backwards from the last one, beginning with *Siegfried's Death*, while he composed the scores in chronological order. Consequently the libretto of *The Rhinegold* knows more about the course of events than *Twilight of the Gods*; musically, however, it is the other way around. I for one find these counter-currents inspiring, as if the music were emancipating itself more and more from the text and indeed from the moment being described.

The libretto of *The Valkyrie* was completed in July 1852, and of *The Rhinegold* in November that year. Then Wagner set about revising the two dramas based on Siegfried's story. He completed the score of *Rhinegold* at the end of May 1854, the score of *The Valkyrie* at the end of March 1856 – and then, in June 1957, at the height of the Wesendonck affair, he put his work aside in the middle of *Siegfried*. There were several good reasons for this interruption: acute lack of money, his unsuccessful search for a publisher, the realization that his mammoth work would be impossible to stage in traditional opera houses, the unsuspected force of his own wish for love. I would add another and musical one. When, in the second scene of the second act, Siegfried sits down 'under a great linden tree' to learn the meaning of fear, Wagner did not know how to go on. The music here, to put it inelegantly, picks its nose and dilly-dallies. Wagner seems to feel that he does not yet know how to link gods and humans in the third act; he has no real idea of the way to fit the Gibichungs of *Twilight of the Gods* into the mechanism of his musical cosmos. So he stepped back and turned to the characters of *Tristan* and *The Mastersingers* for aesthetic advice.

In July 1865, directly after the successful Munich première of *Tristan*, he finally went back to work on *Siegfried*. However, the score was not completed until February 1871. A disagreement with Ludwig II began brewing when, in 1869/70, the monarch insisted on having the premières of *The Rhinegold* and *The Valkyrie* in Munich. Arguing against the idea was useless. To keep the king from any further high-handed actions of that kind, Wagner took his time, and left Ludwig in the dark about the progress he was making. The first two acts of *Twilight of the Gods* were therefore not finished until 1871, the third followed in the spring of 1872, and on 21 November 1874, at about midday, an overworked and weary Wagner announced at Wahnfried that he had completed the whole tetralogy. However, husband and wife spent that 'thrice sacred, memorable day' at odds with each other. Cosima, not realizing that the cycle was finished, tried to cheer her husband with a letter from Franz Liszt – and had to spend the rest of the day hearing him say that all her sympathy for him was 'wiped away' as soon as a word came from her father. Nerves in the Wagner household were jangling. 'If genius was to end its flight on such a high note, what was a poor woman to do?' Cosima tearfully complained to her diary, and at once gave herself the only practical answer: 'Suffer in love and enthusiasm.'

I have already described above how the Bayreuth première of the entire *Ring* cycle was given from 13 to 17 August 1876. Scenically and technically it may have been a disaster, but all the same there was an overwhelming response. The words that Wagner's witness at his wedding, the freethinking Malwida von Meysenbug, is said to have whispered to him are famous and significant: 'Don't see too much in it, just listen!' However, there was still some way to go before the total work of art was fully realized. Three performances of the *Ring* cycle were given in that first year, and then the coffers were empty. The next Bayreuth Festival did not take place until 1882, with the première of *Parsifal*, and the *Ring* was not performed again until 1896, after Wagner's death, but then in a 'model' production by Cosima.

Preliminary evening: *Das Rheingold* (*The Rhinegold*)

The Rhinegold is risky. One must never forget that it is the Overture or prelude to the whole *Ring*. Wagner may put all the instruments of torture on show, the pincers, clamps and thumbscrews, and we feel a touch of them now and then – but they are never really applied. Except perhaps to a slight extent in Alberich's curses, but that is just a foretaste. However, those who are aware of this run the opposite risk of taking the music too lightly, just letting it splash and flow past. That too would be a mistake. The long *parlando* passages that are the lifeblood of the opera must be conducted so that they are as transparent and fluent as possible – and so that the audience begins to guess at the rough, riven mountainous world behind them.

Cast and orchestration

The characters of the 'preliminary evening' are fairy-tale gods, giants, water nymphs and dwarfs. Today, the role of Wotan, father of the gods (baritone) is as hard to cast as the part of Hans Sachs in *The Master-singers*. Beside Wotan, the one-eyed god, stand his quarrelsome wife Fricka (mezzo-soprano); her carefree sister Freia (soprano); the earth goddess Erda (alto); Loge, god of fire (tenor), Donner (baritone) and Froh, the god of spring (tenor). The two giants entrusted with the task of building Valhalla, the citadel of the gods, Fafner (baritone) and Fasolt (bass), are as impressive a pair of brothers as the malicious dwarfs Alberich (baritone) and Mime (tenor). The three Rhine maidens Woglinde, Wellgunde and Flosshilde have soprano, mezzo-soprano and alto voices. Only the Nibelungs exploited by Alberich are silent, walk-on parts.

In its orchestration the *Ring* orchestra shows minimal difference between the four works, but there is considerable difference in the character of the music. It begins brightly and darkens progressively until it reaches *Twilight of the Gods*. On a colour scale I would see *Rhinegold* in my mind's eye as yellow, a radiant golden-yellow. To get this effect, Wagner calls for three flutes and a piccolo, three oboes and a cor anglais, three clarinets and a bass clarinet, as well as three bassoons (the third of which has the option of being a contrabassoon), and in the brass eight horns (including two tenor and two bass tubas) and a contrabass tuba, three trumpets and a bass trumpet, three trombones and a contrabass trombone (or bass trombone), in addition kettledrum, triangle, cymbals, large drum, tamtam, six harps and a large body of strings (16, 16, 12, 12, 8). On stage there is another harp and 16 anvils (*sic*) for the Nibelheim scene.

In *Rhinegold*, *Valkyrie* and *Siegfried* there is no chorus. Not until *Twilight of the Gods*, when human beings feature on the stage, does Wagner call for men and women. Gods, giants, dwarfs and water nymphs obviously do not assemble in crowds.

Plot

The 'preliminary evening' is set in the depths of the River Rhine, on an 'open space on a mountain top' (also near the Rhine), and in the underground caverns of Nibelheim, so all the action is either deep down in the river or high above it. The four scenes are played continuously, without an interval.

Before the opera begins: Wotan has sacrificed an eye for the sake of omniscience (knowledge is power), and is proverbially blind in one eye, or in fact blind to love. He has made his spear out of a branch of the World Ash Tree, and has carved on it all the laws and contracts that ensure his rule of the world.

Scene 1: At the bottom of the river, the beautiful Rhine maidens are guarding the golden treasure, and teasing the Nibelung Alberich (often played as a hunchback), who lusts after them. As a ray of sun lights up the gold, the object of Alberich's greedy desire changes: if he cannot have a woman, at least he will have power. The water nymphs tell him that only one who abjures love for ever and forges a ring from the gold can win mastery of the world. No sooner said than done. The dwarf quickly curses love, seizes the gold and flees with it.

Scene 2: The divine couple Wotan and Fricka view the citadel that Fafner and Fasolt have built for the gods. As a reward, the giants have agreed with Wotan that they are to have Freia. Without her golden apples, however, the gods will lose their eternal youth. Fricka blames Wotan bitterly, while Donner and Froh want to fight for their sister. Meanwhile Wotan has told Loge to find a substitute for Freia. Loge finally appears and gives an account of the ring that Alberich has made from the gold of the Rhine. The giants agree to give up Freia in exchange for it, but the goddess will remain in their power until they have the ring in their hands. Loge and Wotan set off for Nibelheim to steal the ring and the gold.

Scene 3: The underworld is subject to Alberich's rule of terror. He has induced his brother Mime to make him a Tarnhelm, a helmet that will render him invisible and allow him to take on any shape he likes. All the thanks that Mime gets is a beating. Meanwhile Loge provokes Alberich into showing him the magic arts of the helmet. First the powerful dwarf turns himself into a huge snake, then into a toad. Now it is easy for the gods to overpower him, and they bring Alberich up to the world above.

Scene 4: Wotan and Loge blackmail Alberich into giving them the gold of the Rhine to ransom his freedom. As soon as Wotan seizes the ring from him, the dwarf utters a second curse (*Wie durch Fluch er mir geriet, / verflucht sei dieser Ring!* / 'As I gained it with a curse, / cursed be this ring!') The giants return with Freia, and demand as much of the piled-up gold as will cover her entirely. When finally only Freia's eye is left showing, they insist that they want the last of the gold, the ring, to fill the gap. Wotan refuses, and Erda gives him an urgent warning: (*Alles was ist, endet!* / 'All that is, can end!'). When he has let the giants have the ring, Alberich's curse comes true: Fafner kills his brother Fasolt in a quarrel over the gold, the first murder in a story that is not short of corpses. But Freia goes free, and the gods move into their fortress after a mighty thunderstorm. Loge follows at a distance – *Ihrem Ende eilen sie zu* ('They hasten towards their end'), he tells us – while in the depths of the river the daughters of the Rhine mourn for their lost treasure.

What is this really about? The relationship between eroticism and power. The loss of innocence, the defilement of nature, the decadence of an ossified system. Power for power's sake – this cannot turn out well. And as we know, it will not. The opera tells a story of gods, nymphs and dwarfs, a mythical, fairy-tale situation as if divorced from reality. But it might as well be telling the story of, say, Dominique Strauss-Kahn, former head of the International Monetary Fund, in his suite on the 88th floor of a Manhattan hotel, a whirlpool bath bubbling in the background, with three sexy chambermaids entering the room, and events taking their fateful course. The scenes in *Rhinegold* are vivid, and tell their own story: there lies the gold, Alberich snatches it – there lies the enchanted toad, to be overpowered in a trice by Wotan and Loge. Not until we reach *The Valkyrie* does Wagner move on to interweave the present shown on stage with flashbacks and recapitulations, prognostications and anticipations, and question what has happened. The 'stage festival piece' is on its way to such a story.

First Day: *Die Walküre* (*The Valkyrie*)

In my musical theory of colour, *The Valkyrie* is red: bright red. The drama becomes more complex, the action divides into acts and scenes, the music itself takes on the role of an actor. On this 'First Day' there are prominent 'numbers' that are staged spectacularly in musical terms but lead to nothing in the dramatic action, for instance the 'Ride of the Valkyries'. At the beginning of the third act the Valkyries are carrying off to Valhalla heroes fallen in battle, and Wagner makes the Prelude to this act into a tone poem giving off sulphurous vapours: as if the sound of battle all over the world were echoing in the mountains where the gods live, there are sonorous sounds from the brass, while thunder rolls, horses foam at the mouth and the daughters of Wotan fling their cries of *Hojotoho!* into the sky above the stage. What a battle cry of maenads, what a release of wild feeling! And what a motif, putting its imprint on the score here: *ta-taa-tata-taata*! It is not surprising that the 'Ride of the Valkyries' has been used as a theme tune so often in the history of film, from the newsreels of Nazi Germany to Francis Ford Coppola's *Apocalypse Now.*

There are also passages that counteract such extreme tone-painting in *Valkyrie*, illustrating the breadth of its aesthetic horizon. For instance, Wotan's great narrative in Act 2 (*Als junger Liebe / Lust mir verblich* / 'When my joy in young love faded') is one of the main hinges on which the whole *Ring* turns, a positive cornucopia of understanding: the father of the gods reveals his heart, describing what has been and what will be. In theatrical terms not much happens except talk: Wotan talking to Brünnhilde and vice versa. All the same this passage, just under half an hour long, is incredibly exciting, as we can see from the fact that the orchestral accompaniment is minimal over long stretches of it. As we have seen before, this tends to happen at crucial moments in Wagner's work. There are two long general rests, a *piano* passage dying away, and we hear Wotan's wish for 'the end... the end'. In the cinema there would be a close-up shot to show the face of the despairing god at this point. In Wagner it is musical exhibitionism, pure pornography (without any sex, naturally). We learn how to see with our ears and – in the right production – hear with our eyes. And we understand that the world on the stage really exists in our own heads.

Cast and orchestration

Wotan and Fricka, husband and wife, move on from the cast of *Rhinegold*. In addition there are the Wälsung twins, children of Wotan and an anonymous human woman, Siegmund (tenor) and Sieglinde (soprano), as well as Hunding, Sieglinde's boorish husband (bass). Other characters are Brünnhilde (soprano), the daughter of Wotan by Erda. She is Wotan's 'wished-for maiden', the eponymous heroine of this 'First Day', and her sisters are the other eight Valkyries, Helmwige, Gerhilde, Ortlinde, Waltraute, Siegrune, Rossweisse, Grimgerde and Schwertleite. Brünnhilde will determine the end of the tetralogy in *Twilight of the Gods*. Together with Isolde, hers is one of the great dramatic soprano parts in Wagner's operas.

The orchestra does not differ much from its composition in *Rhinegold*. Wagner expands the percussion section slightly by adding a snare drum and a glockenspiel; the only instrument played on stage is an ox horn in C.

Plot

The opera is set in Hunding's hut, on a wild, rocky mountain range, and at the top of a mountain. The three acts are fully through-composed, with an interval after the first and second acts.

Before the opera begins: Wotan fears that Alberich will try to get his hands on the gold again. To prevent that, he plans to bring into the world a free hero who is not bound to the laws of the gods. The twins Siegmund and Sieglinde will be this hero's parents.

Act 1: During a storm, Siegmund seeks refuge in Hunding's hut. Not knowing that she is his twin, he tells Sieglinde his story. His mother was killed, his sister abducted, and in their flight he finally lost his father as well. Hunding informs Siegmund that he is the leader of the marauders who destroyed his family, but he grants him the right to hospitality overnight. Sieglinde gives her husband a sleeping draught so that she can go on finding out about Siegmund's origins. Siegmund's father once promised him a sword that would come to his aid in his hour of greatest need. Sieglinde remembers an old man who, at her wedding, drove a sword into the ash tree around which the hut is built: only the strongest of men will be able to pull it out. Siegmund and Sieglinde realize that the old man was their father Wolfe (Wotan, known to Siegmund as Wälse) and that they are siblings. (*Winterstürme wichen / dem Wonnemond /* 'Wintry storms gave way to the moon of joy'). Siegmund pulls the sword out of the ash tree, and calls it *Nothung* (Needful). Brother and sister fall passionately in love with each other.

Act 2: Wotan tells Brünnhilde to help Siegmund win his forthcoming single combat with Hunding. But the jealous Fricka pleads on Hunding's behalf: she wants revenge for Wotan's adultery and the twins' incest, and demands Siegmund's death. As guardian of the law, Wotan knows his hands are tied; he expresses resignation (*Nur eines will ich noch: das Ende /* 'I want but one thing now: the end') and commands Brünnhilde not to go on protecting Siegmund. In flight from Hunding, the pregnant Sieglinde collapses. Brünnhilde appears to Siegmund to tell him he is to die. However, he says he would rather kill himself and his sister than be parted from her by death. His unswerving love moves Brünnhilde so much that she decides to disobey Wotan, who now intervenes in the single combat himself. Siegmund's sword breaks to pieces, Hunding kills him, and dies as well. Brünnhilde escapes from Wotan's rage, taking Sieglinde with her.

Act 3: While the Valkyries take the fallen heroes to Valhalla, Brünnhilde seeks refuge with them for Sieglinde. She gives the pregnant woman the splintered pieces of Needful, and tells her that she will have a son, Siegfried, who will forge the sword again (*O hehrstes Wunder!* / 'Ah, sublime marvel!'). Then the Valkyrie faces her father. Wotan gives his cruel verdict: Brünnhilde will be cast out of Valhalla and lose her divine status. But when she tells him about Siegfried, the free hero who can save Wotan's power, the god passes less severe judgment (*Leb wohl, du kühnes / herrliches Kind!* / 'Farewell, my brave and lovely child!'). From now on Brünnhilde will lie in a ring of fire. Only a man who fears nothing and no one can break through it, and then Brünnhilde will be his.

What is this really about? Of all Wagner's works, Cosima notes in 1873, *The Valkyrie* is 'the most emotional, the most tragic'. She is probably indicating the classic theory of drama that Wagner was concerned with in the *Ring*. According to that theory, there has to be an intensification of feeling and a first climax to the drama here. It is about putting love above all laws (in the incest of the Wälsung twins and Brünnhilde's defiance of her father). It is about the attempt to turn away from a 'loveless' world devoted solely to political rancour and the cold-blooded pursuit of profit. And it is about an understanding of the futility of that attempt, certain as it is to fail. Although evil in the form of the dwarf Alberich does not appear on stage in *The Valkyrie*, that does not detract from but increases its presence. In addition Wagner introduces a new race of beings here, at least indirectly: Siegmund and Sieglinde are half divine, half human by birth. One day their son Siegfried will overcome Wotan's power and make his way to mankind – although not until the next opera but one.

Second Day: *Siegfried*

From bright red to burgundy in colour: *Siegfried* was the most difficult part of the whole *Ring* for me from the first, and it still is. For four hours there are no more than two characters on stage at a time, and most of those characters have male voices. That can be tiring, and a conductor gets details confused more easily than on the other 'days' of the cycle. In rough outline, the sequence of pairings is: Siegfried and Mime, Mime and the Wanderer, Alberich and the Wanderer, Siegfried and Fafner, Erda and the Wanderer, Siegfried and Brünnhilde. The first act in particular, with its constant changes of rhythm and tempo, is composed with the utmost attention to detail. It is a kind of burlesque, full of grotesque features, with Mime as Siegfried's malicious tutor, the father of the gods (secretly the hero's grandfather) appearing in the guise of the Wanderer, and Siegfried a youthful anarchist who has yet to be initiated into what is going on – a crazy set of circumstances. Then, in the second act, comes Siegfried's fight with the dragon. Siegfried is made a man by tasting its mythical blood, in a turn of events to rejoice the heart of any psychoanalyst.

To me, one of the greatest passages in the entire *Ring* is the short Prelude to the third act (we also get preludes to the third acts of *Lohengrin*, *Tristan*, *The Mastersingers* and *The Valkyrie*). Here the entire orchestra plays together for the first time in a very dark and grandiose manner. Contrary to what has sometimes been said, such *tutti* are extremely unusual in Wagner's operas. Here we have all eight horns playing together – or rather four horns plus four tubas, in addition a bass tuba and trombones, so that the sound is extremely loud, and is meant to be. The walls of the world itself seem to totter, whereas the sound in the first and second acts is, strategically, less of a combined assault on the ears. Because of that effect, and because Wotan's fate is sealed in this third act, the conductor comes up against his own limitations. Something that always fascinates me in Wagner is the way he manages to synchronize art and the realization of art in such a way that you feel it physically and understand what it is about. The means may be simple, but they work: the third act is so long that after a certain point the conductor has to fight against the weakness of his own condition. I realize that I am running out of strength, merely because I don't feel strong enough to go on. I'm finished, just as Wotan is finished, except that unlike Wotan I can't disappear, never to be seen again. I have to stay where I am and conduct the performance to the end – hoping to husband my resources better next time.

Cast and orchestration

The dwarf brothers Mime and Alberich, the giant Fafner who has now turned himself into a dragon, the mother goddess Erda and the Valkyrie Brünnhilde are now joined by the hero Siegfried, one of the most demanding parts for a dramatic tenor that Wagner ever wrote. Wotan is at large in the world as an anonymous Wanderer, and a Woodbird (soprano) raises its voice.

Again, the orchestra is the same as before. The percussion uses the same instruments as in *The Rhinegold*, while a cor anglais and horn are played on stage.

Plot

The 'Second Day' is set in a cave in the depths of the forest, in a wild region at the foot of a rocky mountain and on top of Brünnhilde's rock – an extremely romantic background. The three acts, again, are fully through-composed, and once more there are two intervals.

Before the opera begins: Siegfried has been born in Mime's cave, where Sieglinde died giving birth to him. The dwarf brings up the boy, hoping that some day Siegfried will kill Fafner for him.

Act 1: Mime and Siegfried hate each other. The dwarf makes the young man a sword that he smashes easily. However, Mime cannot re-forge the sword Needful from the broken pieces that Sieglinde gave him. Wotan appears as the Wanderer and challenges Mime to a riddle contest. Asked who will be able to forge Needful again, Mime does not know the answer, to which Wotan scornfully replies: *Nur wer das Fürchten / nie erfuhr* ('Only he who never knew fear'). Siegfried returns, tries re-forging the fragments of the sword himself, and promptly succeeds (*Nothung! Nothung! Neidliches Schwert!* / 'Needful! Needful! Sweetest of swords!'). Mime realizes that it is Siegfried himself who has never known fear, and sends him into the forest to find Fafner. Siegfried brings the sword down on Mime's anvil, cutting it in two.

Act 2: Alberich is lying in wait outside Fafner's cavern. The Wanderer warns him against Mime's greed. Alberich in turn warns Fafner of the coming of Siegfried and, pretending concern on the dragon's behalf, tries to get the Ring away from him. But Fafner feels sure of himself. Mime wants Siegfried to fight the dragon. Siegfried sends Mime away into the forest, and lies down under a linden tree. He rouses Fafner by blowing his horn, and quickly kills him. Tasting the dragon's blood, Siegfried suddenly finds that he can understand the language of nature and the Woodbird, who advises him to take the Tarnhelm and the Ring from the dragon's cave. Alberich and Mime quarrel over the looted items, and finally Siegfried kills his foster-father Mime. The Woodbird promises to lead the hero to a wonderful woman (*Heil! Siegfried erschlug / nun den schlimmen Zwerg!* / 'Aha! Siegfried has now killed the evil dwarf').

Act 3: In the middle of a storm with thunder and lightning, Wotan asks Erda about his future (*Wache, Wala!* / 'Awake, Vala!'), but the earth mother goddess sees no way out for him. Siegfried approaches Brünnhilde's rock, and shatters Wotan's spear when the latter tries to stand in his way. Now the power of the father of the gods is broken at last. Siegfried fearlessly walks through the flames and kisses Brünnhilde awake. The Valkyrie greets the hero (*Heil dir, Sonne!* / 'All hail the Sun!') and tries to explain his responsibility as saviour of the world. But Siegfried, very much the man, prefers to give way to his ecstatic passion.

In *Siegfried*, then, the long-awaited saviour and redeemer of the world finally appears on the stage. Unlike the Dutchman or Lohengrin, however, he does not come from outside, but is born in the course of the action and for the sake of the action. The audience has seen his conception in *The Valkyrie* and will be there to mourn his death in *Twilight of the Gods*. Siegfried's short life is entirely devoted to the *Ring*; it is the litmus test. The fate of the world depends on Siegfried. For a figure of such significance he is curiously sexless, and it is not easy to identify with him. He is a hero who murders without remorse, who rapes and betrays women, and drinks any magic potion put in front of him. Perhaps it is logical for Siegfried to fail in the end. One man alone, Wagner says, cannot save the world, just as no one person can support the weight of the *Ring*. We musicians, singers, set designers and directors, in co-operation with the artistic directors of opera houses, can only do it together, if at all.

Incidentally, I am convinced that Wagner, seeing the necessity of that scene, deliberately made theatricality a part of its composition. In *Siegfried* of all the operas in the cycle, with its long scenes played out between two characters, the conductor and singers have to depend on the director. Music alone will not get you very far here. On this 'Second Day' the conductor is taken not only to the limits of his strength but to the limits of what he can actually do; he is not able to step into the breach if a scene fails. Down in the pit he cannot compensate for any lack of energy and tension up on stage. You notice that in certain recordings: they can have outstanding conductors and excellent singers, all that can be fabulous – but something is still missing in the great confrontations and recapitulations of the music, and that is the stage itself, the hearing eye.

Third Day: *Götterdämmerung (Twilight of the Gods)*

Just as the River Rhine overflows its banks like a tsunami at the end of the 'Third Day', extinguishing the conflagration that threatens the whole world and giving nature back its own – the precious raw material of gold – the opera *Twilight of the Gods* itself bursts its banks. With a playing time of four and a half hours it is the longest of the tetralogy, Wagner wrote a two-part scenic Prelude to precede its three acts, and in five fully developed orchestral interludes absolute music speaks – composed as changes of scene and mood, but also, obviously, as the only way to get to the heart of what has yet to be said. The transitional passages that Wagner created between separate scenes in *The Rhinegold, The Valkyrie* and *Siegfried* now develop a life of their own. And the musical vocabulary that he heaps up in the *Ring*, his network of leitmotifs or 'memory motifs', attains a density in *Twilight of the Gods* that begins to withdraw from the direct dramatic blueprint. As a result the ostensible action, what is happening on the stage, comes to a standstill increasingly often. There is not much future ahead of us, and so memory and reflection, with the epic theme in itself, occupy more space. Nothing simply happens now, it all means something or is laden with significance. It is said that the old live more in the past than the present, and that is the case with *Twilight of the Gods*. In terms of the colours I see in it, by the way, it traces an interesting curve, from the reddish-brown of the opening to the rich yellow of a setting sun in D flat major.

All the same, the conductor – and this is very important – should not fall into the trap of letting solemnity reign over everything. That would be wrong, and indeed Wagner shows that it would. The scene with the Norns in the Prelude, for instance, must not die away, for all its oracular character, particularly not where tempo is concerned. In spite of muted trumpets and strings, it needs a certain airy nonchalance, or the link to the little sisters of the Norns, the Rhine maidens, will not be made and it will look as if *Rhinegold* has been entirely forgotten. Moreover, why would Wagner aim for the orchestral pedal effect in the introduction to the Prelude if everything is already signed and sealed? The tubas and trumpets begin so quietly here, indeed subversively, making listeners feel the thrust of the music deep inside them, entirely without the lustre of overtones and without drawing attention to a single transition, that one feels pop music could learn something from such eroticism. The motif of Brünnhilde's awakening in the third act of *Siegfried* is heard here, and we remember her glance of recognition and love. But now Wagner sets the motif a semitone lower, and at once all its jubilation is gone. What is coming now will be difficult, that modulation tells us. But would it not have been just as easy to reverse the modulation again?

Cast and orchestration

Siegfried, Brünnhilde and Alberich are now joined by the court of the Gibichungs: the weak Gunther (baritone), his sister Gutrune (soprano) and their evil half-brother Hagen (bass), Alberich's son. Another new character is Brünnhilde's sister Waltraute (alto), who sings one of the most beautiful narratives in the entire *Ring*. The three Rhine maidens return at the end of the opera, counterparts to the three Norns at the beginning of the 'Third Day'.

The orchestra remains the same except that the instruments played on stage are supplemented by a horn in F, four horns in C, and three ox horns in C, D flat and D.

Plot

The settings are: the Valkyrie rock, the hall of Gunther's court on the Rhine, an open space outside that hall, and a woodland area on the banks of the Rhine. As before, there are three acts and two intervals.

Prelude: Wotan has decided that the gods must fall. As soon as the Ring is back in the hands of the Rhine maidens, he is going to set fire to Valhalla. The three Norns, Erda's daughters, are spinning the rope of destiny (*weisst du wie das wird?* / 'How will this turn out?'), until it breaks. Meanwhile Siegfried is anxious to perform new feats of arms. Brünnhilde lets him leave, and gives him her horse Grane to take him to the Rhine. In return, he gives her the Ring.

Act 1: Hagen tempts the unmarried Gunther with the idea of a union with Brünnhilde, whom only the strongest of men can conquer. Together, they hatch a plot. Their victim, Siegfried, is welcomed to the Gibichung court with open arms, and Gutrune gives him a potion of oblivion which at the same time makes him fall in love with her. Siegfried is now prepared to try to get the Tarnhelm from Brünnhilde for Gunther. The two men set out for the Valkyrie rock. Waltraute tries to persuade Brünnhilde to give up the Ring and thus prevent the downfall of the gods. However, Brünnhilde refuses to part with Siegfried's pledge of love. Siegfried, disguised as Gunther, snatches the Ring from her, and says she is now the bride of the Gibichung.

Act 2: In a dream, Alberich urges Hagen not to forget their joint aim: to possess the Ring and rule the world after the fall of the gods (*Schläfst du, Hagen, mein Sohn?* / 'Are you asleep, my son?'). Siegfried has hurried ahead of Brünnhilde and Gunther, Hagen and his men blow horns for the double wedding with cries of '*Hoiho! Hoiho!*'. When

Brünnhilde sees the Ring on Siegfried's hand, she knows she has been tricked, and accuses Siegfried of betrayal. He swears his innocence. Brünnhilde's heart is set on revenge, and Hagen worms out of her the secret that Siegfried's back is vulnerable. Together with Gunther, they plan to kill Siegfried.

Act 3: Out hunting, Siegfried meets the Rhine maidens, who prophesy his death if he does not return the Ring to them. But Siegfried remains stubborn. Hagen gives him an antidote to the potion of oblivion, and only now does Siegfried remember everything: the dwarf Mime, his fight against Fafner – and his bride Brünnhilde. With that he shows himself guilty of treachery, and Hagen kills him. Siegfried's body is carried to the hall of the Gibichung to the accompaniment of a funeral march. Meanwhile, Brünnhilde has heard the full truth from the Rhine maidens, and has a funeral pyre built (*Starke Scheite / schichtet mir dort /* 'Build me there a pyre of logs'). She takes the Ring from the dead Siegfried's hand and rides into the flames. The Rhine overflows its banks, the hall of the Gibichungs collapses, the daughters of the Rhine rejoice at regaining their Ring, and pull Hagen down into the depths of the river with them. Valhalla is burning in the firmament – the twilight of the gods has come.

How do we interpret this third and last day? I think we should not go too far here (at least, we musicians). It is well known that Wagner wanted to put his entire ideology into the *Ring*, and that can certainly be explained by its origins in the time around 1848. But did he maintain that attitude over three decades? Are political and philosophical elements really so much in the foreground as he intended, and as we tend to claim today without thinking about it very hard? I have my doubts. Because music conveys nothing political in itself, because E flat minor is always E flat minor, and a simple message such as 'Money rules the world' does not necessarily have anything to do with Wagner's highly artistic sensory skill. Nor do I think he would have used that sensory skill deliberately to promote his ideology. Wagner was a brilliant calculator and stylist, but not a political demagogue. In addition, circumstances changed radically during the long gestation of the *Ring*, and that is something we should not forget. At the beginning Wagner wanted to change the world and enlist art in the cause of revolution; at the end his own revolution was that he changed art.

There were several draft outlines for the close of *Twilight of the Gods*. The first, tinged with the ideas of Feuerbach, suggested a great apotheosis of love in the person of Brünnhilde, the second, more pessimistically Buddhist in tone, dwelt on mankind's dedication to destruction – and a third, a compromise between the other two, was the one that he used. The only question is: do we or do we not all react to it in the same way? There is no character in *Twilight of the Gods* who has not contributed something to the catastrophe: Brünnhilde by taking revenge on Siegfried, Wotan and the gods by disappearing, Alberich through his son Hagen, who becomes a stupid killer, and even Gutrune suffers from malign over-estimation of herself. All the same, Wagner does not believe in the final extinction of the world, or he would have composed differently. In the Old Norse legend of Ragnarök, which he used as a source, the conflagration consuming the world leads to a kind of equilibrium between chaos and order so that everything can be created anew. Unfortunately Wagner is not so clear about it, but he does give us signs. For instance, I have always wondered why the one passage in Siegfried's funeral march in the last act that is in a major key retains the sword motif (slightly expanded, but recognizable)? After all, Siegfried is dead.

Does he raise his fist one last time? Will he return? Does Wagner want to probe a painful subject again? Is the whole thing just the conventional transfiguration of a hero?

On stage, that comes as Hagen is about to tear the Ring from Siegfried's finger. 'He reaches for Siegfried's hand, which rises menacingly,' runs Wagner's stage direction, and he adds 'to the horror of all present.' In the auditorium, this spooky effect regularly provokes hilarity, which is all wrong. It ought to seem like a greeting from the next world, a sign of dignity. Siegfried bears a burden of guilt and has failed, yes, but all the same we should not forget him.

Music

What an opening! First we hear the contrabass instruments in the very lowest registers, then the bassoons and horns, a groaning, a whispering, 'the beginning of the world' in pastoral 6/8 time; only at a late point do the low strings come in, rocking in the waves of the Rhine, later still the high woodwind instruments, like bubbles of oxygen rising to the surface of the water. The Prelude to *Rhinegold* is 136 bars long and takes just under five minutes (it should not be played too slowly), 136 bars of pure E flat major in 'calmly cheerful movement': the birth of the universe from the triad. And the birth, too, of that unique network of signposts that arches over four music dramas, imposing unity, dividing and putting matters in order, looking ahead and looking back, questioning and telling the truth. With the nature motif, the first of an extraordinary number (80 in all) of leitmotifs is heard: motifs running the gamut of subjects from adventure to blood-brotherhood, the magic of fire and flickering flames, atonement, the darkness of force, love between siblings, release and much more (naturally each character also has his or her own motif). The term 'leitmotif', incidentally, was coined by Hans von Wolzogen, editor of the *Bayreuther Blätter*, a representative of the sectarian 'Wahnfried Circle'. Wagner did not like the word, since it suggests a single thread running all the way through the four operas, one that would simply have to be followed by means of stereotypical and easily recognized melodies. However, 'leitmotif' has come to be accepted, perhaps because such a term as 'emotional signposts' sounds too nebulous.

Wagner's leitmotif technique is meticulously calculated, and works by reference to the past, the present and the future. The present is the moment being shown on stage, when the characters interact with each other; the past deals with their origins or history; and the future faces the consequences arising from this or that set of circumstances or dramatic situation. The sum of all this forms the memory of the score of the *Ring*. There is something of the slide rule about the whole thing, something of the demiurge, and there is no denying that it can sometimes be tautological. Deciphering the individual leitmotifs is in fact not so easy. Wagner is not pasting musical labels on them separately and together, but playing a sophisticated game with his audience's attention and powers of deduction. To take one example: we hear the sword motif for the first time as the gods enter Valhalla in the finale of *The Rhinegold*, at the moment when Wotan, 'as if struck by a great idea', greets the citadel of the gods. The sword motif belongs to Needful, the mythical weapon with which Siegfried is to free the world some day from the curse of the gold. However, Needful has not yet featured in the plot as either a subject or a stage prop. All the same, announcement of its presence takes over the music now. Wotan has a plan; he has redemption in mind, even if the action on stage may not suggest that. At this point, as Dieter Holland has said, the orchestra is communicating with the audience 'over the heads of the characters on the stage'. And if you listen closely you will hear that there is something not quite right about the gods' entry into Valhalla and their procession over the rainbow bridge. Interrupted by Loge's cynical comments and by the lamentations of the daughters of the Rhine, the music opens up a shattering sense of emptiness behind all its grandeur.

Of course the question is what the audience, hearing the sword motif for the first time, can and should make of it. Do they understand its dotted rhythm, the rising fourths, as an affect, in this case a signal of hope and a new beginning? Or do they wait, remembering the motif, until it recurs in *The Valkyrie* and reveals it significance in retrospect? Another example will illustrate the opposite case: at the end of *The Twilight of the Gods*, we hear the redemption motif, one of the catchiest and most seductive melodies in the entire *Ring*. Wagner uses it very sparingly, indeed exactly twice: in the third act of *The Valkyrie*, when Sieglinde rejoices in the prospect of bearing her still unborn child, and then in Brünnhilde's final song and the closing chords of the tetralogy. But how is a listener to interpret this message from the past? The world is perishing, capitalism is devouring its children, and are we supposed to cling to something as archaic as unconditional (maternal) love? All around there is murder, treachery, deceit, abuse, avarice, depression, the fires of purgatory – and the final message is that as long as love lasts, life will somehow or other go on?

Wagner himself is said to have commented, 'There is no conclusion to the music.' Why not? Because at the end of the *Ring*, responsibility is left to mankind itself. No god or composer can step in to help. There is not and cannot be any conclusion to the music, because it goes on into life. It has no conclusion because it formulates a Utopian principle of hope overarching everything with the redemption motif. The Utopian concept is that human beings cannot live without love – and that they will always be aware of that, despite all doubts.

With the *Ring*, as I have said already, Wagner once again begins from the beginning. And perhaps everything also begins again *in* the *Ring* (in the sense of a repetition in a new dimension, as Bloch indicates). Wagner pushes aside everything he had done before the tetralogy as if those works were merely random samples bearing witness to the fashions and moods of his time, craftsmanlike journeyman pieces, tracks that he had left behind him. The never-ending melody in the orchestra, the way the drama keeps changing of its own accord, the motifs coming thick and fast – all that lends the music symphonic stature. At the same time Wagner, as always typically bold, paces out the horizon of European theatrical history. The quicksilver *Rhinegold* makes one think of a Shakespearian comedy; *The Valkyrie*, with its drama of relationships, is like a domestic family tragedy; the densely forested texture of *Siegfried* quotes from German Romantic opera; and *Twilight of the Gods* adopts the criteria of Greek tragedy. The *Ring* absorbs all this, and is giving none of it back in a hurry.

But Wagner wants yet more. In 1878, two years after the première of the *Ring*, he made that significantly regretful remark, saying that as creator of the invisible orchestra he would also like to be the inventor of 'invisible drama'. I think that was more than a *bon mot*, more than his usual distaste for theatrical effects depending on costumes and make-up. He saw that his ideas for the realization of music drama on stage were not working, what could be done in the theatre of his time was not adequate, nor was he succeeding in allowing equal weight to the music, the libretto, and the space, acting and lighting available. The stage represented an enormous risk to Wagner, and if we are to be honest, to this day not much has happened to change that. Of course there have been a number of major new productions of the *Ring* since 1876 (for instance, directed by Patrice Chéreau, Götz Friedrich and Ruth Berghaus). Fundamentally, however, what is true of the music applies even more to the staging of the work: Wagner shows us exactly what he wants – and we know that we cannot do it with the powers at our command. However, we also know that we will try, and indeed must try, to do it again and again. I see that as an enormous motivator and a great comfort.

Recordings

At present there are about 30 complete recordings of the *Ring* on the market, ranging from the unusual, like the 'HMV potted *Ring* cycle' (a historic compilation from the years 1927–32, featuring among others Friedrich Schorr as Wotan, Lauritz Melchior as Siegfried and Frida Leider as Brünnhilde, on the Pearl label), to individually typical versions under Georg Solti and Bernard Haitink and the standard recordings under Furtwängler, Karajan and Boulez. Thirty times 15 hours of music comes to 450 hours – how can anyone do justice in detail to all those recordings (leaving aside the fact that I don't know them all myself)?

If the Bayreuth Festival Theatre is often a disadvantage, acoustically speaking, to the *Flying Dutchman* and *The Mastersingers*, it is a gift to the *Ring* – and you can hear that in the recordings. My own Bayreuth recording of 2008 (Opus Arte) is preceded by eight older ones, and they could hardly be more different in spite of being recorded in the same conditions. That in itself says much for the potential of the house. Daniel Barenboim, for instance (in 1992, with John Tomlinson as Wotan and Siegfried Jerusalem as Siegfried, Warner), concentrates very much on flexibility; he is interested in the sound and what becomes of it, as we can sense from his transitions and colours. Pierre Boulez, on the other hand (1980, with Donald McIntyre as Wotan, Gwyneth Jones as Brünnhilde and Peter Hofmann as Siegfried, Philips), exposes more of the bones of the music and is very sensitive, very analytical and extremely instructive. He is showing, so to speak, the negative of many older versions, for instance under Karl Böhm in 1966, but also the recording of Hans Knappertsbusch (whom I revere) in 1956, with Hans Hotter as Wotan, the young Wolfgang Windgassen as Siegmund *and* Siegfried, Astrid Varnay as Brünnhilde and many other great names

(Orfeo). The nobility and craftsmanlike bravura of Knappertsbusch's music drama is always phenomenal. He does a good deal on the spur of the moment, without any overriding concept, but feeling everything even in his little finger. By comparison, to me Joseph Keilberth (1955, Testament) is rather stern and serious.

Of the recordings not made in Bayreuth, Solti's *Ring* in particular is regarded as legendary, and was the first complete recording of the tetralogy to be made for gramophone; it was produced, with considerable gaps in the recording, between 1958 and 1965, in the Sophiensäle Theatre of Vienna. The order in which the operas were recorded was *Rhinegold, Siegfried, Twilight of the Gods, Valkyrie*, and for the first time there is no doubt that the whole recording (Decca) sounds wonderful. With excellent wind and string playing, the Vienna Philharmonic does justice to its reputation, and allows Solti's sometimes over-dramatic interpretation to shine to the best possible effect. Technical sound effects were used to simulate the stage that was not present in the recording, and they are not good for the atmosphere, making it seem both artificial and cold (an impression reinforced by the non-chronological order of recording, but perhaps I am only imagining this). In *Rhinegold* George London sings Wotan and Kirsten Flagstad Fricka, the Bayreuth couple of Nilsson and Windgassen sing Brünnhilde and Siegfried, so the cycle to some extent straddles a generation gap between the singers, which does not help listeners to orientate themselves.

That at least unites Solti and Herbert von Karajan, who made the second complete recording not much later, also over a long period of time (1966–70, Deutsche Grammophon). Karajan began with *The Valkyrie* and varied the casting from opera to opera. Sometimes his Wotan is Dietrich Fischer-Dieskau (in *Rhinegold*), sometimes Thomas Stewart (in *Valkyrie* and *Siegfried*), sometimes Jess Thomas sings Siegfried, sometimes the part is taken by Helge Brilioth. Even though I will happily admit from my own experience that, strictly speaking, it would be good to have several voices available for the big parts in the *Ring*, a game of musical chairs like this does nothing for the coherence of the whole thing. However, Karajan's disposition – he liked to work on the grand scale – helps to make up for that. His infallible sense of drama, as always, is striking. And the Berlin Philharmonic play beautifully – with a silky texture in the strings, homogeneity among the wind instruments, and sensitivity in the approach to dramatic climaxes, the orchestra's achievement could hardly be improved upon.

All the same, my choice for the proverbial desert island would be Wilhelm Furtwängler's 1953 recording of the *Ring*, made over a period of a month, act by act, for Italian radio (EMI). Certainly there are more idiomatic orchestras with more of a Wagnerian affinity than the orchestra of RAI, and technically there are a number of intrusive effects, but the ensemble of singers, with Martha Mödl, Ludwig Suthaus, Ferdinand Frantz, Margarete Klose, Ira Malaniuk and Elisabeth Grümmer, is unbeatable. A bigger red carpet could hardly have been rolled out for the German conductor. And with Furtwängler, believe it or not, all strands of the interpretation of Wagner both before *and* after him come together as if by magic: the Apollonian and the Dionysian, the epic and the dramatic, the musical and the theatrical. No other recording so clearly explains the cycle to me, or enlightens me so much.

10

An Anti-*Tristan* Composed in Violet Ink:
Parsifal

A young person is probably bound to think as I did, I suppose, but today I am a little ashamed of my hubris: I was working as Herbert von Karajan's assistant, and Wagner's *Parsifal* was on the programme for the Salzburg Easter Festival of 1981. So there I was, at the age of 21, sitting in on the pre-rehearsal stages in Berlin, hearing Karajan conjuring up the atmosphere of sanctity with an easy touch, and thinking: I could do that too. Because it all sounded so easy and natural, as if it had to be performed in exactly that way and no other. Later, I realized how difficult *Parsifal* is. You need a plan, above all you have to think hard about the tempi and what you will do with them, or you will be lost. Nothing happens of itself in *Parsifal*, not only in the matter of musicality and intuition. Wagner's 'festival play to consecrate a stage' is a slow piece, but you do not have to slow the tempo down all the time, or the effect will be bleak. I still try to take what Wolfgang Wagner told me to heart: you must have a feeling for it, you are going much too fast – and then it turns out all right. In 2001 in Bayreuth it took me an hour and 44 minutes to conduct the first act. In Vienna in the spring of 2012 it was only an hour and 37 minutes. Part of those seven minutes less may be ascribed to the difference between an open and a covered pit, the rest was experience.

And there is another factor. *Parsifal* is so difficult because here Wagner has torn down the high walls between German and French culture. He wants us to bear in mind Debussy's *L'après-midi d'un faune*, he wants his audience to know Ravel's *Daphnis et Chloë*, he assumes acquaintance with Mendelssohn and *The Mastersingers* anyway – and we are expected to know all this and transfer it, so to speak, inject it into the Passion music of *Parsifal*, so that the opera will shine from within, living and shimmering in an almost Impressionist and very Latin way. It can be terrifying.

Two remarks by Wagner help one to approach *Parsifal*. One was positively prophetic: in 1859 Wagner wrote, in a letter to Mathilde Wesendonck, that he was toying with the idea of a very dark work, one that would go even further than the third act of *Tristan*: Amfortas was Tristan taken to unimaginable extremes. The torment of love as a cross to be borne through life? The second remark dates from the spring of 1878, and it comes down to us from Carl Friedrich Glasenapp. According to him, the Master was playing and singing from *Tristan* one evening at the Villa Wahnfried, and said that his new work 'has a very unusual colour, everything in it is violet, like a deep lilac hue'. That is significant not only because Wagner did indeed write the entire score of *Parsifal* in violet ink, but also because of the time when he said it. According to Glasenapp again, Wagner had just reached that point in the second act when Parsifal attains 'knowledge' through Kundry's kiss, and abjures everything erotic. That would make *Parsifal* a kind of anti-*Tristan* – it is rewarding, in many ways, to follow that trail.

Origin

Soberly considered, the first Bayreuth Festival of 1876 led to disaster. Wagner had not achieved anything like what he wanted to achieve artistically, and in spite of all King Ludwig's contributions the financial situation looked gloomy. Wagner himself was suffering from depression and heart attacks (diagnosed by the doctors as 'chest cramps'). Sometimes he dreamed of a performance of the *Ring* with a cast consisting entirely of the dead, sometimes he thought of emigrating, sometimes he saw, in his mind's eye, the Villa Wahnfried and the Festival Theatre going up in flames. He had to earn money, and in May 1877 set off on a concert tour to London, where he hated everything. He said of the docks along the Thames, very much in a visionary and oracular manner: 'Alberich's dream has come true there – Nibelheim, domination of the world, busy activity, work, steam and fog everywhere.'

Anyone else in that situation would probably have given up, but at the beginning of 1877 Wagner was already contemplating a new work. He felt that he had not yet finished; the universal conflagration of *Twilight of the Gods* was not to be the last opera he left for posterity. On 25 January he told Cosima something that made her 'laugh out loud for joy'. He was beginning *Parsifal*, and said, 'I will not stop work until it is finished.' He did as he had said. Wagner looked out the 20 pages that he had written in haste in 1865, after the première of *Tristan*, the first prose draft of a drama on the subject of *Parsifal*. The subject had been accompanying him for years, ever since his very productive stay in Marienbad in 1845, the period from which *Lohengrin* and *The Mastersingers* date, when he also read Wolfram von Eschenbach's epic *Parzifal*. Wagner now changed the spelling of the eponymous hero's name from the Middle High German *Parzifal* to *Parsifal* (derived, or so he thought anyway, from ancient Persian *fal parsi*, meaning 'pure fool'), and now he made good progress with the libretto. He began composing the music in September 1877, and some four years later, on 13 January 1882, he completed the score in the Hôtel des Palmes in Palermo. As he did with all his works, he was afraid of 'being interrupted by death', as Carl Friedrich Glasenapp tells us.

This was the second winter that Wagner spent in Italy for the good of his health. He stayed in the south of the country for most of 1880, and took inspiration from Siena Cathedral for the Grail Temple in his *Parsifal*; the garden of the Villa Rufolo in Ravello on the Amalfi coast served as his model for Klingsor's domain in the second act. Back in Germany in 1882, Wagner feared that his new work would be defiled by the modern theatre and its 'entertainment business', and he induced Ludwig II to promise that *Parsifal* would be performed only in Bayreuth. He went there for rehearsals on 2 July 1882, on 26 July the 'festival play to consecrate a stage' had its successful première, and 15 more performances followed. During the last of them Wagner himself took up the baton, thus sealing a success that, alone among his operas, also made money. The ticket prices covered the cost of production, certificates of patronage brought in another 140,000 marks, and Schott paid 150,000 marks for the full score and the piano score. As a festival entrepreneur, Richard Wagner was rehabilitated – and set off again for Italy, this time making for Venice. He and his family moved into 15 rooms in the Palazzo Vendramin Calergi. Just under five months later, Wagner died of a heart attack there.

Cast and orchestration

The opera should really be called *Gurnemanz* or *Kundry*, at any rate not *Parsifal*, since the eponymous hero (tenor) has almost less to sing than anyone else, and is not a very grateful part in other respects either. Wagner, who never showed much concern for his singers, seems to have set no store by the conventions here, as if he were finally past any craving for admiration. The Grail society upon which Parsifal stumbles by chance consists of the Grail king Amfortas (baritone) and his father Titurel (bass), and four squires (two sopranos, two tenors). Opposite them stands the magic kingdom of Klingsor (bass) with his magical flower maidens (three solo sopranos and three solo altos, along with two groups of female voices, sopranos on the one hand and altos on the other, 12 of each). Kundry (mezzo-soprano) is the only character who belongs in both worlds, sometimes as a messenger of the Grail and a penitent, sometimes as a whore – and is the sole female protagonist. In the first act we also hear a voice from on high (alto). The chorus plays the parts of Grail knights, youths and boys.

The orchestra is smaller than in the *Ring*: three flutes, three oboes and a cor anglais, three clarinets plus one bass clarinet in A and another in B, three bassoons plus a contrabassoon, four horns, three trumpets, three trombones, a bass tuba, kettledrum, two harps and the large body of strings usual at Bayreuth (16 first violins, 16 second violins, 12 violas, 12 cellos, 8 double basses). Instruments not used by comparison with the *Ring* are tubas, a bass trumpet and bass trombone, in fact the brass instruments in lower registers. Music on stage is provided by two trumpets, four trombones, a snare drum and the Grail bells (in low C, G, A and E), an eternal problem in practice. Photographs of the première show the original monstrosities lying at the back of the stage: gigantic barrels intended to be struck with equally large beaters. At first Wagner had wanted Chinese tamtams; today much more easily handled instruments of the dulcimer type are generally used.

Plot

The opera takes place in the Montsalvat area of the Grail castle and in the castle itself, as well as in Klingsor's magic castle and its garden. The time is a mythological period of the early Middle Ages.

Before the opera begins: Two relics of Christ are kept in the temple of the Grail: the spear that was driven into the side of Jesus as he hung on the cross, and the goblet that received his blood. Amfortas, the Grail king, has let the enchantress Kundry seduce him and has lost the spear. In his fight with a renegade knight, Klingsor, he received from the spear a wound that never heals. Kundry is now atoning for her guilt by secretly finding herbs and balm for Amfortas to alleviate his pain. Only a chaste boy, it is said ('a pure fool made wise by compassion'), can bring back the spear and release the king from his suffering.

Act 1: Preparations for Amfortas's morning bath are in progress in the woods outside the Grail castle. Kundry brings healing herbs from distant lands, and after the bath Gurnemanz tells the squires the story of the Grail knights (*Titurel, der fromme Held* / 'Titurel, the pious hero'). Suddenly a swan falls from the sky, mortally wounded and bleeding. A strange boy, Parsifal, has shot the bird, and Gurnemanz takes him to task. Parsifal does not know that there must be no killing in the vicinity of the Grail – in fact he knows nothing, not even his name or where he comes from. Gurnemanz thinks he may be the 'pure fool', the saviour that the knights long for, and takes him into the Grail temple to be present when the Grail is unveiled. The ritual gives strength to the knights, but means that the torments of Amfortas are prolonged. Parsifal does not understand that it may be up to him to express compassion for the king, and remains silent. Disappointed, Gurnemanz dismisses him from the Grail area again.

Act 2: Parsifal falls into the clutches of Klingsor. Kundry – whom the magician has in his power because she once mocked Christ on the cross – is to seduce and so destroy the boy (*Die Zeit ist da* / 'The time has come'). Flower maidens surround him, the garden beguiles his senses. When Kundry kisses him, Parsifal understands the wound of Amfortas, and pushes the temptress away (*Amfortas! –* / *Die Wunde! – Die Wunde!* / 'Amfortas! The wound! The wound!'). Now he knows what he has to do. When Klingsor throws the spear at Parsifal, it remains hovering over him in the air (this works in the theatre). The weapon has become a relic again and will release Amfortas. Klingsor's world sinks away as Parsifal makes the sign of the cross. *Du weisst – / wo du mich wieder finden kannst!* ('You know where you can find me'), Parsifal calls to Kundry, and sets off in search of the Grail castle.

Act 3: Several years later. Titurel is dead, and the Grail society is living in great want, for Amfortas refuses to unveil the Grail. He wants only to die. On the morning of Good Friday, Gurnemanz meets Kundry in the woods, a changed woman and ready to 'serve' again. A strange knight appears, carrying a spear. Gurnemanz recognizes Parsifal, and tells him about the distress of the Grail society. Then Kundry washes Parsifal's feet, and Gurnemanz anoints him the new Grail king (*Gesegnet sei, du Reiner* / 'Blessed be, O pure one'). As his first act, Parsifal baptises Kundry. Gurnemanz leads him to the Grail castle, where the knights are holding a funeral service for Titurel. Parsifal touches the wound of Amfortas with the spear, and it closes up. Kundry falls 'lifeless to the ground', and a white dove hovers above Parsifal's head. He reveals the Grail.

Obviously this final work is about life. In all Wagner's other operas (with the exception of *The Mastersingers*) the action is making for death: there are characters who die transfigured, characters longing for death, condemned to death, damned and lost souls. There is dying in *Parsifal*, although mainly in the background. Parsifal's mother Herzeleide (heart's suffering) dies when her son leaves her, but that is part of the unseen backstory, and Titurel dies of old age and because the Grail is no longer giving the knights strength. On the other hand, we may doubt whether Klingsor dies at the end of Act 2, in view of his magic powers. As for Kundry, she is condemned to endless reincarnation for laughing at Christ on the cross, but only occasionally falls into a deathlike sleep. That curse and her guilt are lifted from her by baptism, so now she can die. But does she? Wagner leaves that an open question. In the last bars of the opera, the motifs oscillate between promise, Agape (sanctified love), faith and the Grail, as if there were nothing more worth striving for than such transcendence for *everyone*.

Admittedly there is a drawback to the Utopia of communal life together in faith (faith in art rather than in God), and Wagner would have been the last to deny that: it remains infertile. Where men embrace a monastic existence and women disappear, where empathy denotes celibacy and eroticism is to be feared, where a man who refrains from it triumphs over those who love and feel desire, where art has only itself in mind – then the future of music drama is short. Is that why Wagner gives *Parsifal* a conclusion of such unearthly beauty? Is the 'festival play to consecrate a stage' not just an anti-*Tristan* but an anti-opera in general? I think that in *Parsifal* all Christian, psychological and non-musical concerns in general should stay in the background – and once again it is better not to go in for too much interpretation. Wagner's affirmation of life is radically and exclusively an affirmation of art. Art must not die, says *Parsifal*, still to some extent thinking of the end of opera on a large scale. At the age of 69, Wagner dedicated his last opera to art, staking his final throw on it.

Music

Parsifal begins with a rest; 4/4 time, strings and woodwind, very slowly, very expressively, 'the semiquavers always calm and stately', is Wagner's additional direction. But first comes the famous crotchet rest, silence composed as music. All is dark, only the space speaks, rustles, whispers. Then we are off. What a strange timbre, cor anglais with clarinet, oboe with violas and half of the second violins, crude colours, many arpeggios in the strings, *piano, più piano, pianissimo, più piano*, as if the music were fading in and then out again, as if the beam of a searchlight in the pit were moving now one way, then another. And at the end of the Prelude, Wagner takes the colours apart, resolves them into their separate pigments, solo clarinet, solo oboe, solo flute, a spectrum as clear as glass in which the light breaks.

Wagner is aiming to compose a work as his farewell to the world, following the *Ring*, an *opus ultimum*, bringing everything together and yet occupying a special position of its own. You have to take a deep breath before enumerating all the associations conjured up by *Parsifal*. There are the contrasting worlds, the minimal surface action of the opera, the overarching theme of redemption, and a hero who has not become a hero by performing any notable deeds. All this will seem familiar to those who love Wagner. They are, so to speak, the prerequisites that the work establishes – only to strike out in an entirely different direction. The step from a 'festival play' to a 'festival play to consecrate a stage' is not only the step from art to religion (the religion of art), from the profane to the sacred, but also a backward glance. As if Wagner were lying down on his own psychoanalytical couch to investigate his creative origins, and set off again drawing strength from within to make new discoveries.

Consequently the potential similarities of this last opera to its predecessors are less illuminating than the differences between them. What is Wagner doing differently in *Parsifal*? The answer is simple: yet again, everything. The number of leitmotifs is radically reduced – and the use made of them radically refined. Malicious tongues claim that Wagner composed *Parsifal* on just two themes, which is sheer nonsense, although a five-hour opera could be written using two themes if the composer had internalized the principle of the transformation and changing moods of his motifs as well as Wagner did. No one motif appears in the same form twice, everything is always changing as if in a never-ending metamorphosis. *Du siehst, mein Sohn, / zum Raum wird hier die Zeit* ('You see, my son, here time is turned to space'), Gurnemanz tells Parsifal as he takes him into the Grail castle for the first time, and I have always seen this much-discussed riddle in relation to Wagner's mode of composition. His music defines time (in the sense that it is passing in time), it occupies time like a lining and thus constructs a backdrop of sound. Music creates the space in which it is played. Music *is* that space.

Wagner's treatment of his two opposing worlds also feels different and new. You think at first that you recognize it: here is the diatonically fixed pace of the world of the Grail (in the manner of the Wartburg music), there the chromatically sensuous flickering of Klingsor's magic powers (in the manner of the Venusberg music); here is a good deal suggesting the archaic, priestly tone of church music, there an orgy of pure mixed sound. But how does Wagner work on that tension? Not at all; he just leaves it as it is. He puts blocks of sound in place side by side, inserting empty spaces between them – general rests, like that crotchet rest at the beginning, again and again. What moves is moving only within its own sphere; there is no interaction between the two. Because there is only one sphere *or* the other sphere, not one *in* the other? Because mankind has to choose between the intoxication of the senses and a sacred mission? Something similar, incidentally, can be observed in the orchestral setting: here too Wagner works for preference with blocks or groups of instruments, with woodwind, brass *or* strings, as if pulling out the various stops of an organ.

So the *Parsifal* art of an 'extremely fine and gradual transition', as Wagner put it, faces a certain architectural structure. Controversial interpretations of this could certainly be put forward: as an old man's fantasy of liberation from all sensuality and sexuality (Cosima, aged 45, might not have liked that); as expressing devotion to a pure form of art that must not be disturbed by anything or anyone. I don't see it in quite such chaste and Catholic terms. Rather, I think that here Wagner was composing his own composition: the 'transition' is the work – and the architecture is that of the Festival Theatre. *Parsifal* is Wagner's only music drama that was really written for the covered orchestra pit and the acoustics of Bayreuth – it bears their imprint all over it. He could only look forward to those effects in the *Ring*; in *Parsifal* he makes the most of them.

Yet the mystery always remains clearly present. For instance, Wagner often has only half the strings playing, which makes the orchestra sound as if it were about to take off into the air a little way. Or he has different metrical times overlapping: a passage in 6/8 time will suddenly occur in a slow passage of 4/4 time, making everything begin to vibrate. If the conductor avoids rhythmical counting in such passages and instead concentrates on phrasing the music and letting it breathe, he will draw from the orchestra that fine pulsation that has an intoxicating effect, particularly in Bayreuth. But there are also other positively expressionist passages, and their effect develops only in contrast. For instance, Kundry's notorious enunciation of the word *lachte* [the past tense of the verb *lachen*, to laugh] in the second act, when she is telling Parsifal how she laughed at the Saviour hanging on the cross, should really make the audience feel that the Festival Theatre has that moment burnt down. Wagner sets the word as a minor seventh, B minor – C sharp minor, followed by a general rest and a pause in which Parsifal turns away 'in horror'. I would always try to hold that horror, that glimpse of the abyss into which humanity can descend, as long as possible. But that also depends on the singer of the part of Kundry and the intensity she brings to the moment, the kind of shudder she can arouse as the echo dies away. Incidentally, this is another of those places where the orchestra holds back. There are woodwind triplets, a *sforzato*, and then Kundry's C sharp falls into the bottomless depths.

Apart from a few passages, the instrumentation of *Parsifal* is not loud anyway; there are hardly any noisy effects, and even the moments of solemnity sound measured rather than pompous. An opera that takes the middle way for all its extremes, one might say. And there is great art in finding the right degree of moderation. Not freezing to rigidity in the slow tempi, making sure that old Gurnemanz tells a straightforward story in the first act rather than making a meal of it, not holding a magnifying glass over the general rests but keeping the tension going and all the same, when it is necessary, letting all external trappings drop away. This is not something I really like to say, but perhaps *Parsifal* is not for young conductors, who may confuse moderation with power and want to make too much of it. And because its music contains a touch of frailty, as if the composer were gathering his powers together for the last time, that must be observed.

What might have come after *Parsifal*? Perhaps Wagner really would have written a symphony. In Venice, Cosima noted that he wanted to 'spin a melodic thread right to its end,' adding, as if it were not to be taken for granted, 'only there will be no drama in it'. Even if Wagner had lived longer than he did, he would probably not have written any more operas.

Recordings

Hans Knappertsbusch's very favourite work was Otto Nicolai's *Merry Wives of Windsor* – I always think of that when I see in my mind's eye the list of his Bayreuth recordings of *Parsifal*, an incredible 11 in all, from 1951 to 1964, almost a new one every summer. Knappertsbusch was the *Parsifal* conductor of the post-war New Bayreuth period, which supports my hypothesis of the maturity needed by a conductor for this work. He was 63 when he first conducted Wagner's 'festival play to consecrate a stage' on the Green Hill, and 76 when he raised his baton to conduct it for the last time. Naturally his cast of singers varies. In the first years, the young Martha Mödl certainly promises a stormier experience of Kundry than Irene Dalis and Barbro Ericson in the early 1960s, and in the title part, while Wolfgang Windgassen was already presenting himself as the Heldentenor of the future in 1951, later singers of the role such as Hans Beirer and Jon Vickers left something to be desired. Over the years, however, Knappertsbusch himself became increasingly fluent and agile – and also faster. He developed a way of chiselling out the climaxes of the music, yet proceeding at a good pace. The action never comes to a standstill, the thread of tension never breaks, he never becomes stolid – his are masterly performances. (The 11 recordings are on a number of different labels, the first with Naxos, the last with Orfeo.)

Apart from the recordings by Knappertsbusch, there were not many others at first. Mahler's assistant Fritz Stiedry is represented by three recordings of 1952 to 1956 at the New York Met, and a curiosity that works surprisingly well is Vittorio Gui's studio production of 1950 in Rome – sung in Italian, with Maria Callas as Kundry, Rolando Panerai as Amfortas and Boris Christoff as Gurnemanz (Opera d'Oro). Rudolf Kempe is always reliable (Covent Garden in 1959, on the Testament label), and Erich Leinsdorf is rightly regarded as one of the great conductors of Wagner in the New World, both before and after the war. Herbert von Karajan appears in the *Parsifal* discography for the first time in 1961, with a live recording from the Vienna State Opera, notable not least for having such prominent flower maidens as Gundula Janowitz, Hilde Güden and Anneliese Rothenberger (BMG). Karajan did not make a studio recording of the work until 20 years later, when he was already over 70. His recording with the Berlin Philharmonic, produced before the Salzburg Easter Festival, as was Karajan's custom, was made in December 1979 and January 1980. It is clearly slower than Knappertsbusch's recordings in many ways, but no less fluent. Karajan was, in principle, imitating the sound of conditions at Bayreuth in his interpretation, and that is the brilliant aspect of it: the homogeneity of the strings, the rounded brass, the immaculate *legato*. Anyone who wants to hear the magic that can exist between an orchestra and a conductor who know each other inside out should listen to this recording (with Peter Hofmann as Parsifal, Kurt Moll as Gurnemanz and Dunja Vejzovič as Kundry, Deutsche Grammophon).

Nine years earlier, Pierre Boulez took a very different approach, again in Bayreuth. His tempi may be extremely brisk and French (10 minutes 27 seconds for the Prelude, almost two minutes shorter than the fastest Knappertsbusch recording), but they work very well for the music. I have seldom heard a more exciting, coherent, logical and at the same time freer and more unencumbered *Parsifal*. And the conducting of Boulez is masterly. I must admit that listening to his recording was a road-to-Damascus experience for me. It was as if the old spirit of Bayreuth had been given fresh oxygen – many of the musicians with whom Boulez was working had still been playing under Knappertsbusch a few years earlier. And that may be the secret: if the conductor's approach is lean and slim, and the orchestra traditionally has something of a paunch, well and good; if his approach is the same but the orchestra is metaphorically on a diet, it will all be rather too skinny. Boulez avoids this drawback by using a fine cast of singers, including James King as Parsifal, Gwyneth Jones as Kundry and Donald McIntyre as Klingsor (Deutsche Grammophon).

In 2004 and 2005 Boulez returned to Bayreuth to conduct *Parsifal* in Christoph Schlingensief's production, and it was as if the relationship between the stage and the pit had been reversed. In 1970, Boulez was still dealing with the old aesthetic of Wieland Wagner: the notorious disc on an empty stage, extremely stylized costumes, few props. Schlingensief, on the other hand, heaped the stage high with the throwaway products of civilization and mythological junk, dead hares and voodoo priests, so that the music seemed quite small and thin beside it all. I have noticed a tendency to the (historically) excessive since 2008 in the production on the Green Hill by Stefan Herheim, Schlingensief's successor as director of *Parsifal*: as if these directors knew what wealth Wagner had left in his last opera but did not feel able to control it and make it fertile. I think we should not be too complicated, nor always think of history before and after Wagner and show it on stage. As Lars von Trier said: if we want Wagner, then Wagner is what we want.

Conclusion

Sometimes I have nightmares. I dream that artistic quality is out of tune. I dream that art and music are destroying themselves because the quality has gone wrong. Because far too much that is trivial, empty, superficial and indifferent is rife, and is tolerated. And because none of us can find genuinely creative time to spare any more, either for ourselves or for such great work as Richard Wagner's. Was everything better in the old days? For a long time I thought such doom-laden prophecies were the talk of frustrated old folk, and I did not take it seriously. Now I understand it myself. Yes, a good deal *was* better in the old days, even if we idealize much of it. In the same way as the glaciers in the Alps are melting, so is the quality of art. We have learned to function perfectly; we have not learned *not* to function or to say no. That is what gives me nightmares. What was it that Ronald Wilford once said about Carlos Kleiber? 'He doesn't function.' What a great compliment. Do we still understand that art is not there to function, but so that it can come into being?

Perhaps it is for my generation to identify what is wrong, so that young people can do better. It would really be so easy. The artist determines the market, not the other way around. And why do we take such an interest in Richard Wagner if we are not going to learn from him? If we can't summon up the slightest courage to resist, and the least little confrontation terrifies us out of our lives?

Learning from Wagner, for me, means above all going deeply into the subject. The more closely I know his music dramas, the more curious, courageous and sensitive I feel. To that extent, I am fairly sure that he will accompany me for the rest of my musical life. Of course it can be said of any great art that it is inexhaustible in the variety of its interpretations and the ways of approaching it. A conductor interpreting Wagner, however, also has to deal with dimensions and complexities that lead straight to the limits of what can be done. If he is not to lose the battle with himself, he must be able to look over his shoulder. He ensures that the audience is enthusiastic, and is enthusiastic, too; he castigates himself, he enjoys himself. The heroine up on the stage, at her best moments, is almost beside herself; the conductor down in the pit is wrestling with his powers and discovering how much sensitivity, humility and love there can be in a certain kind of incorporeality that comes from exhaustion.

And sometimes then the real joy of Wagner comes to the interpreter, and cannot be compared to anything else in the world, because it arrives full of self-assurance and means everything. Because there is no more fundamentally significant experience than in the music of Wagner. The waves may close over you, but you always stay above them. And then the divine sparks of Schiller's 'Ode to Joy' fly, and you don't really know if you are seeing the light of understanding or it is just the reflection of the lights of a good restaurant somewhere ahead. I am sure that Richard Wagner would be glad of both.

Acknowledgements

My thanks, first and foremost, go to my parents, who first introduced me to Wagner.

This book is based on conversations that took place between August 2010 and July 2011 in Bayreuth, Berlin, Salzburg and on the Attersee. Warm thanks to Christine Lemke-Matwey for the illuminating intensity of those long conversations, and for making the often complex strands of them into the text of this book. In addition, I would like to thank Stefanie Hölscher for her always quiet but firm interventions, Carlo Wolf for his hospitality, and the Bayreuth Festivals for their support in so many ways.

And I must not omit to mention that I have been involved for many years with Kilian Heck, Katharina Wagner, Dieter Borchmeyer and Joachim Thiery in an intensive exchange of opinions about the music of Wagner.

Appendix

⚜

Bibliography

Books mentioned in the text, and a small selection of other works consulted during the writing of this book, are listed below.

Richard Wagner, *Sämtliche Werke*, ed. Carl Dahlhaus and Egon Voss (Mainz, 1970 ff.)

Cosima Wagner, *Die Tagebücher*, ed. with comments by Martin Gregor-Dellin and Dietrich Mack, 2 vols (Munich, 1976 f.)

Udo Bermbach, *Der Wahn des Gesamtkunstwerks. Richard Wagners politisch-ästhetische Utopie* (Stuttgart/Weimar, 2004)

Dieter Borchmeyer, *Das Theater Richard Wagners. Idee – Dichtung – Wirkung* (Stuttgart, 1982)

Fritz Busch, *Aus dem Leben eines Musikers* (Zurich, 1949)

Carl Dahlhaus, *Richard Wagners Musikdramen* (Velber, 1971)

Wilhelm Furtwängler, *Aufzeichnungen 1924–1954*, ed. Elisabeth Furtwängler and Günter Birkner (Wiesbaden, 1980)

Martin Geck, *Richard Wagner* (Reinbek bei Hamburg, 2004)

Carl Friedrich Glasenapp, *Das Leben Richard Wagners*, 6 vols (Leipzig, 1910–23)

Martin Gregor-Dellin, *Richard Wagner. Sein Leben, sein Werk, sein Jahrhundert* (Munich/Zürich/Mainz, 1995)

Brigitte Hamann, *Winifred Wagner oder Hitlers Bayreuth* (Munich, 2002)

Norbert Heinel, *Wagner als Dirigent* (Vienna, 2006)

Fanny Hensel, *Tagebücher*, ed. Hans-Günter Klein and Rudolf Elvers (Wiesbaden/Leipzig/Paris, 2002)

Oliver Hilmes, *Cosimas Kinder. Triumph und Tragödie der Wagner-Dynastie* (Munich, 2009)

Tobias Janz, *Klangdramaturgie. Studien zur theatralen Orchesterkomposition in Wagner's 'Ring des Nibelungen'* (Würzburg, 2006)

Joachim Kaiser, *Leben mit Wagner. Der Komponist, das Werk und die Interpretation* (Munich, 1992)

Ingrid Kapsamer, *Wieland Wagner. Wegbereiter und Weltwirkung* (Graz, 2010)

Jürgen Kesting, *Die grossen Sänger unseres Jahrhunderts* (Düsseldorf/Vienna, 1993)

Joachim Köhler, *Wagners Hitler. Der Prophet und sein Vollstrecker* (Munich, 1977)

Frida Leider, *Das war mein Teil. Erinnerungen einer Opernsängerin* (Berlin, 1959)

Heinz-Klaus Metzger and Rainer Riehn (eds), *Richard Wagner – Wie antisemitisch darf ein Künstler sein?* (Munich, 1978 = Musik-Konzepte, 5)

Stephan Mösch, *Weihe, Werkstatt, Wirklichkeit. Wagners 'Parsifal' in Bayreuth 1882–1933* (Kassel, 2009)

Hans Neuenfels, *Wie viel Musik braucht der Mensch? Über Oper und Komponisten* (Munich, 2009)

Peter P. Pachl, *Siegfried Wagner, Genie im Schatten* (Munich, 1988)

Lars von Trier, *Abtretungsurkunde*, published from time to time on the director's homepage (www.zentropa.dk), quoted here from: *Das schwarze Theater*, in: *Der Tagesspiegel*, 2 June 2005

Nike Wagner, *Wagner-Theater* (Frankfurt am Main/Leipzig, 1998)

Wolfgang Wagner, *Lebens-Akte. Autobiographie* (Munich, 1994)

Peter Wapnewski, *Weisst du, wie das wird...? Richard Wagner: 'Der Ring des Nibelungen'* (Munich/Zürich, 1995)

Hartmut Zelinsky, *Richard Wagner, ein deutsches Thema. Eine Dokumentation zur Wirkungsgeschichte Richard Wagners, 1876–1976* (Frankfurt am Main, 1976)

Photo credits

Index

NOTE: Works (musical and written) by Richard Wagner (RW) appear directly under title; works by others under author's/composer's name

at Bayreuth, 17, 65, 67; author
conducts in Chicago, 17–18;
Beckmesser harp in, 27–8; words,
32–3; difficulty to perform, 66–7;
and German ideology, 91, 94;
Friedrich's production (1995),
113; interpreting, 123; plot and
themes, 132, 204–7; characters
and orchestration, 133–5, 203–4;
qualities, 187, 201; origin and
writing, 201–3; première, 203;
music, 207–10; at Bayreuth, 209;
length, 210; recordings, 210–12
Masur, Kurt, 10
Matačić, Lovro von, 53
Mayer, Hans, 88, 180
media: effect on Bayreuth tradition,
52
Meistersinger von Nürnberg, Die
(RW) *see Mastersingers of Nurem-*
berg, The
Melchior, Lauritz, 118, 235
Melles, Carl, 53
Mendelssoh-Bartholdy, Felix: RW
misjudges, 24; as conductor,
36–7, 40, 167; as prodigy, 38, 141;
appearance, 80; musical style, 80;
Wagner's hostility to, 82–8; cor-
respondence with Wagner, 84–5;
RW quotes in music, 86–7; later
reputation, 87; Wagner observes,
167; *Calm Sea and Prosperous
Voyage* (overture), 83, 85; *Elijah*,
87; *The Fair Melusine*, 86–7;
Hebrides (overture), 86; *Midsum-
mer Night's Dream* (overture), 87;
St Paul (oratorio), 86
Merz, HG (architectural firm), 96
Messerschmidt, Franz Xaver, 133
Metternich, Josef, 185
Meyerbeer, Giacomo: in Paris, 82,

151; RW dislikes, 82, 85, 178; and
RW's *Rienzi*, 153, 158; and *The
Flying Dutchman*, 158; attends
Lohengrin performance, 177;
death, 876; *Les Huguenots*, 152;
Les Patineurs, 177; *Le Prophète*,
77
Meysenbug, Malwilda von, 216
Milan: La Scala, 98
Millington, Barry, 129n
Mödl, Martha, 118, 198, 237, 248
Moll, Kurt, 249
Mortier, Gerard, 73
Moscheles, Ignaz, 124
Moser, Thomas, 198
Mottl, Felix von: in Wagner School,
39; portrait, 42; death, 43;
diaries, 43; discovers Balling, 45;
conducts *The Flying Dutchman*,
159; conducts *Lohengrin*, 184
Mozart, Wolfgang Amadeus: and
musical theatre, 35; operatic
singers audible in pit, 107; Jacobs
conducts, 122; as infant prodigy,
141; *The Magic Flute*, 146
Muck, Dr Karl (Carl), 45, 47–8
Müller, Maria, 164, 185
Munich: theatres, 97
Muti, Riccardo, 53

Nazis: and Furtwängler, 48; and
Tietjen, 50; anti-Semitism, 86;
antipathy to Mendelssohn, 87;
misuse Wagner's music, 94;
disfavour Knappertsbusch, 512
Nelsons, Andris, 186
Neuenfels, Hans, 56, 108, 186, 190
Neumann, Bernd, 76
New York: Metropolitan Opera
House, 64, 72, 95
Nibelungenlied, 214